# WHO IS THE ASIANIST?

## The Politics of Representation in Asian Studies

# WHO IS THE ASIANIST?

## The Politics of Representation in Asian Studies

Edited by
**Will Bridges,
Nitasha Tamar Sharma,
and Marvin D. Sterling**

Published by the Association for Asian Studies
Asia Shorts, Number 14
www.asianstudies.org

**The Association for Asian Studies (AAS)**

Formed in 1941, the Association for Asian Studies (AAS)—the largest society of its kind, with over 5,500 members worldwide—is a scholarly, non-political, non-profit professional association open to all persons interested in Asia. For further information, please visit www.asianstudies.org.

Published by Association for Asian Studies, 825 Victors Way, Suite 310, Ann Arbor, MI 48108 USA.

Cover Image: Photo of Mrs. Marguerite McCraven in China. Photo credit to Marcus McCraven, April 1987. Grand Canal, a UNESCO site, China.

Cataloging-in-Publication Data is available from the Library of Congress.

# ASIA
## SHORTS

Series Editor: David Kenley
Dean of the College of Arts & Sciences, Dakota State University

ASIA SHORTS offers concise, engagingly written titles by highly qualified authors on topics of significance in Asian Studies. Topics are intended to be substantive, generate discussion and debate within the field, and attract interest beyond it.

The Asia Shorts series complements and leverages the success of the pedagogically-oriented AAS series, Key Issues in Asian Studies, and is designed to engage broad audiences with up-to-date scholarship on important topics in Asian Studies. Rigorously peer-reviewed, Asia Shorts books provide cutting-edge scholarship and provocative analyses. They are jargon free, accessible, and speak to contemporary issues or larger themes. In so doing, Asia Shorts volumes make an impact on students, fellow scholars, and informed readers beyond academia.

**For further information, visit the AAS website: www.asianstudies.org.**

AAS books are distributed by Columbia University Press.

For orders or purchasing inquiries, please visit

https://cup.columbia.edu

COLUMBIA
UNIVERSITY
PRESS

# CONTENTS

INTRODUCTION: *Do Black Lives Matter for Asian Studies?*
WILL BRIDGES, NITASHA TAMAR SHARMA,
AND MARVIN D. STERLING / 1

1: *Who Is a South Asianist? A Conversation on Positionality*
HODA BANDEH-AHMADI AND ISABEL HUACUJA ALONSO / 23

2: *A Different Way of Seeing: Reflections of a Black Asianist*
CAROLYN T. BROWN / 39

3: *From Bhagdād to Baghpūr: Sailors and Slaves in Global Asia*
GUANGTIAN HA / 53

4: *The Asianist is Muslim: Thinking through Anti-Muslim Racism
with the Muslim Left*
SOHAM PATEL AND M. BILAL NASIR / 75

5: *Racial Capitalism and the National Question in the Early
People's Republic of China*
JEREMY TAI / 89

6: *Science without Borders? The Contested Science of "Race Mixing"
circa World War II in Japan, East Asia, and the West*
KRISTIN ROEBUCK / 109

7: *Toward an Afro-Japanese and Afro-Ainu Feminist Practice:
Reading Fujimoto Kazuko and Chikappu Mieko*
FELICITY STONE-RICHARDS / 125

8: *Black Japanese Storytelling as Praxis: Anti-Racist Digital
Activism and Black Lives Matter in Japan*
KIMBERLY HASSEL / 139

9: *From Black Brother to Black Lives Matter: Perception of
Blackness in Viet Nam*
PHUONG H. NGUYEN AND TRANG Q. NGUYEN / 159

10: *"We Have a Lot of Names Like George Floyd":
Papuan Lives Matter in Comparative Perspective*
CHRIS LUNDRY / 183

# Acknowledgments

This volume largely originated with a petition submitted by Levi McLaughlin, Kimberlee Sanders, Jolyon Thomas, and Michelle C. Wang in June 2020 to the AAS Board of Directors. The letter, written in response to the tragic killings of African American men and women at the hands of state-sponsored and other forms of violence, encouraged the Board to act on a series of proposals intended to address the state of the field, including issues of racial, gendered, and other forms of inequity in Asian Studies. The AAS Board responded by initiating a webinar series, AAS Digital Dialogues. Two of the co-editors of this volume participated in one of these webinars—"Asian Studies and Black Lives Matter"—on issues of diversity and representation in the field. The edited volume emerged principally from this event. We would therefore like to thank the petitioners for their letter, the AAS Board of Directors, and especially Executive Director Hilary Finchum-Sung, for their combined efforts in producing this volume.

We would like to thank former Asia Shorts Series Editor, Bill Tsutsui, and current Series Editor, David Kenley, for their guidance and encouragement, as well as AAS Publications Manager Jon Wilson for his attentive and patient stewardship of the volume. We would also like to thank the Connecticut-based McCraven family for their permission to use the photo of Marguerite McCraven's visit to China for our cover image.

Special thanks to consulting editor Keisha Brown of Tennessee State University, also a participant in the "Asian Studies and Black Lives Matter" webinar, for her close involvement in the conceptualization and development of the edited volume, as well as for her review of several essays submitted for the project.

The co-editors would also like to thank the attendees of the eponymously titled AAS 2022 Roundtable Session in Hawai'i, during which we presented an overview of the project, for their thoughtful suggestions and support.

## INTRODUCTION

# DO BLACK LIVES MATTER FOR ASIAN STUDIES?

## Will Bridges, Nitasha Tamar Sharma, and Marvin Sterling

*Who Is the Asianist?*—an Asia Shorts edited volume—is both a call from and response to the movement for Black lives that demands a reckoning with race and a deep acknowledgement of the humanity and value of Black life. This reckoning by our field is now urgent, if not belated. The reverberations of the unconscionable 2020 Minneapolis police murder of George Floyd—yet another state-sanctioned murder of a Black person in the United States—were felt across the country and around the globe, in the streets and in the academy. University departments released statements in support of BLM and detailed their commitments to challenging institutional racism. Academic disciplines responded to this global movement by acknowledging and seeking to learn more about racism and by interrogating their practices. Critical geographer and prison abolitionist Ruth Wilson Gilmore defines racism as "the state-sanctioned and/or extralegal production and exploitation of group-differentiated vulnerability to premature death."[1] But do Black lives matter for Asian Studies?

Black scholars in Asian Studies have insisted upon the field's obligation to undertake a serious consideration of our hiring practices and curricular content, and of race's entanglements with the historical roots of the discipline. This field was among those called upon, from within its ranks and by the general pause across the academy, to self-reflect, to consider how scholars in this area of knowledge both practice and contend with anti-Blackness. This volume amplifies the call to take on this form of work while it is also its result. We feature scholarship that emerges from critical self-reflection by Asian Studies scholars who are interrogating their field, its colonial roots, its hiring practices, its politics of representation, and its areas of legitimated focus and silence.

We disseminated a call for papers that approached the questions of positionality, race, Blackness, and the movement for Black lives by Asianists. The response was overwhelming. We are heartened to be able to curate a collection that includes self-reflections on various Asianists' experiences in the academy, multilingual and transregional scholarship on race and Blackness, and studies on the effects of BLM movements across Asia. The contributions in this volume theorize race, consider the discipline's gatekeeping practices that circumscribe ideas about who an Asianist *is*, discuss the experiences of Black scholars in Asian Studies, and center the study of Blackness and Black people in Asia.

The contributors to this volume provide intersected African and Asian diasporic perspectives on Asian Studies. They speak, directly and otherwise, not only to this work as a coherent, increasingly established body of knowledge within Asian Studies (even as there is a continued need for institutional support for such scholarship, including through hiring, curricular design, mentorship, and the other approaches indicated above). These perspectives that are attuned to diasporic intersections in Asian Studies also illustrate the collaborative possibilities between scholars of African and Asian descent who, along with other ethnically and racially minoritized scholars and white collaborators, advocate on behalf of marginalized scholars and areas of research within Asian Studies. Placing race at the center of analysis calls into question Asian Studies "itself" as a field of academic knowledge production. In the two sections that follow, we highlight themes that emerge when we center race, concluding with a synopsis of the contents of our volume that, as a whole, urges Asian Studies scholars to address this question: Do Black lives matter for Asian Studies?

## Toward Unfragmented Epistemologies, or Do Black Lives Matter for Asian Studies?

This volume of essays is, among other things, a record of the transformative reverberations of the Black Lives Matter movement as they undulate throughout Asia. It is also an invitation to consider the transformations these reverberations might occasion for Asian Studies. In other words, this volume asks: Do Black lives matter to and for both Asia and Asian Studies? And if they do matter, in what way does the constitutive importance of Black life for Asia and Asian Studies make itself manifest?

Black Lives Matter, Laurie Collier Hillstrom writes, is a movement that began as a moment, namely the moment in which social justice activist-organizers

Alicia Garza, Patrisse Cullors, and Opal Tometi created and shared the hashtag "#BlackLivesMatter" on social media.[2] The immediate inspiration for the hashtag's creation was Alicia Garza's 2013 Facebook post entitled, "Love Letter to Black Folks." Prompted by the announcement of the acquittal of George Zimmerman in the fatal shooting of Trayvon Martin, Garza wrote, "We don't deserve to be killed with impunity. We need to love ourselves and fight for a world where Black lives matter. . . . We matter. Our lives matter."[3] Cullors shared Garza's love letter on social media alongside the hashtag "#BlackLivesMatter." In the wake of the death of Michael Brown at the hands of the Ferguson Police Department, and the subsequent Ferguson protests of 2014, #BlackLivesMatter became a digital rallying cry for the activist work of Garza, Cullors, Tometi, and members of what would ultimately become the Black Lives Matter (BLM) movement, a decentralized, global network of activists "whose mission is to eradicate white supremacy and build local power to intervene in violence inflicted on Black communities by the state and vigilantes."[4]

The emergence of BLM is informed by a sentiment—namely, the sentiment that Black life is a beautiful, constitutive expression of our shared humanity and thus is just as deserving of protection from undue legal and extralegal modes of eradication as any other expression of humanity—with a deep intellectual and political history. In *The Making of Black Lives Matter*, philosopher Christopher J. Lebron writes that the political ethos of BLM amalgamates four tributaries of Black intellectual and activist history: the tactic of "shameful publicity" practiced by Frederick Douglass and Ida B. Wells; the "countercolonization of the white imagination" proffered by Langston Hughes and Zora Neale Hurston; the "unconditional self-possession" embodied in the protests of Anna Julia Cooper and Audre Lorde; and what Lebron calls the "unfragmented compassion" of James Baldwin and Martin Luther King, Jr.[5]

For the purpose of this volume (read: the purpose of articulating how Black lives matter to and for Asian Studies), BLM's promotion of unfragmented compassion is particularly revelatory. Unfragmented compassion refers to a commitment to empathetic relationships defined by reciprocity and mutual regard. This commitment is coupled with a refusal to cede one's rightful claim to self-respect and the pursuit of the good life. Such compassion is "unfragmented" insofar as it is extended to both the self and the other: unfragmented compassion entails good faith attempts to understand the humanity of one's interlocutor alongside a non-negotiable vision of one's own existential value. To the degree that the political ethos and tactics of the Black Lives Matter movement are informed by the civil rights movement—think here, for example, of the "Freedom Ride" to Ferguson, Missouri, organized by BLM in 2014 to protest police brutality—BLM political action often features the revivification of the unfragmented compassion of King,

Baldwin, and other intellectual leaders of the civil rights era. To be sure, there is no one-to-one correspondence between the imaginative and actual infrastructures of BLM and the civil rights movement: BLM's founding by Black queer women, its decentralized leadership structures, and its digital activism are all examples of the transformations ushered in with the changing of the guard from the civil rights movement to the BLM generation. There is a way in which, however, these shifts speak to a continuity between the movements: BLM represents the emergence of a movement better equipped to make good on the former's promise of expanding, rather than fracturing, epistemologies.

This is one reason why Black lives matter to Asian Studies: Black Lives Matter serves as a model and reminder of Asian Studies' need for what we might call unfragmented epistemologies. We are quickly approaching a grim anniversary: it has been almost two decades since Andrew Jones and Nikhil Pal Singh assessed Asian Studies as "characterized by a studied failure to consider the question of race in the constitution of . . . modernities . . . throughout Asia."[6] There has been relatively little reckoning with this state of affairs in the intervening years. This continuing "studied failure" is not a coincidence. Rather, it is an organic by-product of the historical formation of area studies in the American academy, in which the study of race is sequestered into ethnic studies; area studies functions as the equivalent of an intellectual safe haven for those who other their objects of study by other means. In turn, this historical formation emerges as a present in which, to borrow comparative literary scholar Shu-mei Shih's articulation, Asian Studies rarely investigates its racial unconscious or the "open secret"—"that there is a dearth of African American or other non-Asian minority scholars in Asian studies"—underwritten by the unspoken racial logic through which Asian Studies organizes itself.[7]

Shih writes that the emergence of a new Asian Studies, one which speaks consciously to the question of race in the constitution of modernities throughout Asia, requires a response to the "ethical demand" of recognizing "interlocking racial formation[s]."[8] Such recognition would mean seeing race as an intellectual issue that Asian Studies "need[s] to bring over here and set . . . in active confrontation and dialogue, that is, in a relation" with the epistemological concerns typically privileged by the field.[9] To say that Black lives matter for Asian Studies is not to ask Asian Studies to do Black Studies any favors. Instead, the creation of a relationship between Black Studies and Asian Studies provides—as the essays in this volume attest—the field of Asian Studies with an opportunity to make whole its fragmented epistemology, and in so doing, to come closer to the fulfillment of the promise of its intellectual endeavor.

## Centering Race in Asian Studies

How shall we interrogate the politics of identity in Asian Studies? This volume features work by Asianists who analyze the gatekeeping practices and presumptions that scholars hold about who studies what, how, where, and why. The scholars who have taken on this task, at least in these pages, include those who are minoritized and who have experienced marginalization and gatekeeping. We hope to expand an awareness of these dynamics by calling upon the broader membership of Asian Studies—particularly those who act as gatekeepers due to their prominence in the field or their backgrounds that make their position as "Asianists" seemingly self-explanatory—to undergo a similar self-assessment. What does it mean to curtail our understanding of "Who is an Asianist?" based on the presumption that the scholar is either white or else shares the background of the places and people whom they study? How are we to be accountable to scholars—such as the Latina and Iranian South Asianists in our first chapter, or the Black Asianists across several of these contributions—for erecting roadblocks, challenging, and otherwise not mentoring those whom we consider "outside" the realm of Asian Studies?

Whereas the scholars in this issue discuss their individual experiences as "unlikely" Asianists who work outside of their expected interests or presumed expertise, we connect these experiences as patterns of racism that structure area studies. It is our hope that this volume speaks not only to scholars whose experiences parallel those of our authors; we intend for this Asia Shorts publication to make Asianists—writ large and *especially* including those who have not considered these dynamics—pause and take stock of the politics that shape the production and dissemination of knowledge about Asia, particularly within US universities. Part of this process begins with an engagement with this volume. The more necessary task, however, is to *center race* and extend this knowledge to the practices that shape the field, including hiring and promotion, mentorship, as well as research and publishing on Asia.

The chapters in this volume include cutting-edge research by a new generation of scholars who are informed by national and global events, including the inequalities that have led to the rise of the movement for Black lives and a recognition of global anti-Blackness. Among them are researchers who have engaged ethnic studies in their pursuit of knowledge about Asia and who incorporate Black Studies scholarship, for instance, along with, in some cases, their own experiences as people racialized as Black in the US in their study of Asia. A more accurate analysis of the world emerges from centering race as a globally and historically relevant phenomenon, one that intersects with culture, religion, ethnicity, caste, and other markers of difference and community. Additionally, considering the positionality of the Black Asianist, for instance, complicates taken-for-granted assumptions within the field by the presentation of new questions and different approaches to inquiry. Stated in the obverse, the refusal of Asianists to center or even consider race in researching "the other," the "elsewhere" of Asia, the politics of knowledge production, and the overall understanding of how racialized concepts of difference have shaped life is an inadequate approach to the study of Asia or, indeed, any part of the world.

This volume is one small response to the urgent call to center race and analyze the development of racial difference within Asian Studies alongside the field's strong emphasis on culture, language, religion, and history. This includes attention to figures and concepts of Blackness, darkness, and difference within the archives; various languages and literatures; and the scholarship on slaveries, colonialism, and domination across the Indian Ocean and Pacific worlds. The contributors present ambitious, theoretical, and urgent knowledge that emerges from a sustained engagement with ethnic studies, theories of race, and attention to Blackness and African-descended people. They highlight what a deeply local study of people and places provides, especially when they are analyzed through a transregional and *longue-durée* perspective.

An Asian Studies reckoning with race will require that we provide undergraduate and graduate training in theories of race; courses on the development of the global concepts of race, including its social constructivism and very real consequences; and an analysis of political economy that takes race *and* class, or racial capitalism, into account. It includes a careful delineation of how structures of inequality may be informed by, for instance, caste and race, as distinct yet intertwined historical human formations. What would it mean, therefore, to require coursework in ethnic studies and its subfields by our graduate students as they embark on their studies of Asia? And how would teaching this volume shape the universe of ideas and research pathways for students pursuing Asian Studies? The production of knowledge by scholars trained in interdisciplinary fields, including those published here, reveals how the geographic and foundational parameters that once informed various disciplines can be undisciplined to greater effect. Imagine the research questions and methods that emerge, for example, when Asian Studies scholars read closely the work emerging from trans-Pacific Asian Studies that centers diaspora, militarism, and migration *along with* theories of race, gender, and sexuality developed in Asian American studies? This volume has selected chapters that reflect our support of deeply interdisciplinary studies of Asia and its diasporas.

In addition to illustrating the importance of an engagement with Black Studies and areas including trans-Pacific, Asian diaspora, Asian American, and Amerasian studies within Asian Studies, we highlight the analytically rich and politically imperative work that continues to develop out of several emergent, increasingly established and overlapping fields. The editors of this volume have contributed scholarship to these areas, including our research on African diasporic music and literature in Japan, Black and South Asian relations in the US, and Blackness across the Pacific.[10] Scholars in these areas explore the sociocultural, political, economic, and other relationships between African and Asian diasporas and include the growing subfields of Black Internationalism, the Black Pacific, and Afro-Asian Studies.

The term "Afro-Asia" has been mobilized to service a range of intellectual and ideological projects. Political scientists and activists have explored this conceptual space as one inhabited by peoples who share common experiences with Western colonialism as well as the postcolonial effort to contend with its legacies.[11] Other scholars have traced how Western colonialism created global encounters of African and Asian diasporic peoples through the movement of imperial labor.[12] These include Chinese and Indian indentured servants who supplanted the newly freed African labor in the Caribbean and other regions in the mid-nineteenth century. Later, several newly independent African and Asian nations met during the Bandung Conference of 1955 to chart a collective path forward in the face of continued Euro-American dominance of international politics and economics. In the United States, Nation of Islam leader Elijah Muhammad invoked the figure of "the Asiatic Black man" as allied with Asian peoples, such as the Japanese during World War II, in the struggle by people of color against Western oppression. These politics have since been invoked by figures like heavyweight boxing champion Muhammad Ali, who identified himself using this term in his famous refusal to be drafted to fight the Vietcong, with whom he said he had no quarrel.[13] More recently, they have been called upon by figures in popular music. The Wu-Tang Clan, Rakim, Nas, and other hip-hop artists who are drawn to the Afrocentric theology of the Five Percent Nation of Islam sometimes lyrically self-identify, as Ali did, as the revolutionary figure of the Asiatic Black man.

In addition to the long histories of interpersonal interaction between the two groups, African and Asian people today indeed exercise their racial imaginings of each other in the spaces of global popular culture. Scholars of Asia have described the popular cultural traffic between the African and the Asian by explicitly invoking the concept of Afro-Asia.[14] Other works, though not analytically centered on the concept, nevertheless engage exchanges across African and Asian diasporas.[15] Recent scholarship on transnational sonic dialogues describes the rooting of African diasporic musical genres, including hip-hop and reggae in Asia, the Pacific, and the United States.[16] Several chapters in this volume also rest squarely within Afro-Asian Studies, in light of their focus on questions of representation in mass media and social media. They reflect how some Asianists engage race, Blackness, and diaspora. For instance, whereas Muhammad Ali's proclamation of himself as an Asiatic Black man embodied an African American embrace of the radical possibilities of Afro-Asian affinity, in this case with the Vietnamese, Ngyuen and Nguyen's chapter in this volume on BLM social media activism in Vietnam reciprocates that gaze, offering rare insight into the imagination of Blackness in the country. (We show, too, how Afro-Asia overlaps with the Black Pacific—discussed in our final article by Lundry—illustrating how both subfields have spoken to issues like the Vietnam War that have been important to Asian Studies.)[17]

Afro-Asia is also a rubric for considering other recent developments in international economics, politics, and society. This includes China's increasing status as a neoliberal rival to the Western world through the country's capital investments in Africa, Latin America, and the Caribbean; the presence of continental Africans in China such as in Guangzhou; the national debates surrounding the identities of multiracial Black and Japanese tennis player Naomi Osaka and Miss Universe Japan 2015, Ariana Miyamoto; and similar debates surrounding Black and Chinese talent show contestants Lou Jing and Winnie Zhong Feifei in China.[18] The essays by Kimberly Hassel and Guangtian Ha, while in many ways reflecting different intellectual projects, each provide an important sociohistorical context for understanding Blackness in Japan and China respectively.

Black Internationalism has been another framing of Black-Asian encounters that further speak to the possibilities of Asian Studies as a more fully race-cognizant and global enterprise. It reflects an African diasporic (and often specifically African American) gaze toward the possibility of anticolonial or postcolonial kinship with the peoples of the non-Western world, including Asia. In this and other ways, Black Internationalism overlaps with Afro-Asian, Black Pacific, and Indian Oceanic studies. Political scientist Robert Vitalis compellingly argues that the field of International Relations was based in a profound presumption of, and an effort to institutionally validate and sustain, Western dominance over people of color around the world.[19] He describes Black Internationalism as an academic movement significantly centered on the Howard School, a contingent of Howard University scholars including Alaine Locke, E. Franklin Frazier, Ralph Bunche, Eric Williams, and Merze Tate. This "counternetwork" within International Relations sought to shift the field from its Euro-American center toward an African American scholarly engagement with social movements in America and around the world that were seeking Black political, economic, cultural, and other forms of self-determination. "Du Bois and his heirs in the Howard school would begin to insist that history, not biology, explained hierarchy, specifically the history of colonial and mercantile capitalist expansion and the transatlantic slave trade that secured Western people's dominance and African, Asian, and Caribbean people's subordination."[20]

Black Internationalism indeed intersects with Asia in significant ways; two brief examples might suffice. In the past, China and Japan held positions of great respect and admiration in the minds of many African American scholars and activists. W. E. B. Du Bois, for instance, was a staunch supporter of the countries' rising place in the world as bulwarks against Euro-American tyranny, such as after Japan's defeat of Russia in 1905.[21] Historian Marc Gallicchio charts this African American interest in the racial dimensions of world affairs as predating the Civil War. He describes the increasing view among many Black Americans that the racism of the American empire increasingly created the possibility of solidarity between African Americans and the world's "dark-skinned people." "What might be called 'black internationalism' was unusual in that it reached beyond the world's Black Belt to embrace nonwhite peoples everywhere as allies in the cause of liberation," writes Gallicchio.[22]

As a second example, humanities scholar Selina Lai-Henderson explores conversations across Chinese and African American literary worlds, centering on the reception to Langston Hughes's visit to China in the 1930s. She argues for Hughes's importance in stimulating later generations of exchanges between African American and Chinese writers. Lai-Henderson further explores how Hughes himself used his poetic writings on China, a country he viewed as inevitably becoming "a major player in the worldwide proletarian revolution," to provide himself with a way of thinking through and ameliorating through communism the traumas of his racialized existence in the United States.[23] This particular work stands in interesting dialogue with, for example, Felicity Stone-Richards's chapter in this volume. Much like Lai-Henderson, Stone-Richards explores the literary dialogue between African America and East Asia, even as the relationship is inverted (and more explicitly gendered) given Stone-Richards's focus on women Japanese writers' engagements with the work of African American women authors.

The chapters that speak to issues commonly articulated within Afro-Asian studies and Black Internationalism are clearly represented in this volume. However, we also present a chapter on the Movement for Black Lives in West Papua, a Pacific province of Indonesia, raising the question of how far Asian Studies journeys into the Pacific. Chris Lundry's chapter, "We Have a Lot of Names like George Floyd," explains the resonance of the Black Lives Matter movement for those West Papuans in the Pacific who identify as Black and who are struggling for self-determination in the face of Indonesian rule. We end this volume with Lundry's research not as a closing to our broader inquiry but as a geographic, political, and racial opening, extending the geographic boundaries of Asian Studies and Afro-Asia into the Black Pacific. Like Afro-Asian Studies, yet newly emerging, the Black Pacific is an intellectual, relational, and theoretical area of study that pulls together scholars of politics, region, culture, race, and society. Indonesia's extension into the Pacific recalls the vast expanse of Japanese imperialism across Oceania, where its effects upon places like Guam, Okinawa, and the Marshall Islands are still felt. A politically attuned Asian Studies that analyzes race, imperialism, and colonialism across regions makes the Black Pacific directly relevant to scholars of Japan, Korea, Okinawa, as well as Vietnam, whose refugees have found temporary homes in many Pacific Islands. Asian Studies analyses of diaspora consider the migration of various Asian groups to plantations across Oceania, including the Hakka Chinese in French-controlled Tahiti and, in the case of Hawai'i's plantation economy, the arrival of laborers from China, Japan, Korea, and the Philippines in the nineteenth and twentieth century. More recently, the economic insertion of capital by Japan in the 1990s, and now China into Pacific societies, including the purchasing of land and businesses in Hawai'i, similarly extends the regional and analytical reach that Asian Studies scholars may achieve.

Centering a theoretical analysis of race and racial theories as they develop in locally specific ways means that we do not intend to impose US racial formations upon the globe. At the same time, the US empire has exported its racial ideologies alongside its economic, cultural, and military might to influence the world, primarily through its military but also through popular culture including soundwaves, news outlets, television, and film. Notions of Blackness, including racist conceptions of criminalized masculinity, for example, circulate internationally and stick to various bodies, including Black Pacific Islanders like West Papuans. At the same time, scholars in this volume have conducted deep dives into linguistic and historical archives from across Asia to reveal how various Asian societies conceptualized difference in phenotypic ways, thereby constructing hierarchies based on their own concepts of racialized difference that intersected with caste, region, class, and color.

A call for and response to the need for a racial reckoning in Asian Studies motivated by the movement for Black lives and the relentless onslaught of fatal racial violence faced by members of the African diaspora by no means begins in the twenty-first century. The establishment of area studies, including Asian Studies, as colonial fields rooted in disciplines like anthropology, history, and religion has long required an engagement with race and a confrontation with racism. By this, we refer both to the politics of race within the field as well as the production of knowledge by its scholars. We feature a range of contributions that articulate these vexed issues in several ways. First, we encourage a reckoning with race in how we view who an appropriate Asianist is—we may take for granted our white students' interests in Asia; we also can comprehend why, for instance, a South Asian scholar may want to study the 1947 Partition of the subcontinent. But how committed are we to nonwhite and non-Asian scholars who wish to embark on a career in Asian Studies? How does our questioning of their interests and expertise reflect gatekeeping that shuts the door on these areas of study in ways that not only mimic colonial actions but also deepen *racist* experiences within the academy? Who are we hiring, in what areas, and for what compensation? The reflection pieces in this volume uncover the racial politics of gatekeeping and mentorship that can make or break careers.

Second, the belated and thus-far inadequate contending with who the Asianist *is* goes hand in hand with the need to center race *analytically* as a locally emergent, globally dynamic, and historically produced phenomenon in the study of Asia, alongside other significant and overlapping categories of caste, religion, and ethnicity. This, we insist, requires a greater intellectual engagement with theories in Black Studies, Asian Diaspora Studies, and other ethnic studies. It calls for an emphasis on the freedom—even perhaps the necessity—of asserting a *political impetus* behind our work as scholars.

Race already is and has always been central to Asian Studies. This refers to the whiteness of Asian Studies and area studies more broadly. The colonial disciplines, like anthropology, that it draws from, the tiered and unequal racial and gendered patterns in hiring tenure-track versus teaching-track language instructors—these all reveal the material effects of racism upon the production of knowledge and knowledge producers. We hope this introductory essay illustrates one way of engaging with race intellectually as we also express our political desires to critique imperialism, move toward decolonization, and acknowledge anti-Black racism in Asia and in Asian Studies. Motivated by a similar impetus, our volume includes chapters that analyze anti-Black racism in Japan, Vietnam, and West Papua; interrogate the centrality of anti-Muslim racism to notions of race; and provide insight into the meanings of Blackness and darkness in early Asian texts. These are among the ways in which this volume becomes most compelling in its attempts to grapple with Asian Studies today: when it evokes a politics that might propel the study of people, places, and languages in the service of comprehending, and therefore addressing, inequalities across the globe.

## Overview

Our volume offers ten chapters representing the vast and deep scholarly interest in positionality, race, and Blackness in Asian Studies. We begin with a pair of essays that address the collection's eponymous concern—*who* is the Asianist? In theory, the answer to this question is infinite: insofar as the moniker "Asianist" is one earned by way of the accrual of credentials and intellectual capital, there is, in theory, no predetermined restriction on who might become an Asianist (or who the Asianist might become). In practice, however, the answer to this question has been much more finite: insofar as the accrual of credentials and capital (intellectual or otherwise) cannot be divorced from the way racial logics police access to the institutions and resources required to earn the moniker "Asianist," a limited set of racial and ethnic identities have come to define what it means to embody—to "look the part"—of the Asianist. The first pair of essays question how this limitation cuts both ways, undercutting the plentiful potential of both Asianists and Asian Studies.

In the opening essay, "Who Is a South Asianist? A Conversation on Positionality," anthropologists Hoda Bandeh-Ahmadi and Isabel Huacuja Alonso provide a compelling discussion about their experiences as nonwhite, non-South Asian scholars of South Asia. Long-term collaborators, they reflect upon the troubling experiences they confronted during their training, including other scholars' reactions to their positionalities (Iranian American and Mexican American, respectively). Structured as a conversation in response to four questions, the authors address what motivates their focus on South Asia; how their identities and backgrounds shape their research; barriers they have faced as "non-South Asian but minoritized scholar[s] in South Asian Studies"; and what their experiences say about who can and should be a scholar of South Asia. Through parallel experiences that reflect a troubling state of the field resulting from gatekeeping, assumptions about the link between a scholar's ethnic and racial background and their area of study, and the importance of mentors, this honest dialogue provides much for Asian Studies scholars to reflect upon with regard to our approach to the question of research, identity, and authority. While anthropology has come some distance in addressing the "insider" and "outsider" dynamics of "native" and white scholars, anthropologists have not yet contended with or cultivated nonwhite, non-Asian Asianists more broadly. Bandeh-Ahmadi and Huacuja Alonso outline the very questions this volume seeks to address. They center the effects of positionality by highlighting not so much its impact on the quality of research but rather the productive ways non-South Asian and nonwhite scholars trouble the fields' assumptions about "Who Is the (South) Asianist?"

Carolyn T. Brown's "A Different Way of Seeing: Reflections of a Black Asianist" is many things: it is a history of a career of service to the field of Asian Studies; it is a love letter to an academic field that at times refuses to love you back; and it is an auto-theoretical exploration of how Brown's lived experiences informed her writing of *Reading Lu Xun through Carl Jung* (Cambria Press, 2018). Much like the career of Brown herself—which begins with a PhD in literature and culminates in directorships of the Area Studies Collections and John W. Kluge Center of the Library of Congress—Brown collects the various strands of thought pursued in "A Different Way of Seeing" and reconfigures them into something with a collective force beyond that of any individual skein. Namely, she argues that "originality in the choice of subject matter" is a definitive characteristic of many Black Asianists. This originality is not the product of happenstance; it is an upshot of their attunement to the significance of putatively anomalous existences. Nor is this originality irrelevant; rather, it—when not attenuated by yesteryear visions of the way Asian Studies "should be"—facilitates the re-envisioning and expansion of the scope of the field. Taking her own scholarship as a case study in which she reads Lu Xun alongside the likes of Carl Jung and W. E. B. Du Bois, Brown considers how a more inclusive Asian Studies enables the field to see its objects of study in heretofore unforeseen ways.

Taken together, the next two chapters encourage Asian Studies scholars to think with race as a category on par with space, time, and society, as well as class. This commitment is central to ethnic studies but is a move that, according to contributor Guangtian Ha, "has barely caught on in Asian Studies for which the potentially transformative theoretical innovations of ethnic studies are at times reduced to studies of marginalized 'ethnic minorities' in postcolonial and postsocialist regimes." Ha and, in another essay, coauthors Soham Patel and M. Bilal Nasir provide two chapters that turn our attention to deeply historicized and transregional questions of Blackness and race.

Ha's piece, "From Baghdād to Baghpūr: Sailors and Slaves in Global Asia," encourages Asian Studies scholars to focus on transregional inter-Asian connections that "can contribute to a broadened understanding of global blackness that at once encompasses and transcends trans-Atlantic slavery." His multilingual research into Persian and Chinese texts and images from the fourth and seventh centuries reveal references to slavery and depictions of Blackness, such as the Chinese term "kunlun," that contribute to underexamined areas in both Asian Studies as well as Black Studies. Ha, a religious studies professor, considers "(1) the intellectual contribution and the political work Asian Studies may be capable of in addressing the entrenched racial bias that structures the field itself (white people studying non-whites, Black people studying themselves, and Asians finding anti-Black racism a matter not directly relevant to their existence and scholarly pursuit), and (2) the under-theorization of race as it pertains specifically to blackness in transregional Asian Studies." This fascinating chapter, which spotlights Black sailors and slaves, expands our understanding of slavery beyond the Middle Passage and West Africa, offering a broadened analysis of Blackness in Asia "without displacing or belittling the unique brutality of European colonialism and trans-Atlantic slavery." Blackness throughout this intertextual and transregional study refers to several things, including references to darkness and enslaved status, as well as to members of the African diaspora. In this way, Ha brings together matters of interest and concern that connect Asian Studies to ethnic studies.

The coauthored chapter by Patel and Nasir, "The Asianist is Muslim: Thinking through Anti-Muslim Racism with the Muslim Left," picks up on this same cross-field theme, linking the concerns and strengths of Islamic studies to Asian American studies in their analysis of the central role "the Muslim" has historically played in the development of race. That is, they argue that "the Asianist is Muslim." They draw on Edward Said's theorization of Orientalism to "address the limitations of Asian Studies regarding the question and representation of Muslims and Islam." Through a sweeping and theoretically acute account of the development and deployment of the Muslim, Patel (trained in American studies) and Nasir (an anthropologist) denounce the erasure of Muslims from both the categories of the Asian and the Asian American. Rather, they offer to Asian Studies a "reflection upon European Orientalist discourse as a way to return to the centrality of Muslims and Islam in bridging Asian and Asian American histories and politics." At the center of their contribution is how the figure of the Muslim unsettles not only diaspora studies but also area studies. Like Ha, they call for a transregional—a global, in fact—and historicized study of categories and processes including the Muslim, race, and slavery that we urge Asian Studies to engage more deeply. Patel and Nasir argue that "anti-Muslim racism and global Muslim politics can bring about a *critical* Asian Studies that connects region, broadly conceived, and its diasporas in solidarity with the Global South and its ongoing political struggles against imperial racism, empire, and the violent conditions brought on by coloniality." Their chapter's charting of the centrality of Muslims to modern racial formation ends with a clarion call to acknowledge radical Muslim politics and Muslim decoloniality.

Jeremy Tai's "Racial Capitalism and the National Question in the Early People's Republic of China" explores the comparative politics entailed in both the PRC and the West's "instrumentalization" of the ideologies of socialist ethnicity and racial capitalism. Socialist ethnicity for the PRC denotes the multicultural project of Han and non-Han belonging within a cohesive nation, while in the West it is represented as justifying the surveillance, incarceration, and genocidal disappearances of ethnic others within the body of the nation. If capitalism for many Westerners naturalizes assumptions about merit in an equitable pursuit of profit, *racial* capitalism for the PRC foregrounds how this pursuit has actually entailed a profound Western exploitation of peoples of color around the world. Tai astutely argues, however, that it is important for scholars of China to interrogate these sharply drawn distinctions in which both China and the West have been invested and through which each defines itself and the other. Acknowledging this divide is important because of how it echoes and compounds *academic* divides between area studies (such as the international political study of "the Chinese nation") on the one hand, and studies of ethnicity and race on the other. In his chapter, Tai explores the archives on Chinese socialism for how racial capitalism might not be considered as "just so" denoting of Western exploitation in contrast to the PRC's project of socialist ethnicity, but rather for its disclosures of the actual, ideological labor through which the PRC mobilized race to carve out the clear, moral, economical, and geopolitical domain of the People's Republic of China.

"Science without Borders? The Contested Science of 'Race Mixing' Circa World War II in Japan, East Asia and the West" by Kristin Roebuck similarly addresses the imaginary of race in the construction of Asian national identities. An historian, Roebuck interrogates scholarly characterizations of the global scientific thinking about race in the postwar era as defined by its recession, one facilitated by a Western scientific establishment invested in liberal notions of progress beyond the eugenicist, genocidal horrors of World War II. Roebuck asserts that these claims about a supposedly global scientific rejection of race—stress on the global—are, among other failings, provincially Western, often made without regard to scientific knowledge production in non-Western regions such as Asia. Focusing on the Japanese instance, Roebuck explores a shift in the Japanese scientific community's rhetorical embrace of Japanese and Asian race mixing before the war, one that served the goals of empire by arguing for the robustness of mixed-race people born from Japanese colonial encounters to a vision of race mixing as posing an existential threat to the purity of a defeated nation. Roebuck traces this ideological shift as expressed in the careers of several Japanese scholars. This chapter represents an important point of reference for scholars conducting research on mixed-race identities in East Asia past and present.

In "Toward an Afro-Japanese and Afro-Ainu Feminist Practice: Reading Fujimoto Kazuko and Chikappu Mieko," Felicity Stone-Richards situates her scholarship as a contribution to "a practice that is coming to be defined in the academic world as Afro-Japanese exchange." If a foundational premise of Afro-Japanese studies is that the interdependencies of Black Studies and Japanese studies has been overlooked and understudied by previous generations of Asianists, then Stone-Richards (alongside other contributors to this volume, including Kristin Roebuck and Kimberly Hassel) provides a sense of the potential avenues available for future generations of Afro-Japanese scholars. Stone-Richards, a political scientist, does this by advancing a heretofore understudied facet of Afro-Japanese politico-philosophical exchange. This chapter addresses how the art and thought of Black women such as Alice Walker and Toni Cade Bambara have informed the cultural practices of Japanese thinkers, with a focus on translator Fujimoto Kazuko and Ainu activist and clothwork artist Chikappu Mieko. In her analysis of the transcultural bridge the act of quilt-making forms between Chikappu and Black American culture, Stone-Richards notes that the quilt "has the dual purpose of enveloping a loved one and transmitting cultural history through the images, materials, and methods of sewing." Stone-Richards's scholarship itself has a quilt-like quality, as its methods weave together histories and artists who are otherwise regarded as cut from different (academic) cloths.

As a "born-digital" movement with an aversion to hierarchical organization and a commitment (in the words of Garza's love letter) to "a *world* [our emphasis] where Black lives matter," it should come as no surprise that the transformative potential of BLM has traversed both Asia and Asian Studies at the speed of the Internet. The final three essays in this collection—Hassel's "Black Japanese Storytelling as Praxis," Nguyen and Nguyen's "From Black Brother to Black Lives Matter," and Lundry's "We Have a Lot of Names Like George Floyd"—take up the travel of BLM to Asia and consider the methodological experimentation required of Asian Studies in order to do justice to the study of this transnational, transmedia movement. In the wake of the March 2020 killing of George Floyd, protests by the Black Lives Matter movement erupted not only across the nation but also internationally, including in Asian countries like Japan. Ethnic majority Japanese, African Americans living in Japan, and mixed-race Black Japanese individuals were among those who organized and attended protests. These developments raise the question of the Japanese histories and politics of race and ethnicity through which the BLM movement came to be locally inflected, especially as centered on the imagination of racial Blackness, Black Japanese peoples, and other mixed-race identities in Japan.

Kimberly Hassel's essay, "Black Japanese Storytelling as Praxis: Anti-Racist Digital Activism and Black Lives Matter in Japan," explores Black Japanese people's lived experiences of the friction between Blackness and Japaneseness as two identities around which fictions of absolute difference and incommensurability have been woven. Although fictions, their status as social reality significantly evidence themselves in the ideological investments many Japanese (as well as Black, white, and other peoples) have had in notions of Black Japaneseness as an improbable conjunction of exemplary difference. In her essay, Hassel historicizes Blackness in the Japanese context, including the ways it was reflected in mainstream media commentary during the 2020 BLM protests, and traces the early development and current moment of social media activism in Japan. Principally by drawing on interviews with Black Japanese interlocutors and by analyzing their digital activism, but also through a brief but compelling reckoning with her own positionality as a mixed-race ethnographer of Dominican descent, Hassel reflects insightfully on the possibilities for change in majority Japanese attitudes towards Black, Black Japanese, and other mixed-race peoples that these activists labor to bring into being.

In "From Black Brother to Black Lives Matter: Perception of Blackness in Viet Nam," Phuong Nguyen (an urban ethnographer) and Trang Nguyen (a cybersecurity engineer) consider the creation and reception of media spaces in Viet Nam inspired by BLM. Nguyen and Nguyen interviewed the members of three prominent youth activist groups stationed in Hanoi and Ho Chi Minh City: Viet Activism, Viets for Change, and Black Lives Matter Hanoi. The coauthors also collected some 898 comments left on the Black Lives Matter Hanoi Facebook page and identified thematic tropes across the comments by way of "web scraping techniques." When viewed through this methodological lens, the digital life of BLM in Viet Nam takes on a bifurcated, asymmetrical shape. Members of organizations such as Black Lives Matter Hanoi see BLM as a two-fold opportunity to "raise awareness and educate Vietnamese youths on the issues of systemic racism and police brutality," issues which begin abroad but—in the eyes of BLM Hanoi—have reverberating significance for contemporary Vietnamese life. Such affinity, however, is met with "a tsunami of negative responses," with some commenters arguing "that anti-Black racism has nothing to do with Vietnamese." In this regard, the response to BLM in Viet Nam is not unlike the response to BLM in the United States, and so Nguyen and Nguyen gesture toward the need for a transnational, unified approach to the study of anti-Blackness.

Addressing many of the questions raised by Nguyen and Nguyen, Chris Lundry shifts our attention to West Papua and PLM—Papuan Lives Matter, a movement inspired by BLM. Pace the arguments posed by the detractors of BLM Hanoi, the concerns of BLM are straightforwardly germane to West Papuans, for "West Papuans share many of the same grievances expressed by African Americans through BLM," including a history of slavery and its afterlife and violence at the hands of the police. Given the affinities in the activist grammars of BLM and PLM—in tandem with the contemporary turn toward richer transnational approaches in Asian Studies scholarship—one might assume that Asian Studies would have much to teach us about the intersecting histories of these two movements. As Lundry (citing Indonesian anthropologist Veronika Kusumaryati) notes, however, "the place of Black Melanesians in Asian Studies is still ambiguous, as they are not considered to be proper 'Asians.'" Thus, PLM has yet to receive the scholarly attention it merits. Lundry's corrective—which considers the dialogue about race in Indonesia opened by PLM with an eye toward how PLM is just as interested in the creation of Papuan futures as it is in Papuan pasts and presents—returns the volume to the idea with which it begins. Reminiscent of Carolyn Brown, Lundry, a Southeast Asianist, sees in PLM a provocation "for those of us who study Asia to more deeply interrogate how race and racism fit into our work and acknowledge the marginalized minorities who are frequently overlooked."

## Conclusion

The essays in this volume are part of long histories of interdiasporic engagement between the African and the Asian, between race and other modes of societal organization. The diversity of those encounters indexes a complex set of cartographies and temporalities through which Asia and Asian Studies emerge as dynamic and interpenetrated, and in which race is recognized for having been, and for remaining, undeniably critical. The movement for Black lives has impressed upon us that these cartographies and temporalities must be more fully and globally explored for the empirical, theoretical, methodological, pedagogical, restorative, and other possibilities they hold.

Weaving through the epistemologies of an Asian Studies fragmented by its circumventions of race have been, among other elements, the liminal epistemologies of Afro-Asian Studies, Black Internationalism, and studies of the Black Pacific. Emerging over the course of decades, born of the relationships—realized and aspirational—between subaltern scholars, artists, and activists across continents and diasporas, these epistemologies must be recognized as more than supplementary to, or excesses within, the body of Asian Studies as a predominantly white discipline. They suggest the possibility of a discipline in which they, institutionalized, do not so much bind the fissures running through "Asian Studies" now rendered as a happily inclusive domain of academic knowledge production. Rather, these epistemologies might become more fully acknowledged but still dynamic vectors of inquiry within Asian Studies, a field whose integrity, in every sense of the term, critically depends on the kinds of explicit engagement with race they evidence. And yet, although these epistemologies significantly inform the essays in *Who is the Asianist?*, their authors gesture, each in their own way given their diverse perspectives and training, toward still newer intellectual imaginaries in their reflections on how Black lives matter to Asian Studies.

## Notes

[1] Ruth Wilson Gilmore, *Golden Gulag,* 247.

[2] Laurie Collier Hillstrom, *Black Lives Matter: From a Moment to a Movement.*

[3] See Carly Jennings, "The Love Note that Launched a Movement," *ASA Footnotes* 48, no. 4 (2020), 15–16, https://www.asanet.org/sites/default/files/attach/footnotes/footnotes_july-august_2020.pdf.

[4] "About Black Lives Matter," https://blacklivesmatter.com/about, accessed May 5, 2022.

[5] Christopher Lebron, *The Making of Black Lives Matter: A Brief History of an Idea.*

[6] Andrew Jones and Nikhil Pal Singh, "Guest Editors Introduction," *positions: east asia cultures critique* 11, no. 1 (2003), 1–9.

[7] Shu-mei Shih, "Racializing Area Studies, Defetishizing China." *positions: asia critique* 27, no. 1 (2019), 45.

[8] Shih, "Racializing Area Studies," 58.

[9] Shih, "Racializing Area Studies," 57.

[10] Will Bridges, *Playing in the Shadows*; Marvin Sterling, *Babylon East*; Nitasha Sharma, *Hip Hop Desis*; Nitasha Sharma, *Hawai'i Is My Haven.*

[11] Vijay Prashad, *Everybody Was Kung-Fu Fighting.*

[12] Lisa Lowe, *The Intimacies of Four Continents.*

[13] Nathaniel Deutsch, "'The Asiatic Black Man': An African American Orientalism?" *Journal of Asian American Studies* 4, no. 3 (2001): 193–208.

[14] Crystal S. Anderson, *Beyond the Chinese Connection: Contemporary Afro-Asian Cultural Production*; Thorsten Botz-Bornstein, *The Cool-Kawaii: Afro-Japanese Aesthetics and New World Modernity*; Tamara Roberts, *Resounding Afro Asia: Interracial Music and the Politics of Collaboration*; Marvin Sterling, *Babylon East.*

[15] E. Taylor Atkins, *Blue Nippon*; Ian Condry, *Hip-Hop Japan: Rap and the Paths of Cultural Globalization*; Warren A. Stanislaus, "From Cool Japan to Cold Japan: Grime Cyborgs in Black Britain," in *Japan Forum* (February 9, 2022), https://doi.org/10.1080/09555803.2022.2033300.

[16] Marvin Sterling, *Babylon East*; Nitasha Tamar Sharma, *Hip Hop Desis*; Brent Clough, "Oceanic Reggae." In *Global Reggae*, edited by Carolyn Cooper (Kingston: University of the West Press, 2012), 265–283; and G. Solis, "The Black Pacific: Music and Racialization in Papua New Guinea and Australia." *Critical Sociology* 41, no. 2 (2015), 297–312.

[17] See Douglas Allen, "Antiwar Asian Scholars and the Vietnam/Indochina War." *Bulletin of Concerned Asian Scholars* 21, nos. 2–4 (1989): 112–135.

[18] Among several scholars who have written on the experiences of people of both East Asian and African ancestry are Michael C. Thornton, "Black, Japanese, and American: An Asian American Identity," *The Sum of Our Parts: Mixed-Heritage Asian Americans* 231 (2001): 93; Mitzi Uehara Carter, "Mixed Race Okinawans and Their Obscure In-Betweenness," *Journal of Intercultural Studies* 35, no. 6 (2014): 646–661; Ping Su, Yuejian Lin, and Mingying Zhou, "Identity Negotiation and Segregated Integration of African-Chinese Mixed-Race Children in Guangzhou, China," *Journal of Contemporary China* 31, no. 134 (2022): 186–201; and Ji-Hyun Ahn, "Rearticulating Black Mixed-Race in the Era of Globalization: Hines Ward and the Struggle for Koreanness in Contemporary South Korean Media," *Cultural Studies* 28, no. 3 (2014): 391–417.

[19] Robert Vitalis, *White World Order, Black Power Politics.*

[20] Robert Vitalis, *White World Order, Black Power Politics*, 21.

[21] Gerald Horne, *Race War: White Supremacy and the Japanese Attack on the British Empire*; Nahum Dimitri Chandler, "A Persistent Parallax: On the Writings of W. E. Burghardt Du Bois on Japan and China, 1936–1937," *CR: The New Centennial Review* 12, no. 1 (2012): 291–316.

[22] Marc S. Gallicchio, *The African American Encounter with Japan and China: Black Internationalism in Asia, 1895–1945*, 11.

[23] Selina Lai-Henderson, "Color Around the Globe: Langston Hughes and Black Internationalism in China." *MELUS* 45, no. 2 (2020): 88–107.

## Bibliography

Ahn, Ji-Hyun. "Rearticulating Black Mixed-Race in the Era of Globalization: Hines Ward and the Struggle for Koreanness in Contemporary South Korean Media." *Cultural Studies* 28, no. 3 (2014): 391–417.

Allen, Douglas. "Antiwar Asian Scholars and the Vietnam/Indochina War." *Bulletin of Concerned Asian Scholars* 21, nos. 2-4 (1989): 112–135.

Anderson, Crystal S. *Beyond the Chinese Connection: Contemporary Afro-Asian Cultural Production* (Jackson: University Press of Mississippi, 2013).

Atkins, E. Taylor. *Blue Nippon* (Durham: Duke University Press, 2001).

Botz-Bornstein, Thorsten. *The Cool-Kawaii: Afro-Japanese Aesthetics and New World Modernity* (Washington, DC: Lexington Books, 2012).

Bridges, Will. *Playing in the Shadows: Fictions of Race and Blackness in Postwar Japanese Literature* (Ann Arbor: University of Michigan Press, 2020).

Carter, Mitzi Uehara. "Mixed Race Okinawans and Their Obscure In-Betweenness." *Journal of Intercultural Studies* 35, no. 6 (2014): 646–661.

Chandler, Nahum Dimitri. "A Persistent Parallax: On the Writings of W. E. Burghardt Du Bois on Japan and China, 1936-1937." *CR: The New Centennial Review* 12, no. 1 (2012): 291–316.

Clough, Brent. "Oceanic Reggae." In *Global Reggae*, edited by Carolyn Cooper (Kingston: University of the West Press, 2012), 265–283.

Collier Hillstrom, Laurie. *Black Lives Matter: From a Moment to a Movement* (Santa Barbara: Greenwood Press, 2018).

Condry, Ian. *Hip-Hop Japan: Rap and the Paths of Cultural Globalization* (Durham: Duke University Press, 2006).

Deutsch, Nathaniel. "'The Asiatic Black Man': An African American Orientalism?" *Journal of Asian American Studies* 4, no. 3 (2001): 193–208.

Gallicchio, Marc S. *The African American Encounter with Japan and China: Black Internationalism in Asia, 1895-1945* (Chapel Hill: University of North Carolina Press, 2000).

Gilmore, Ruth Wilson. *Golden Gulag: Prisons, Surplus, Crisis, and Opposition in Globalizing California* (Berkeley: University of California Press, 2007).

Horne, Gerald. *Race War: White Supremacy and the Japanese Attack on the British Empire* (New York: NYU Press, 2004).

Lai-Henderson, Selina. "Color Around the Globe: Langston Hughes and Black Internationalism in China." *MELUS* 45, no. 2 (2020): 88–107.

Lowe, Lisa. *The Intimacies of Four Continents* (Durham: Duke University Press, 2015).

Prashad, Vijay. *Everybody Was Kung Fu Fighting: Afro-Asian Connections and the Myth of Cultural Purity* (Boston: Beacon Press, 2002).

Roberts, Tamara. *Resounding Afro Asia: Interracial Music and the Politics of Collaboration* (Oxford: Oxford University Press, 2016).

Sharma, Nitasha Tamar. *Hip Hop Desis: South Asian Americans, Blackness, and a Global Race Consciousness* (Durham: Duke University Press, 2010).

Sharma, Nitasha Tamar. *Hawai'i Is My Haven: Race and Indigeneity in the Black Pacific* (Durham: Duke University Press, 2021).

Solis, G. "The Black Pacific: Music and Racialization in Papua New Guinea and Australia." *Critical Sociology* 41, no. 2 (2015), 297–312.

Stanislaus, Warren A. "From Cool Japan to Cold Japan: Grime Cyborgs in Black Britain." In *Japan Forum* (February 9, 2022), https://doi.org/10.1080/095558 03.2022.2033300.

Sterling, Marvin. *Babylon East: Performing Dancehall, Roots Reggae and Rastafari in Japan.* (Durham: Duke University Press, 2010).

Su, Ping, Yuejian Lin, and Mingying Zhou. "Identity Negotiation and Segregated Integration of African-Chinese Mixed-Race Children in Guangzhou, China." *Journal of Contemporary China* 31, no. 134 (2022): 186–201.

Thornton, Michael C. "Black, Japanese, and American: An Asian American Identity." *The Sum of Our Parts: Mixed-Heritage Asian Americans* 231 (2001): 93.

Vitalis, Robert. *White World Order, Black Power Politics* (Ithaca: Cornell University Press, 2016).

# 1

# WHO IS A SOUTH ASIANIST?

## A CONVERSATION ON POSITIONALITY

### Hoda Bandeh-Ahmadi and
### Isabel Huacuja Alonso

Who is a South Asianist? To answer this question, this essay traces the personal and professional experiences of two women scholars of South Asia in academia in the United States: a Chicana/Mexican American media historian and an Iranian American anthropologist. Isabel Huacuja Alonso's book project traces the history of radio broadcasting in India and Pakistan, focusing on the late colonial and early post-independence era. Hoda Bandeh-Ahmadi studies academic institutions, and her current book project is an ethnography of three anthropology and sociology departments in Delhi and Lucknow, India. The two scholars met in 2010 and have remained in contact since.

Both Bandeh-Ahmadi and Huacuja Alonso consciously resisted pressure to become experts of what are perceived to be their "own cultures" and bonded over their shared experiences in South Asia-related academia. Their interest in the region stemmed in part from a simple desire to learn about cultures, histories, and places beyond what was familiar to them—a scholarly pursuit still, in many ways, conceived as the domain of white students and scholars.

In this essay, the authors propose that their shared experiences shed light on how expectations about who is, who can be, or who should be a scholar of South Asia are enforced and reproduced, and they reveal the ways these expectations shape the creation of knowledge in South Asian Studies in US-based academia. The essay is structured as a conversation or a co-interview revolving around four main questions, and it stems from many informal discussions that have taken place over more than a decade of friendship and scholarly collaboration. The authors hope that the essay's conversational format not only creates a space for frank consideration of personal experiences but also decenters the very idea of scholarly authority in academia, embracing instead a more collaborative model.[1] In the interest of space, they focus specifically on their experiences and on issues of positionality in US-based, South Asia-related academia and, as a result, they must inevitably leave out other important issues. They hope that what they discuss here will also be relevant to other specialties and places and will open up further conversations within and beyond Asian Studies.

## Tell me about your research and how you became a scholar of South Asia

HODA BANDEH-AHMADI (HBA): My research, broadly, is on institutions, particularly academic and scientific institutions. I'm interested in their cultures, how and what they reproduce, and how power operates and is experienced in them. My first book project is an ethnography of anthropologists and sociologists in North Indian universities, focusing on several generations of scholars in three departments from 1947 to 2015. I found that what I call scholars' "intellectual kinship"—understandings of who one's kin are in an academic context (like academic lineages)—molds academic cultures and worlds in important ways, shaping interpersonal relationships, hiring practices, disciplinary boundaries, and international academic hierarchies.

I didn't enter grad school planning to become an expert in South Asia as a region. Instead, I eventually chose to work in India because of my research questions, which were then framed around how anthropologists do anthropology, how ethnographic knowledge is made. Some of what influenced these research questions was that I was coming out of an undergraduate anthropology program at Berkeley where department centennial celebrations had me thinking about the history of anthropology. Discussions about the militarization of anthropology after 9/11 helped me connect that history to the present. I was surrounded by faculty who were investigating questions about power, controlling processes, and the anthropology and ethnography of science. I also had a work-study job in my department, so I was seeing "behind the scenes" of academic life. Finally, I was troubled by some narratives of the history of anthropology as a march of progress that began with ancient Greek philosophy.

I wanted to help challenge Euro-American-centric views of the history of anthropology and to combine the anthropology of science with the history of anthropology so that we could ethnographically study the present of anthropology as well as its past. In anthropology, though ethnography is "our thing," it's extremely rare to ethnographically study ethnographers. Anyone considering this focus gets told that they're committing "academic suicide," something I've personally heard many times. Because these were unusual interests, for a long time, I felt frustrated that I didn't know what I wanted to study, but in reality, I did know; I just didn't know if it would be considered acceptable. I finally talked to my undergraduate mentor, Laura Nader, and she told me: you know what you're interested in, write that. That was how I got up the courage to propose this project to graduate programs.

In graduate school, I realized that I was unusual in not already having a specialization in a particular area or region. I was unsure what part of the world I wanted to study. I think many of my colleagues had traveled much more than I had, or had spent some time in a place, or had some personal connection to it, and made that part of their identity to the point of introducing themselves first as an area"-ist." I didn't come from a family where we were able to travel much and had barely been outside the US (which, of course, also relates to questions of class). That made the idea of traveling someplace alone where I didn't know anyone all the more daunting.

Some people suggested I should work in Iran because they imagined it would be "easier" for me. It's also a place most Americans can't access to study. Though I've never been there, I am fluent in Farsi, so perhaps there was a bit of an underlying sense of a "waste" of an opportunity for some. But I was also aware that the task of representing Iran to US academics would be a fraught one. When something is your area of expertise, you have to respond intellectually to scholarship about it, but there was a lot written about the Middle East and Islam that I found offensive, orientalizing, and personally upsetting just to *read*. I value the work people do to counter that, but I wasn't sure I wanted to take on that responsibility. It wasn't what was motivating me as a scholar, and I thought people would just use the fact of my "subjective" position to dismiss anything I might say anyway. I also couldn't imagine going to Iran, meeting my extended family there for the first time, and managing the emotions and politics of that all while simultaneously attempting international ethnographic fieldwork in a country that hasn't had regular diplomatic relations with the US since before I was born. Nothing about that seemed "easier" to me.

In the context of a discipline that has historically emphasized studying the unfamiliar, I also saw the suggestion that I work in Iran, not for intellectual reasons but *because* my family is from there, as an insult that both pushed me into a "native" role and denied me the same presumption granted to white colleagues that my choice of field site be intellectual rather than familial. I wanted and felt I deserved a chance to learn *how to learn* about an unfamiliar place, culture, and language as much as anyone else. I took the decision of field sites very seriously, recognizing it as a huge personal, emotional, and intellectual commitment. I knew how I felt about some scholarship about Iran or Muslims that hadn't taken that commitment as seriously as I would have liked, and I didn't want to make other people feel that way. But I also respected how challenging that would be.

I initially wanted to do a comparative project in multiple countries, but that wasn't feasible for a variety of reasons. I considered places that have larger, institutionalized traditions of anthropology like Mexico, Brazil, Russia, South Africa, China, and, of course, India. An advantage of working in India was that in addition to having large, institutionalized traditions of anthropology and sociology, it also has English-language scholarship. Practically, it was easier for me to jump in and think about scholarship and work. Intellectually, that also made moot those arguments that use language barriers to explain Euro-American scholarship's tendency to not engage with work from outside its own institutional networks.

Ultimately, I chose to work in India because it was a particularly relevant and interesting place to address the research questions I had. About a year into graduate school, I was leaning toward India enough that I took a preliminary trip there—they had some funding for preliminary fieldwork trips in my department.

**ISABEL HUACUJA ALONSO (IHA):** That's when we met.

**HBA:** Yeah, that's right! During my first trip to India in Summer 2010. I visited different cities and tried to figure out if this was a place where I could do fieldwork. By the end of the summer, I had decided that, yes, I was going to work in India. And that is how I came to study South Asia. So, now, Isa, tell me about your research project and how you became a scholar of South Asia.

**IHA:** My current book project is a history of radio broadcasting in Hindi and Urdu in North India and Pakistan. I study how radio contributed to the making and unmaking of the Indo-Pak border (1920–1980). But more broadly, I am interested in the role of the media, and specifically sound media, in the making and unmaking of borders in South Asia. My research combines archival work (including written and aural sources) and oral history, namely interviews with retired broadcasters and radio listeners. Trained as a historian, I am committed to the idea that the study of media, and specifically mediated sound, is not ancillary to our understanding of past societies but fundamental, and that a perspective from South Asia, one of the world's most prolific media-producing regions, is critical.

Now, in regards to how I came to study South Asia. In college, I found it very fulfilling to learn about places different from my own. I grew up on the US-

Mexico border in Laredo, Texas, and Nuevo Laredo, Tamaulipas. I visited my extended family in Mexico City regularly, but other than that, the only world I really knew before attending college was the US-Mexico border. So it felt like a thrilling opportunity to be able to learn about places so different from where I had grown up. I became very interested in learning about South Asia after I wrote a paper on Pakistan in a history class about US-foreign relations and 9/11. I remember writing to the professor late at night to ask if I could change the topic of my paper from a project on US foreign policy toward Latin America to a project on Pakistan. He responded, "Sure." Also, one of my closest mentors in college, a sociologist, was Indian, and she went out of her way to make me feel comfortable in her classes, and she became a source of support in a majority white university. Her long-standing mentorship certainly increased my interest in the region.

When I decided to return to graduate school, I planned to pursue a comparative project between South Asia and Latin America. I was unsure of the discipline at the time. I had completed a BA in economics but had liked and had been much more successful in my history and humanities classes. A mentor recommended that in preparation for a PhD program, I should first get a solid background in South Asia and learn a South Asian language. This would also give me time to figure out what discipline might best allow me to combine my technical training and humanistic interests. So I applied for an MA in South Asian Studies at the University of Texas at Austin and was fortunate to earn a scholarship. There, I fully dedicated myself to learning Hindi and Urdu, which I loved, and I traveled frequently to India for language courses. I gradually dropped the idea of doing something comparative and decided to focus solely on South Asia. Also, while pursuing my MA, my interest in history, particularly twentieth-century South Asian history, grew, and I gave up plans of pursuing disciplines closer to my BA training in economics.

**HBA:** I find it interesting that we both first intended to pursue "comparative" projects and later settled on South Asia. I suspect that by virtue of our backgrounds, we had sort of a built-in comparative perspective in which our questions and thinking were naturally influenced by an awareness of more cultural contexts than just American and South Asian ones. It's unfortunately easy for many of our colleagues to forget that their projects are also comparative. It's impossible for anyone to avoid making implicit comparisons to what is known or familiar. Our comparisons are more likely to be *marked* as comparative because they're informed by cultural knowledge of more than one place that is foreign to some audiences. On the other hand, comparisons are less visible for people who belong to dominant or *unmarked* cultural groups and whose imagined audience is people like themselves.

**IHA:** That is so true. That doesn't mean that their projects are not comparative; it means that their comparisons are less likely to be interrogated. I think there is great value in having comparative perspectives but even more so in being aware of why and how we make comparisons.[2]

A number of times in graduate school, my professors and classmates asked, often indirectly, why I was not working on something more closely related to my background, where I would automatically have some advantage (fluency in Spanish, lived experience, and family connections). I always said I did not want to but couldn't explain why. Now, with some distance, I see I was then dealing with trauma related to my own personal experiences, and having to talk about my own identity and take on a "native informant role," as minoritized academics are expected to do, made me uncomfortable. It would not have been "easy," as you say about studying Iran. In my last year of high school, I had moved back with my mother to the Mexican side of the border after my parents divorced. For a period of time, I had to cross the border every day, and my immigration status and financial situation in the US became precarious. Amid that personal life crisis, I was accepted to Cornell University and was offered financial aid as a Mexican citizen, which was the only way I was able to attend college in the US. I left my mother to go to college, but my departure and her precarious situation deeply affected her physical and mental health. While in graduate school, I was still processing all those things, but I did not want to do so publicly. It doesn't mean that I wasn't dealing with difficult issues in my own research and study of South Asia, but like you, I wanted to carve a different path for myself. I found learning a new language especially fulfilling and even liberating during that difficult time of my life.

**HBA:** It seems we both came to South Asian Studies because we did not want to be pigeonholed into representing a "native" voice or writing about ourselves. Other people's ideas of what was "easy" or "advantageous" didn't necessarily fit our experience. We also both genuinely enjoy learning new languages and about different places, and we did not want that to be denied us.

## How have your identity and background shaped your research?

HBA: I think growing up with parents who immigrated from Iran made me more likely to develop the concept of intellectual kinship—to be able to "see" it and take it seriously. I want to be careful not to reinforce stereotypes of the Middle East or India as more "traditional," especially because forms of intellectual kinship exist everywhere. But it was something I'd been exposed to in different ways, that I'd occasionally heard referenced more openly and without the stigma that exists in many academic contexts, like ideas that one has moral obligations to one's teachers that are similar to what one owes one's parents. A second influence I've come to recognize in retrospect is growing up in a college town as the daughter of research staff at a major research university. I was surrounded every day by the hierarchies and inequalities that are taken for granted in communities around universities. Experiencing that certainly made me more sensitive to seeing and addressing how some people's voices and intellectual contributions are not valued.

**IHA:** It's taken me nearly a decade to understand the connections between my work and my background, although it seems rather obvious now. The experience of growing up on the Mexican border made me very attuned to how borders could be simultaneously rigid and porous. I think that was why I was always so committed to studying both India and Pakistan and both Hindi and Urdu, despite being advised repeatedly against "trying to do too much" in a single dissertation. In my research (both archival and ethnographic), I paid close attention to what the ethnomusicologist Alex Chávez calls "sounds of crossing," or the ways ordinary people push and pull at the "real and metaphorical edges of the nation-state."[3] Of course, that ability to travel back and forth from India to Pakistan was made possible by my foreign passport, a privilege so often denied to South Asian-origin scholars. I am also poignantly aware that being based in the Global North—and the access to resources that entails—made it possible for me to travel for research to India. (The difficulties that scholars based in the Global South face, the ways these restrict research topics, and how that is related to a longer history of imperialism are hugely important issues that we cannot do justice to in this brief essay.) But what I wish to emphasize here is that the sensibility and commitment to understanding border-making was one that undeniably stemmed from my own personal experience. Yet, as I said earlier, as obvious as it might seem now, I did not really realize this connection until after I completed my dissertation. It was not something that I could explain in grant applications that would be immediately valued as a strength.

As you know, I became poignantly aware of the connections between my research and my background while teaching South Asian history at California State University, San Bernardino, where the majority of the students are Latinos and where many had similar border experiences to mine. I hope seeing me as a professor of South Asia was empowering to them. Frankly, though, I benefited the most. I owe much of my recent growth as a scholar to Cal State students; being in the classroom with them enabled me to see value in my positionality.

**HBA:** Absolutely. This reminds me of how crucial mentorship is to counteracting challenges like the ones we faced. In both of our stories, having even a couple of mentors who supported and encouraged our interests made an enormous difference. Our stories are also connected in that our positions bring important contributions to our field of study, but because we were not fulfilling expected roles (to become experts of what is perceived as "our culture"), it was very hard for others (and sometimes for ourselves as well) to see our possible contributions and to find value in our work early on.

**IHA:** I also want to add that finding value in my own positionality has also allowed me to respond to other types of queries. For example, I am often asked by family, friends, and academic colleagues alike why I "abandoned" my identity— as a Latina, Chicana, and fronteriza—to study South Asia. (Sometimes, this is phrased more aggressively, as betrayal—that I somehow betrayed my community or that I am not proud of "my roots.") I get that from my parents and family a great deal, but also from Chicanx/Latinx and Latin American academics. In the past, I had no answer to that. I now respond that I have not abandoned anything, and that I couldn't, because whether I like it or not, I will bring my identity and background to my scholarly work.

### Describe some of the barriers that you have faced in the field as a non-South Asian but minoritized scholar in South Asian Studies

**IHA:** First, I am now speaking from a position of considerable privilege, as an assistant professor at Columbia University. But when you and I started our conversations on this topic, I certainly wasn't. It took a long time for my research to receive recognition. Given that I now have access to a platform of sorts, I think it's more important than ever that I talk openly about the challenges I faced. And the whole thing about waiting until I am tenured: well, I am not going to do that because that mentality is precisely what hinders much needed changes in academia.

I am not sure where to start, but let's begin with graduate school. The questions I would ask in classes, the comparisons I wanted to make, often seemed odd in a classroom with only white and South Asian students. Once, I overheard a classmate in a seminar calling me "crazy" because I had said that we should consider the state of indigenous languages in Latin America when studying language politics in South Asia. I also felt a difference in the ways some faculty treated me. These were subtle things, but they had significant consequences. To give you an example, I would gather courage to approach a famous professor at a conference, and they'd say, "You have an accent, where are you from?" and start telling me about their trip to Teotihuacan or about middle-school Spanish classes. Here was a missed opportunity for connection and conversation about research. So much academic networking happens through the sense of connection from shared experiences and backgrounds, and I didn't have much of that.

Even after finishing my PhD, these types of interactions continued. For example, during a campus visit, I was asked if I planned to pursue research on Latinx things later since the city where the university is located had a large Latinx community (and particularly Mexican American/Chicanx). I was being interviewed for a South Asia history job and was taken aback. I responded that I had other ways of connecting with Latinx students and did not need to change my research trajectory. The professor's facial expressions showed he felt my response was defensive. Maybe it was because it was a terrible question. I didn't get that job, and I don't know if that exchange had anything to do with it. But my point here is that I had to constantly explain myself and my presence in South Asian Studies in ways that my white and South Asian-origin classmates and colleagues did not have to do.

Conversations with you and other minoritized, non-South-Asian-origin scholars of South Asia have allowed me to see my experience as part of a pattern. A dear friend of mine who is also Latinx and studies South Asia has similar experiences. He noted that when he mentions studying Indian history, people would ask him again and again, "Indians [i.e., native peoples] from Latin America, right?" He would then have to spend the next half hour justifying his presence in South Asia-related academia.

**IIBA:** That's happened to me too. After I'd completed three years of fieldwork in India, a well-known anthropologist asked me about my fieldwork in Dearborn (which is known for its large Arab American and Muslim communities), assuming that I must have studied other Muslims.

**IHA:** Yes. This might all seem innocuous, but subtle expectations about who is, who can be, or who should be a scholar of South Asia can make or break a career. Another friend, a climate change scientist who specializes in India and is neither white nor South Asian, had two (white) senior professors and research collaborators who forced her to include Indian scholars as coauthors even though they had not contributed to the research or writing of the article. When she pointed out the tokenism, these (white, not Indian) senior professors retaliated and almost successfully kept her from graduating with her PhD. Over and over, we have heard from our non-white, non-South-Asian-origin friends who study South Asia that their ability to speak for and about South Asia has been questioned more than that of colleagues who do not share that positionality. Not being taken seriously as a scholar can have major consequences.

As you know, I had a particularly awful experience that almost derailed my career. The last year of my PhD, two academics, both white and with secure tenured positions at an elite university, had access to my research by means of their institutional position. They appropriated key ideas from my work, publishing them later as their own without citing me or giving me any credit. It was a difficult situation that affected me emotionally and professionally in more ways than I can describe here. In reflecting on why and how that happened, though I can never know for certain, I believe these academics might have treated me differently had I been white and male or if something in my background signaled that I would later be in a position of power. Intersectionality is key here; one can't parse out the roles of gender, racialization, ethnicity, class, and so on, as these all work together. But I also think they would have been more conscious and careful if I had been South Asian. These scholars teach and research South Asia and deliberately perform allyship with South Asian colleagues. Robbing a South Asian colleague, whose "culture" they are studying, would have seriously endangered their "ally" image. I have come to realize that these scholars saw me as an easier target because I ultimately did not fulfill expectations of who is, who can be, or who should be a scholar of South Asia. I recognize that some of this might have been unconscious, but that doesn't make it any less damaging to me.

Now, I want to make it clear that all minoritized scholars, including those who take on representative roles in academia, face difficulties, as do white scholars in vulnerable positions. At the same time, being a minoritized scholar who studies what is perceived as their "own" culture can provide some limited protection in academic circles in the US. Presently, there is at least an acknowledgment that we must listen to people's lived experiences and that there should be a place in academia for these voices, however restricted this space is. (I fully recognize that comes at the cost of often being the target of people and institutions that are resistant to change.)

Second, being a minoritized scholar who takes on a representative role often gives one access to a network of people who can understand one's struggles, even if it is a limited network. It can be isolating to navigate academia without such a network, even when one has sympathetic and caring mentors. One of the issues I faced during and after the appropriation issue is that I did not have a strong network that could help me make sense of the specific ways the dynamics of race and ethnicity played into my experience. In particular, I was surprised at the unwillingness of some of my South Asian classmates and some colleagues, who themselves had experienced discrimination in academia, to even try to see racial and power politics at work in my case. But I also struggled to get support from Latinx/Chicanx colleagues as well. After much hesitation, I finally gathered the courage to approach the Latino caucus of a professional society. Initially appalled by my experience, they promised to help, but they ultimately recommended I seek the advice of the Asian group instead, which left me feeling terribly alone. Thankfully, I was able to eventually build a network of support and a community through meeting people like you, but it took a tremendous amount of work to do so.

In any case, the point I wish to make here is that minoritized scholars without access to the two things I mentioned—(1) some existing, even if reluctant, acceptance of the necessity of including your voice and (2) access to a network of support of people with similar life experiences—can become even more vulnerable to all kinds of abuses. This can also have repercussions in the classroom, on the job market, during the tenure process, and for the review process of academic publications. I could detail some equally difficult experiences with review processes where some of the same patterns seem to have been at work, and the core issue was that scholars who could not (or did not wish to) see me as a scholar of South Asia put me under a greater level of scrutiny, and their opinions were ultimately given more weight than they merited.

**HBA:** Like you, I also encountered gatekeeping as a graduate student. Though anyone may encounter gatekeeping, gatekeeping is also central to reproducing social inequalities like gender and class hierarchies or white supremacy because it's a tool for people to set themselves apart as superior, or, as Toni Morrison put it, for people to "only be tall because somebody is on their knees."[4] I think at least some of the gatekeeping I encountered was influenced by the fact that I am an Iranian American woman. For example, one way I experienced gatekeeping was having my choice of field site turned into a debate on which faculty (some of whom barely knew me) could opine. I was actually told that some faculty did not believe I was doing what I really *wanted* to do and questioned whether I was "committed" to working in India. This came after I'd had to defend my decision of not wanting to work in Iran or the Middle East—even after I'd spent a summer in India developing relationships and learning to navigate a new place alone, enrolling in South Asian Studies courses, studying Hindi, and after personally finally committing to a field site (something I'd been considering for over a decade of studying anthropology). I find it hard to imagine that I would have had my legitimacy as a *student* (not yet then even a "scholar") of South Asian Studies thrown into question, or that I would have been forced to defend my commitment to doing fieldwork in India in these ways, had I been white and male or if I had been filling a "native" South Asian representative role.

I also faced challenges in applying for fieldwork grants. On one grant, a reviewer classified me as a "native speaker," refusing to award points for learning a non-native language for fieldwork (for me, Hindi) because of my native fluency in Farsi. With another grant, my application was sent to an Indian reviewer I'd met whose institutional position created a conflict of interest. Interestingly, some of the reviewer's comments seemed to be trying to put me in my place while positioning themself as having more appropriate area knowledge. For example, they asserted that I hadn't needed to study Hindi because they believed (incorrectly) that all the teaching in the departments I studied was done in English. Like you, I had to put a lot of energy into making sense of this experience with little information. I think there was a reason the granting agency knew of this person and reached out to them; they were part of American academic networks and, even if in restricting ways, benefited and gained legitimacy through representing India and Indian academics to those networks. Perhaps they unconsciously saw a non-white person from the US writing about Indian academia as a threat to their "territory." I can't ever really know, but I think it's important to recognize that, regardless of positionality, even the best-meaning of us can fall into structures that encourage gatekeeping.

When you're just entering a field as a student, you look to senior scholars for guidance, for help making this massive body of scholarship feel more approachable, and for a social space where you can safely learn from mistakes as you attempt to engage with ongoing discussions your own way. If you instead find the opposite when you're in such a vulnerable position, it can be truly terrorizing. I was fortunate to have had a couple mentors who were there for me through this. Even now, I worry about talking about these kinds of experiences. The professional power dynamics are difficult to navigate; there's the fear of stigma, of being labeled a problem, the fear that some may shun you to preserve relationships with more powerful colleagues or that others may take any sign of vulnerability as an opportunity to pounce. All of this greatly exacerbates the problem, making people experiencing it feel isolated and alienated from the academic community. Like you, it's taken conversations like ours for me to be able to see these kinds of experiences as part of broader patterns. If we don't make them visible, it's too easy to internalize negative messages or, even worse, one day participate in perpetuating the systems or processes behind gatekeeping ourselves.

I see the risk of becoming complicit as serious because, as in your case, I think some of how I was perceived was unconscious. For example, I might have been read as less "committed" to working in South Asia for a number of reasons that were influenced by my background: I approached working in India out of an intellectual interest more akin to how anthropologists design projects in the US. In some ways, I rejected regional classifications (like "South Asia") inherited from Cold War foreign policy, which are now also social groups with their own academic cultures. While I'm certainly interested in India, my interest was and is less about understanding India as an object in itself than about understanding and thinking about anthropology and institutions through research *in* India. Finally, the fact that I felt and expressed humility about the intellectual and personal commitment that I was taking on by studying India made people think I was not serious, in ways that are probably also gendered.

**IHA:** Yes, I think that our extra caution in approaching our field of study, which stems from knowing what it feels like to be "studied" and how hurtful it can be when that work is not thorough, is often interpreted as lack of competence and confidence. US academia, I feel, fetishizes confidence, authoritative voices, and self-promotion, but that confidence often comes from a lack of self-awareness. It is, frankly, overrated.

HBA: And like you've said, these perceptions have serious impacts. That issue of how I'm read is very much related to how my scholarship is read as well because it's also about my position relative to an audience that is, at least in the US, still largely assumed to be white American or sometimes South Asian-origin academics. That means that you and I may have to work harder to show that our findings are important or interesting because what we notice and find in our research is less likely to be framed around the questions that those audiences already recognize as the important ones. It also makes it harder to participate in the kind of "reflexivity" that anthropologists commonly include in ethnographic writing. The reflections on the impact of positionality in the field that white anthropologists might share in their writing are something they assume most of their audience will understand, if not identify with and at least be interested in. If I reveal information about what it meant to be a practicing Muslim during fieldwork, I can't assume an understanding audience at all due to the Islamophobia I've experienced in both India and the US. I know colleagues with other identities, like Dalit ethnographers, also struggle with the greater vulnerability involved in revealing sometimes stigmatized information.[5]

## What do you think your own personal experience reveals about who can or should be a scholar of South Asia in US academia and about the study of South Asia in US academia as a whole?

HBA: Well, I think our experiences make visible unacknowledged but deep-seated expectations about who can or should be a scholar of South Asia. That it is often difficult for colleagues to make sense of us and others in similar positions as scholars studying South Asia shows how, for many in US academia, knowledge of the region continues to be imagined as stemming from two kinds of scholars: an unmarked white (usually male) scholar and a "native" scholar. In this imagination, whereas the white scholar's authority derives from his supposed objectivity from being unmarked, the "native" scholar's authority derives from his proximity and intimate relationship to the region. Although these assumptions are often implicit and, as we noted earlier, never fully uniform, the truth is that they continue to profoundly shape this and other fields of research.

IHA: Exactly. Also, the point is not really whether South Asian scholars embrace a "native" scholar identity or whether white scholars consciously present themselves as unmarked or "objective." Many actively reject these categorizations. The point, however, is that there is an implicit and often unacknowledged benefit in conforming to these expectations, just as there are disadvantages to not conforming to it.

It is also important to note that this dichotomy of the "native" scholar versus the "white"/unmarked scholar ultimately hurts all minoritized scholars, including South Asian scholars, as it centers whiteness (imagined as European and/or American) and ensures whiteness unconsciously remains the point of comparison, departure, and/or arrival in scholarly research. The dichotomy in its own way also ultimately upholds white supremacy. I think the struggles that you and I faced stemmed, at least in part, from a refusal, sometimes conscious and sometimes unconscious, to center whiteness. When that student in that graduate class called me "crazy," he was calling me crazy for demanding that Anglo-American world to which he belonged, but which he saw as the unmarked "norm," not be the implicit place of comparison.

Moreover, the dichotomy of the "white" versus the "native" scholar has also had other consequences in South Asian Studies that might not be immediately obvious. It is, for example, an open secret that even though caste is a well-studied topic, the representation of Dalit and lower-caste scholars in USA-based South Asian Studies is abysmal. South Asian academics in the USA are overwhelmingly upper caste. I have long wondered how it is possible that the very field that produced "subaltern studies" has such poor representation of low-caste scholars and, more importantly, how it is possible we have had so few conversations about it. While Dalit scholars have long noted the caste politics of South Asia-related academia, it is only recently that upper-caste scholars have felt an urgency to address the issue directly and to openly talk about their positionality and caste privilege. There are many dynamics at play here, including a much longer history of systemic erasure and oppression of Dalit intellectuals in South Asia itself that we cannot possibly adequately address here. But in all truth, I think this dichotomy of unmarked/"white" scholar versus "native" scholar has distracted us from (and enabled) pervasive inequalities in this field of study, preventing tougher discussions (and reckonings) with positionality. This silence can only continue with the complicity of South Asia scholars of all backgrounds.

**HBA:** That's true. I think often upper-caste South Asian scholars in the US have helped preserve, even if unconsciously, the silence around caste because it protects their authority to represent a "native" voice. Similarly, white scholars may be reluctant to alienate some upper-caste, South Asian-origin colleagues whose "native" authority they rely on for legitimation as regional experts.

We've got our work cut out for us. I can only hope that this short conversation will challenge us all to reimagine what a colleague looks like, what value we think people of different positions can bring to our fields, to what extent our beliefs about whether particular ideas are "important" have more to do with *who* they're important to, and whether our idea of who a "South Asianist" is, is defined more by social in-groups than scholarship. While there may not be easy solutions to many of the issues we've mentioned, I think we can begin to see some possible directions and lessons.

First, we've both learned that having conversations with scholars who also don't fit into imagined or expected roles is a crucial way to counter social processes that isolate us and push non-South-Asian-origin scholars of color away from research in South Asia. I know that for me, conversations like this one have been very helpful to see that experiences that felt intensely personal were in some ways not even really about me. Building community—conversations with you, but also with many others—is what has enabled us to collaboratively develop the realizations and ideas we've shared here. Second, perhaps the greatest challenge that we faced in putting together this essay was how to not make our conversation about individuals but about larger issues at stake. That made us intensely aware that one of the greatest challenges facing academia right now is how to create a space for honest discussion that can create change. We hope that this essay is a small step toward that. Finally, as I mentioned earlier, complicity is an issue that greatly concerns us, and it is a central theme in this essay. It is, after all, much easier to see the patterns of power at work when you are at the receiving end; the trick is to be able to take those lessons with you when you're in a different structural position. It is for this reason that our goal should be to make that space for conversation and for conflict and discomfort but also a space for self-reflection.

## Notes

1. So in some ways, what we are doing here is lending "an ear," or better yet, a "feminist ear," to borrow Sara Ahmed's words, to each other. Ahmed, *Complaint!*, 3.

2. Laura Nader's work on comparative consciousness is particularly relevant here. Nader, "Comparative Consciousness."

3. Chávez, *Sounds of Crossing*, 33.

4. Morrison, *Charlie Rose*.

5. There is, of course, so much to discuss about our experiences and positionality during fieldwork, but these complex issues are difficult to meaningfully address in this conversation about US-based academia.

## Bibliography

Ahmed, Sara. *Complaint!* Durham: Duke University Press, 2021.

Chávez, Alex. *Sounds of Crossing: Music, Migration, and the Aural Poetics of Huapango Arribeño.* Durham: Duke University Press, 2017.

Morrison, Toni. Interview. By Charlie Rose. *Charlie Rose.* Aired May 7, 1993. Video, 55:11.

Nader, Laura. "Comparative Consciousness." In *Assessing Cultural Anthropology,* edited by Robert Borofsky, 84–96. New York: McGraw-Hill, 1994.

# 2

# A DIFFERENT WAY OF SEEING

## REFLECTIONS OF A BLACK ASIANIST

## Carolyn T. Brown

My career as a "*Black* Asianist" is long and intermittent. Sometimes being African American mattered, sometimes it did not, and at times it probably mattered to others more than it mattered to me. Such are the complexities and nuances of being in a field where one fundamental element of your being—your race—is rare and unexpected. As is the case with every human being in our time, at each moment in my life's journey, I have been embedded in a national and international social context way beyond my own; have carried my accumulating biography into every situation; have perceived the world and been perceived through the lenses of group identity (race, class, gender, and so forth); and—this may be somewhat unique to me—have at times been confused, and often amazed, by how instances of individual and group behavior in real-life exhibit archetypal patterns that I first discovered in Chinese literature and that seem to transcend culture. Let me explain.[1]

## A Moment in Time: The Context

My "career" as a Black Asianist began in the early days of the field. When I took my first course in Chinese studies at Cornell University, most of my professors had lived in China prior to the 1949 revolution. One of them, Harold Shadick, regaled me one evening with stories of playing strip poker with Zhou Enlai. When, as undergraduates, we signed up for Chinese language classes, we were given reel-to-reel tape recorders so heavy that I could hardly carry mine to my dorm room. The Chinese program was, I believe, funded by the 1958 National Defense Education Act (NDEA), which among other things, supported studies in "lesser-known languages." At that time, understanding other nations on their own terms, via their language, history, and culture, was considered essential to national security. Studies of China, for whatever purpose, were part of this larger enterprise known as area studies. To this day, I am convinced that if US policymakers and businesspeople had absorbed the lessons of Chinese history, they would never have imagined that the internet would democratize China or that China would easily accept the current international economic system without severe pushback. Thus, for example, both the government's admiration for the First Emperor Qin Shi Huangdi (259–210 BCE), who is said to have banned and burned books, and its ongoing attempt to excise knowledge of the Tiananmen protests of 1989, should have suggested to anyone paying attention that the Chinese government would almost certainly limit the free expression of ideas whatever the medium. A major government-sanctioned reevaluation of Qin Shi Huangdi in the 1970s recast his actions of censoring and destroying books, an action that Chinese historians had condemned for millennia, as an element of his admirable accomplishment in unifying China.[2] Another example: had American business and financial communities understood the deep humiliation the Chinese felt in the wake of nineteenth- and early twentieth-century European and American economic imperialism, would they really not have anticipated challenges to the very mindsets that had engendered that humiliation—that is, to the assumption that an economic order created in the West should become accepted worldwide? Area studies, with its humanist emphasis, had been a good approach for anyone truly wanting to understand China.

I received my BA in Asian Studies and MA in Chinese literature from Cornell University in the 1960s, and my PhD in literary theory from American University in 1978. When I attended the Association for Asian Studies (AAS) conferences, I was usually the only Black person there. Over the years, I have only met two or three other Black scholars of my generation, although there probably were a handful more. Furthermore, at that time, Americans could not go to China, and language programs in Taiwan for Americans only got started in the 1970s. With little chance to study in a Chinese-speaking environment, I learned to read Chinese far better than I could speak it.

Then as now, most research on Asia focused on the external, collective dimensions of human life, in fields such as history, political science, international relations, economics, and more recently, national security, the environment, and so forth. Even those fields that are potentially more amenable to queries about the inner life, such as philosophy, religion, literature, and art, tended to—and I think still do—approach these studies through their external dimensions. In my own field, literature, literary works are most often treated as expressions of intellectual or literary history or as expressions of the author's biography or thought. I am deeply indebted to this very important work. Nevertheless, comparatively little attention is given to literature as art, with all of its literary and rhetorical devices, which include, for example, reported versus dramatized action, irony, images, metaphor, etc. Nor is there sufficient recognition that these formal elements also communicate the meaning, feeling, and emotion that is integral to understanding and that distinguish literature from discursive writing. In the field of religion, Huston Smith provides an exception to normal academic approaches to religion. In his preface to *The Religions of Man* (1958), Smith describes his aim as helping the reader to "feel why and how" religions, including Confucianism, Daoism, and Buddhism, "guide and motivate the lives of those who live by them."[3] Of course, I have only noted tendencies, which means the exceptions are also numerous. Nevertheless, those approaches were not my interests, which hew to the inner life, especially psychology and literature.

The contributions of many Black Asianists are defined by their originality in the choice of subject matter hitherto neglected. In this, they make a major contribution by expanding the scope of the field. At one point in the 1980s, I actually assembled a short bibliography about people of African descent in Chinese history that began, as I recall, in the Tang Dynasty (618–907 CE). However, I never pursued that study. Introducing new subject matter was not to be my role. Rather, I followed my passion for the stories of Lu Xun (1881–1936), the most famous writer of twentieth-century China, whose life and works are the subject of thousands of volumes, drawings, paintings, films, and even several tourist destinations. What has been unique in my approach, informed in part by my biography and my race, is a different way of viewing this well-worn territory.

## Reflections from My Biography

No one ever really knows why he or she chooses one career path versus another. The retrospective story I tell myself suggests that my motivations for entering the field of Chinese studies were driven by a young person's attempt to make sense of a rigorous but badly misguided high school history curriculum. That curriculum postulated, implicitly, that African Americans had no role in United States history except during the Civil War period, and that "world history," as it was called, appropriately narrated the doings of the Great White Men of Western Europe, who apparently dominated the world from the time of the ancient Greeks up through the present. Even to me as a teenager, the omissions were thunderously loud.

I knew enough of my family's history, which can date our earliest identified Black ancestor to late eighteenth-century Virginia, to know that this US history was so distorted as to constitute lies. It never occurred to me, however, that there was a fuller, truer history yet to be told. I barely knew that Latin America existed. I did know that ancient Egyptian civilization was grand and glorious. However, in some vague way, visual evidence notwithstanding, I had been led to infer that these Egyptians were white. That Egypt was located in "Africa" was beyond imagining because Africa, it seemed, at best was peopled by the dark, disorganized, poverty-stricken recipients of European largesse, and there was nothing more to know. I did perceive a tiny bit about East Asia from the Chinese rugs and vases and chinoiserie wallpaper with which my mother decorated our home and somehow surmised that whatever Europe had by way of civilizational greatness, East Asia had as much of it or more, and it was of indisputable excellence. The distinction, though, between China and Japan was still murky. I did want to study history, but I did not want to study lies. By the end of my freshman year of college, I resolved to study all things Chinese. I was too naive to know that to some degree, every culture lies about its past!

Few American universities taught Chinese in the 1960s.[4] Thus, signing up to study the Chinese language at Cornell was easy. The classes were so starved for students that being Black was not an issue. Had I been a Martian, I would have been welcomed with similar enthusiasm. In the course of my undergraduate years, I developed a more sophisticated understanding of bias in history, both inadvertent and intentional. But it felt too late to give up Chinese studies: I had invested too much time to simply throw it over. I had also learned by then that my inclinations ran more toward literature than toward history; toward the questions of the human heart that resonate across different times and places, rather than toward those elements of more public human experience that are unique to their own historical moment. Without recognizing it, I was beginning to identify my special lens.

Whatever its deficits, my high school education had given me a firm chronological framework on which to locate human activity and the initial analytic capacities with which to critique what I had been taught. I am truly grateful for that rigor. Turning these tools on the implicit racial and colonialist distortions that characterized that curriculum directly launched me into the field of Chinese studies. Years later, I met an African American scholar, whose name I have since forgotten, who had been catapulted into Japanese studies for similar reasons. Apparently, I was not as unique a creature as I had imagined myself to be.

## A Different Lens: Doubleness of Vision

Fast forward several decades to the 2018 publication of my book on Lu Xun's modern short stories.

Undoubtedly, multiple factors lie behind the unique way I came to understand these stories. Some are deeply personal and involve my encounter with the works of Carl Jung (1876–1961). Others seem to arise from a capacity that Lu Xun and I share, if I may be so presumptuous—he as a writer whose family's fortunes had dropped precipitously and I as a Black American from an educated, middle-class background, a capacity to experience the world from both above and below, from a place of privilege and a place of disadvantage. Over time I have come to believe that he had a kind of "double consciousness," somewhat analogous to that which W. E. B. Du Bois (1868–1963) described as characterizing the mental life of African Americans. The parallels are suggestive, not exact.[5] Here, I mean only a sense of two contending ways of being within one's inner life, with one deemed lesser and consigned to the shadows but each having powerful claims on the whole psyche.

Any course in modern Chinese literature in translation logically begins with the short stories of Lu Xun, which mark the beginning of a literary era. He was a central figure in the tumultuous decades of the twentieth century, a famous intellectual and literary pioneer in his own time, and a writer launched into the stratosphere of recognition when Chairman Mao Zedong proclaimed in 1940—after Lu Xun was safely dead—that he was "the chief commander of China's cultural revolution," "a hero without parallel in our time."[6]

Lu Xun's works were available throughout the Cultural Revolution (1966–1976) when those of other writers from the 1920s and 1930s were not. They remained part of the official school curriculum into the early twenty-first century. Although Mao's encomiums had legitimate grounding in his writings, they also badly distorted the subtle genius of a sensitive soul whose small corpus of short stories contains some of the most brilliant, probing literary works in modern China. Lu Xun's stories have typically been read as an essential part of Chinese intellectual and literary history or as expressions of his personal life and thought. My way of reading them as a kind of autobiography differs from both.

In my undergraduate Chinese literature class, we probably read "Medicine" ("Yao"), "The True Story of Ah Q" ("Ah Q Zheng Zhuan"), and others. However, it was the conclusion of "The New Year's Sacrifice" ("Zhu Fu"), discussed later, that hit me viscerally, a recoiling that felt more physical than metaphorical. How could any piece of literature, and one in translation, produce such a stunning impact? At the time, I had relatively modest knowledge of China, and except for my language teacher, no more than a passing acquaintance with anyone Chinese. I definitely could not attribute such a shattering response to anything inherent in Chinese history or culture. The explanation had to be deeper. In fact, it required several decades of deep living, deep reflection, and considerable scholarship to arrive at an answer.

I stayed on at Cornell to earn an MA, married, moved to Washington, DC, had two children, earned a PhD, and joined the faculty of Howard University— family obligations confining me to the Washington, DC, area. I rejoiced in my first total immersion in Black culture. However, for reasons too complex to explain, Howard was not an institution where I could thrive long-term. Further, the salary was mediocre, and I had no intention of being pressed financially. I wrote several academic articles on Lu Xun's works and left academia for a career at the Library of Congress.

At that time, before internet-based research, the library's Asian collections were essential to scholars in the US who studied Asia.[7] As head of the area studies collections and later in other capacities, I guided the division's direction and selected, or helped select, the division's chiefs. When Congress was concerned that the Chinese collections, which were magnificently strong in history and culture, might not support the US government's requirements for information about politics, economics, and national security, I testified before a congressional committee about the library's plans to address this deficiency. Subsequently, I spearheaded an application for a grant to revamp the library's acquisition processes in China. I ended my career as director of the Kluge Center, a center for advanced research in the library's collections, which provided research fellowships for scholars, including those studying Asia. My responsibilities there included managing the selection process for the $1 million Kluge Prize, whose winners included Romila Thapar and Yu Ying-shih, for Indian and Chinese history, respectively. After retirement, I returned as a scholar to complete my book, *Reading Lu Xun through Carl Jung*. I have no idea what people thought about a Black woman in these roles. The library had given me position and power, and I did my job as conscientiously as I could. Recent PhDs take note: there are multiple career paths outside of the academy.

At least once I forgot that I was supposed to "be Black." I failed to attend a library function that lay outside of my portfolio because I was busy with what I considered "my real job." Belatedly, appalled, I remembered that politics sometimes demanded the appearance of a "Black face." In fact, although everyone denied it vociferously, I had been hired in part because I was Black. The African American chair of the library's congressional oversight committee had demanded a change in the all-white profile of senior management. This inconvenient fact never bothered me: my father and my ancestors had been denied innumerable positions because they were Black, so it seemed like an appropriate "balancing out." Besides, I was qualified.

Those years in academia and early years at the library were also marked by a crisis in my personal life that eventually led to my encounter with the works of Carl Jung, one of the founders of modern psychology and a contemporary of Lu

Xun's. During those years, I was searching my psyche in hopes of understanding the underlying psychological patterns that were shaping my life and causing me suffering. In my professional life, I was living with Lu Xun's stories, searching below the surfaces for patterns that shaped them. While rethinking these structuring features of my own life, I found myself drawn even more fully into Lu Xun's rewriting of the narrative of his contemporary Chinese reality as he interrogated cultural patterns inherited from the past that, to his mind, accounted for China's inadequate response to the challenges of Western imperialism and caused the Chinese people needless suffering.

I had been fortunate in completing my PhD in the late 1970s, a period when scholars of Chinese literature were just beginning to appreciate the value of literary theory in reading a text, the importance of clarifying the presuppositions that one brings to a work and articulating the variety of questions that one might pose. Thus, I had at my disposal a set of newly available tools that made it even possible to ask about the structuring patterns in Lu Xun's texts.

Lu Xun was writing stories at a time when the old dynastic system was collapsing, the Chinese Republic had barely come into reality, and the founding of the People's Republic of China was a few decades in the future. In the face of the West's economic and military aggression and technological superiority, many feared for China's future. Among intellectuals, who by tradition felt a moral imperative to address the nation's threats, the call was to "save China." But how?

Initially, Lu Xun anticipated that the answer would lie in modern science, and he enrolled in medical school. He left without finishing and took up a career in literature, believing that what the Chinese people most needed was not to have their bodies healed but to have their spirits changed. His comparison of physical healing to social change caused me to wonder whether he had an implicit medical model for his social ambitions: did he have a diagnosis of the illness; an etiology, an analysis of the causes; a course of treatment; and a vision of the healed state? A close reading of the texts of his two short story collections, *Call to Arms* (*Nahan*) and *Hesitation* (*Panghuang*), provided evidence that indeed he did. As I read and reread these texts, I found myself examining literary structures, such as the ordering of events in a story, the structure of images, the various tricks of the literary trade, a process analogous to the tasks I was performing in my own life. I found in Carl Jung's theories a language that helped articulate my patterns of thought and behavior. Astonishingly, the Jungian insights that were helping me understand my own journey provided a language for articulating what I was discovering in the structures of Lu Xun's texts.

In writing my book, I drew on essential elements of Jung's thought, but necessarily oversimplified his ideas, which he developed over a sixty-year career. Here, I describe just enough of these ideas to suggest why the notion of "double consciousness," as structured into Lu Xun's work and implied in his biography, might have relevance.

Unlike Sigmund Freud, who focused on psychological pathologies, Jung tried to understand how the normal human psyche functions. He proposed that the human psyche, the self, is composed of the conscious mind (or the ego self) and the unconscious mind (or the unconscious self). As humans grow to adulthood, the psyche pushes into unconsciousness those parts of the total self that the person or society finds unacceptable. These become the shadow, which is the part of the unconscious self that is most accessible to consciousness. (Other dimensions of the unconscious need not concern us here.) This is not necessarily a problem unless the split generates conflict. This arises when the shadow seeks acknowledgement by the conscious mind and reincorporation into the whole. A minor example of this is the "Freudian slip," the embarrassing moment when an imprudent unconscious thought breaks through and speaks in public. In Jung's system, the shadow possesses knowledge that the larger self, the whole self, needs in order to alleviate inner conflict, in order to function better in the world—a teleological thrust toward healing. Roughly stated, denying the shadow and its knowledge constitutes illness; incorporating the shadow's knowledge into awareness leads to the cure. This process liberates the self to draw on the resources of both dimensions of the psyche so that it can adapt with greater acuity and power to the challenges of the external world.

We apply a simplistic version of this idea in our contemporary American lexicon for discussing political and racial issues when we talk of "the other" and the tendency of the ego-self, the part of the social order with the money and power, to "otherize," to deny the full humanity of and right to full participation by some group that seeks to be recognized as a full and equal partner in the body politic, the societal self. Any side, of course, may "otherize," "dehumanize" the opposition. We speak of social healing but rarely with sufficient awareness of the enormity of effort and the degree of psychic pain required to become whole and liberated from the past.

Carl Jung directed his attention toward healing individual patients through therapy, but he also believed that the same principles applied at the societal level. Lu Xun initiated his reflections at the national level. Although he attacked Confucianism as an outworn system that facilitated national disaster and individual suffering, as a youth, he had been schooled in its tenets. Naturally, his analysis initially presupposed Confucian categories of thought. These assumed that heaven (the metaphysical realm), nation, community, family, and interior self would all be aligned, be shaped by the same patterns.

Lu Xun had no interest in heaven. However, within his short stories, he tested his hypotheses about societal illness through the other four areas of human life.

For Lu Xun, the privileged men who dominated this patriarchal society constituted the social self; women and peasants constituted the social unconscious, the "other" that needed to be heard and incorporated. Over time, he concluded that this would only be accomplished through revolution. A man given to scrupulous self-examination, he questioned whether he, himself, as a male intellectual, one born into modest privilege, was positioned inside or outside of this system. One can easily see how the class-conscious Maoist interpreters of his work found support within these stories.

The story that nearly knocked me out of my chair when I was about twenty years old embodied all of these dimensions. In "The New Year's Sacrifice," the story's first-person narrator returns to his hometown, where he fails to answer with human honesty the straightforward questions of a starving peasant woman. The next day, hearing that she has died and reflecting on her life, he recounts how the archaic family system had exacerbated her suffering; he even acknowledges that he and she are similarly trapped within the same encompassing system. Her descent into extreme poverty had been marked by her preparations for celebrations of the New Year. Yet, when the narrator awakens to celebratory sounds on the morning of the festival, he forgets all he had understood of her suffering and responds as if the encounter had never happened.

Deploying the symbolic forms of literature, the story encodes the split in the body politic, in the national psyche: male/female; intellectual/peasant; social ego/social shadow; and remembering and incorporating the shadow/forgetting and denying its existence. Taken as a whole, Lu Xun's corpus of modern short stories examines all four social levels in terms of illness and healing: the diagnosis, etiology, therapeutic process, and vision of the healed state. He could imagine healing within the family and individual psyche, however rarely it might occur, but in the arenas of nation and community, the shadow's attempt to be heard would result in its death. The only solution he could imagine in the public sphere was for the shadow voices to demand incorporation into the body politic. The ego forces would resist. The revolution that would likely ensue would be, he suspected, violent and bloody.

Although Carl Jung began with a focus on the psyche, and Lu Xun began by interrogating society and culture, they both arrived at analogous conclusions with respect to psychic illness and its cure. Jung and Lu Xun were contemporaries. Lu Xun knew a bit about Jung through translating *Symbols of Agony* by Kuriyagawa Hakuson (1880–1923), a study that briefly mentions Jung three or four times but says a good deal about Freud, whom I believe remains far better known in China than Jung. However, there is no evidence that Jung influenced Lu Xun in even the slightest way. Rather, both Lu Xun and Jung participated in the late nineteenth-century European *zeitgeist* that interrogated the unconscious in human life within the secular realm. Lu Xun read works of Western thought and claimed to have read some one hundred works of European fiction before writing his first short story. Both men were much taken with Friedrich Nietzsche's *Thus Spoke Zarathustra*. To a degree, both drank from the same well. Thus, Lu Xun undoubtedly knew the philosophical and literary precursors to the insights into the psyche that Freud and Jung, working in a psychoanalytic medical context, drew on in formulating their theories.

The analyses of both Lu Xun and Jung resonated with my own life experience.

In *Reading Lu Xun through Carl Jung*, I largely restricted my analysis to the short story texts. This gave me confidence that I was not imposing a Western framework on Chinese material but rather using a vocabulary of concepts to bring to awareness patterns that already existed. Nevertheless, it is also true that every text in some way reflects the author's mind at the time of composition. Therefore, I was willing to speak about the mind that produced them and even guess about the man himself as long as I explicitly acknowledged the degree of speculation that I was bringing to the evidence.

Lu Xun's short stories revealed, without ambiguity, that he deeply understood the privileges of being part of the Chinese intellectual male elite, and the psychological resistances to giving up the prestige and protection of that position. Simultaneously, he also recognized that those in his position, including himself, were morally culpable for the suffering of the social shadow, and he threw his weight into destroying that system. What enabled him to see and then act in this radical way? Let me speculate.

Lu Xun's grandfather had been a high government official whose fall into disgrace nearly bankrupted the family. Lu Xun observed cryptically that anyone who suffers such a fall will come to know what the world is really like. More concretely, in his late teens, Lu Xun had set aside his training in the Chinese classics, the established path to wealth and prestige in dynastic China, embraced knowledge flooding in from the West, and traveled to Japan to study. Japan had embraced modernization in the mid-nineteenth century and was much further along than China in mastering the tools of the modern world. Further, in Japan, Lu Xun was viewed in part as a citizen of an aging empire, an outsider; he was also positioned to see his own nation with foreign eyes and from a distance. Unlike his brother, who embraced Japanese culture and married a Japanese woman, Lu Xun retained his singular identification as a Chinese. Thus, it would seem that family decline and foreign experience facilitated in Lu Xun a capacity to experience that doubleness of vision, to see simultaneously with awareness of the suffering "other" and the privileges of "self."

Now I had acquired the tools to answer my own question. Why had "The New Year's Sacrifice" and Lu Xun's other short stories exerted such a hold on me? My hypothesis: When as an undergraduate I first read that story, even in translation, something of that twoness of vision seized my soul. The grating gap between the woman's suffering and the narrator's morally repugnant refusal to absorb its meaning resonated with my own doubleness. Some of this was personal; some was racial and social; the combination was overwhelming.

Not only had the curriculum of my high school violated my experience; the school was also mean-spirited to most students and would have proven lethal to me without my parents' interventions. Further, the white friends from my childhood at puberty drew the mandatory social line against interracial dating. Naturally, I knew theoretically about such taboos, but it had not fully occurred to me that they would affect me personally. Those high school years had forced a painful awareness of society's insistence on racializing my being. For several years of my young adulthood, I even absorbed aspects of Du Bois's "double consciousness," in part seeing "one's self through the eyes of others."[8]

Until recently, it had been possible for white Americans to see themselves as default "Americans" and to remain oblivious to the evidence that they too have a racial identity. Members of minority groups, particularly any group whose physical features limit the capacity to "blend-in" as white, are well aware that although they are individuals, they are also defined by their racial designation. Over time, I developed a deepening awareness that taking pleasure in my privilege, even those elements I could justly claim that I had earned, did not release me from culpability for the system that was rewarding me but denigrating others. Lu Xun's focus on the ego/shadow dynamic at all four social levels and his self-awareness of benefiting from the system he sought to destroy were also wrapped up in the conundrums of my life.

I now feel confident that in reading that story, I was gazing into the mirror. Jung proposed that the key psychological task at midlife would be to retrieve parts of the self that had been left behind, to integrate the shadow into fuller awareness so as to achieve a less divided, more integrated self. As that process unfolded in my personal life, I came to embrace my responsibility for the social whole, to alleviate the social shadow's distress and overcome the exclusion of people not designated as white. For my younger self, Lu Xun's story had articulated the tensions that I would need to resolve as I matured.

The struggle to incorporate the unconscious into the conscious was so profound that in midlife, I had a series of Jungian dreams. In the earliest of these, I was terrified that water, a frequent symbol of the unconscious, would rise up and sweep me away—that is, the conscious "me," the only part of which I was fully aware. In the final version of the dream, I am in a low-slung boat, Lu Xun is poling the boat, and he guides it safely through a towering wave of the unconscious. Instead of drowning me, the wave deposits me safely on another shore where "one self" assures the "other self" that both parts can live together without conflict. An image of psychological healing.

## The Archetypal Self, Scapegoating

The ubiquitous human pattern of scapegoating can be viewed from one perspective as an extension of the ego/shadow dynamic. In scapegoating, the ego-self, rather than relieving a severe inner conflict by absorbing the knowledge offered by the shadow-self, rejects that unrecognized, unwanted part of the self and projects it onto a third party, typically one without sufficient power to retaliate. Thus, the ego-self tries to eliminate its own internal conflict by "finding" the problem in that "other" and expelling the shadow recipient via exile or death. When perpetuated on a societal scale, those who enact the violence may well be unconscious of their role in this brutal "performance." In fact, scapegoating only succeeds in its purpose of restoring the experience of unity within the ego-self group when the dynamic is covert.

Lu Xun's masterpiece, "The True Story of Ah Q," demonstrates his clear understanding of the psychological mechanism of scapegoating, the processes by which it transpires, and the social circumstances that precipitate it. When he worried that his famous story might be about events decades in the future, Lu Xun was revealing his suspicion that some archetypal pattern was at work in his story. Jung had hypothesized that the ego/shadow dynamic was a universal phenomenon but had no way of testing this view.[9] My reading of "The True Story of Ah Q" as an intricate, accurate anatomy of a scapegoating, documented with details from the text, is radically unique in the long, complex history of interpretations of this masterpiece.

I may have had heightened sensitivity to this broadly human dynamic because the Southern lynchings of Black people offer up such perfect, violent examples of the scapegoating syndrome. The radical insufficiency of the pretexts for torture and murder of other human beings cries out for an explanation of the impetus for these horrific acts. Others have documented the historical contexts. At the psychological root, I believe, was a visceral terror of having to acknowledge the humanity of the despised Black "other." Given the history of violent suppression of Black human beings in slavery and beyond, if this shadow-other were fully human, that would make monsters of the perpetrators, the ego-self of society. That possibility was too awful to contemplate. Better to eliminate the purported cause of the fear.

I am no longer surprised that the white faces that gaze at the camera in photos of lynchings seem empty of emotion. Their lack of affect seems no different from the moral numbness of the crowd that Lu Xun evokes at the scapegoating of Ah Q. Those lynchings are part of my inheritance as an American. Undoubtedly, being Black elevates that history in my consciousness and heightens my sensitivity to the scapegoating syndrome.

As a Black American who has lived both as the social ego, a person of economic privilege who can "do" mainstream white culture, and one who simultaneously lives as a Black person with awareness of the killing costs of social exclusion and psychological projection, I have acquired a particular, complex way of seeing the world. Could a non-Black American scholar marshal the same literary tools and, reading Lu Xun's short stories, arrive at the same insights? Perhaps. Yet it seems to me that the parallels between Lu Xun's life and the full context of my biography made it far more likely that I would see this corpus through a different lens and make a uniquely "Black" contribution to modern Chinese literature.

## Notes

[1] Parts of this essay draw on my publication, *Reading Lu Xun through Carl Jung*, Amherst, New York: Cambria Press, 2018.

[2] *New World Encyclopedia*, accessed January 7, 2022; see also Li Yu-ning, "Introduction," *The First Emperor*, International Arts and Sciences Press, 1975; reissued by Routledge, 2018.

[3] *The Religions of Man*, New York: Harper & Row, 1958, ix.

[4] As I recall, Harvard, Yale, Princeton, Cornell, and perhaps other "Ivies," taught Chinese language, along with the University of Michigan, probably several California universities, and a scattering of others. The situation is dramatically different today, with educational institutions at all levels teaching Chinese.

[5] Each of these three men, Lu Xun, Jung, and Du Bois, was a complex thinker in his own right and deeply embedded in his own culture. All left substantial bodies of written work. My use of the term "double consciousness" for all three merely points to evidence that in nineteenth-century Europe, discourse about "doubleness" in the human psyche occurred frequently in works of philosophy and literature, entered the medical realm, and factored into the development of modern psychology. See Henri F. Ellenberger, *The Discovery of the Unconscious: The History and Evolution of Dynamic Psychiatry*. New York: Basic Books, 1970.

[6] Mao Zedong, "The Culture of New Democracy," 1940.

[7] Many of the library's unique Asian materials may still not be digitized. Consult the division for details. https://www.loc.gov/research-centers/asian/about-this-research-center/.

[8] From "Strivings of the Negro People," *The Atlantic*, August 1897, https://www.theatlantic.com/magazine/archive/1897/08/strivings-of-the-negro-people/305446/. Here Du Bois suggests that the "shadow" element in Black consciousness involved incorporating white

views into the Black psyche. In this, Du Bois differs from both Jung and Lu Xun. For them, the shadow carries important knowledge that the whole self needs, and integrating the ego-self and the shadow-self is necessary to the well-being of the entire psyche.

[9] In chapter 3 of *Violence and the Sacred*, Rene Girard offers a credible reading of Sophocles's *Oedipus Rex* as an exemplary literary rendition of scapegoating. In *Reading Lu Xun through Carl Jung*, I argue that "The True Story of Ah Q" offers an even better example. Among studies that imply that scapegoating is a universal phenomenon are Girard's *Violence and the Sacred*, *The Scapegoat*, and his other works. See also Eric Neumann's *Depth Psychology and a New Ethic*.

## Bibliography

Brown, Carolyn, T. *Reading Lu Xun through Carl Jung*. Amherst: Cambria Press, 2018.

Du Bois, W. E. B. "Strivings of the Negro People," *The Atlantic,* August 1897, https://www.theatlantic.com/magazine/archive/1897/08/strivings-of-the-negro-people/305446/.

Ellenberger, Henri F. *The Discovery of the Unconscious: The History and Evolution of Dynamic Psychiatry*. New York: Basic Books, 1970.

Li Yu-ning, "Introduction," *The First Emperor*. New York: International Arts and Sciences Press, 1975; reissued by Routledge, 2018.

Smith, Huston. *The Religions of Man*, New York: Harper & Row, 1958, ix.

# 3

# FROM BAGHDĀD TO BAGHPŪR

## SAILORS AND SLAVES IN GLOBAL ASIA

### Guangtian Ha

برانگیخته موج از او تندباد      حکیم این جهان را چو دریا نهاد

همه بادبانها بر افراخت      چو هفتاد کشتی بر او ساخته

*When the Wise God of the World created the sea*
*Raise He did by soaring wind massive swells*
*There He set on them seventy ships*
*All with sails hoisted high*

— Ferdawsī, *Shāhnāmeh*, trans. by the author

教門從西一隻船
金幫銀底幾千年

*Our religion is a ship from the West*
*With gold hull and silver keel it had sailed for millennia*

—a saying from China's Jahriyya Sufis (figure 3.1),
trans. by the author

Figure 3.1. Relief at the Jahriyya Banqiao Sufi Lodge, Banqiao, Wuzhong, Ningxia Hui Autonomous Region, China. Source: Photo by author.

This article explores how Asian Studies, in particular works with a focus on transregional inter-Asian connections, can contribute to a broadened understanding of global blackness that encompasses and transcends trans-Atlantic slavery. The title of the article, "From Baghdād to Baghpūr," uses two rhyming words to draw attention to the extensive connection between Asia—Central and East Asia in particular—and the Perso-Arab Islamic world, via the maritime routes through South and Southeast Asia. Both words originate in Persian: Baghdād, the capital of the Abbāsid Empire, means "God-given" (*bagh* means "God," while *dād* is derived from the Persian verb *dādan*, "to give"), and *baghpūr*, meaning "God's son" (*bagh* + *pūr*; *pūr* meaning "son" in Persian), is the title medieval Persians gave to kings and emperors in Inner Asia and China.[1] The latter, of course, is likely a Persian rendition of the Chinese term *tianzi*, "son of heaven." Thus, when the Arab and Persian merchants left Baghdād and sailed across the Arabian Sea, the Indian Ocean, and the South China Sea in their junks or dhows, they were practically moving between the city of God and the land ruled by the sons of God.

In recent years, inter-Asian connections, premodern global connectivities, and the wider Indian Ocean world have drawn a considerably amount of attention from historians and anthropologists.[2] While this article shares the same passion in laying stress on the transregional, it also attempts to sketch out what might have remained less visible in this latest round of research keen on refashioning area studies theoretically as well as geographically. While transregional mobilities often animate cosmopolitan imaginaries, they at times create a differential of positions where some can move at the expense of others' enforced immobilities. Scholarly attention paid to transregional trade or universalist *jihād* may also conceal the transregional structures that enabled these mobilities in the first place while imposing movements on those with the least power to resist.[3] In other words, behind each network of transregional mobility, do we find numerous networks of immobilities and involuntary mobilities—an infrastructure that is as essential to transregional flows of people, languages, commodities, and ideas as it is invisible?

It is with these questions in mind that I write this article. To demonstrate their substance, I will focus on the intersection of race, slavery, and seafaring in medieval inter-Asian exchanges that linked the Perso-Arab Islamic world to East and Southeast Asia. The scale is colossal, the time span is vast, and the languages involved are multiple. Yet I hope in this short article to indicate the directions this research can pursue in the coming years and the ways in which it may help us reconsider: (1) the intellectual contribution and the political work Asian Studies may be capable of in addressing the entrenched racial bias that structures the field itself (white people studying non-whites, Black people studying themselves, and Asians finding anti-Black racism a matter not directly relevant to their existence and scholarly pursuit), and (2) the under-theorization of race as it pertains specifically to blackness in transregional Asian Studies.[4]

A principal suggestion this article makes is that we expand our understanding of blackness beyond the extant focus on Africa and the African diaspora without displacing or belittling the unique brutality of European colonialism and trans-Atlantic slavery. The proposal is rather that we use the category of blackness—in lower case—and its referential expansiveness in Asia-Pacific to bring into focus the interconnection among otherwise disparate notions and structures of racialized hierarchy where people considered "black" have been subject to exploitation or enslavement. I thus use "blackness" in lower case in this article to refer to this often ambiguous color scheme (for who is considered "black" by whom and why varies across historical and societal contexts), and "Blackness" in upper case when the discussion pertains specifically to Africa and the African diaspora. In so doing, I hope both to highlight the continuity of the proposed project with current academic convention in Black Studies and draw attention to the unique contribution this research aims to make to this field. This article is written with the general hope that a new Afro-Asian solidarity can be reimagined and hashed out via rigorous work while keeping the crevices and ruptures running through that solidarity squarely in vision.[5] The conclusive section of this article will clarify the pertinence of the research in question to this political vision.

## Global Blackness

The preliminary idea that propelled me to propose this essay to *Who Is the Asianist?* is an enduring interest in investigating the global creation of notions of blackness that at once encompasses and transcends the trans-Atlantic slave trade. While it is true that the amalgam of imperialism, capitalism, and nineteenth-century pseudobiology has given racism in the Euro-American world a particularly cruel form, it is still essential to acknowledge that anti-blackness both has a longer history and a more varied existence than can be accommodated by a singular framework. A recent article by Rachel Schine titled "Race and Blackness in Premodern Arabic Literature," for instance, shows with conclusive evidence from early Islamic literature that anti-black racism, akin in its intensity to a certain biological determinism, evolved during the high Abbāsid period to the point where a stronger association of blackness with slavery began to take root in classical Arab-Islamic societies from the thirteenth century onward, if not earlier.[6]

The very significance of race as an essential prism for rewriting global history has not gone unnoticed in transnationally oriented Asian Studies. Already, twenty years ago, in a private exchange between Amitav Ghosh and Dipesh Chakrabarty, which was later published in *Radical History Review*, Ghosh contemplated that "[r]ace was much more than just a tool of Empire: it was (in the Kantian sense) one of the foundational categories of thought that made other perceptions possible."[7] Admittedly the context wherein he made this postulation is when Ghosh recounted the British response to the Japanese invasion of Malaya and Burma: "In Malaya while evacuating their government from the north, they stuck absolutely resolutely to the principles of race: trains were forbidden to transport 'non-Europeans.' . . . Similarly, in northern Burma in 1942, in a moment of total crisis, with hundreds of thousands of civilians heading for the mountains, the British still found time to set up 'white' and 'black' evacuation routes."[8] In addition to the most obvious, Ghosh's remark exposes a quintessentially binary racial mindset that afflicts more than the colonial Britons: in both medieval Perso-Arabic and Chinese accounts, we find the color black being used to refer to a wide range of populations—often other than oneself—and the color white invariably celebrated as a marker of (one's own) beauty and nobility.

If indeed one is to take Ghosh's suggestion seriously—that race ought to be considered a category on a par with, say, space and time in Kant, or "society" à la Emile Durkheim—then confining it only to modern empire or European colonialism may well dull the edge of an intriguing provocation, a theoretical as well as political challenge to think with race and to treat race as Marx does class or Lacan does sexuality. While this conceptual move has been definitive to the discipline of ethnic studies, it has barely caught on in Asian Studies, for which the potentially transformative theoretical innovations of ethnic studies are at times reduced to studies of marginalized "ethnic minorities" in postcolonial and postsocialist regimes. Some recent works on Sinophone Muslims in China, for instance, while aware of the numerous transregional and multilingual religious networks that animated the histories of Islam in China, still tend to portray their objects of study as monolingual "minorities" under a reigning nation-state framework.[9] Treating race as a category with its own conceptual integrity may help us explore an alternative, premodern, subaltern transregionalism: the fact that both coastal East Africans and coastal Southeast Asians are referred to as being "black" in medieval Arabic and Chinese accounts, and that both are employed in different legs of the trans-Indian Ocean journey to staff the ships of seafaring Muslim merchants, cannot but lead us to contemplate the prospect of theorizing a certain "Black Pacific"—a là Paul Gilroy[10]—where the simple black/white binarism, precisely because of its referential fluidity across histories and geographies, can be employed as a dynamic hinge to connect multiple structures of racial exploitation and subversion.[11]

Is this expansive elaboration on race unduly a conceptual overreach, even an epistemic imperialism that generalizes a specifically Euro-American problematic—with a distinct US American tint—into a spurious universality? The answer to this question depends on whether we would be willing to entertain the possibility that there may have been other transregional mobilities comparable in their historical ramifications to the trans-Atlantic slave trade—mobilities that have created and entrenched alternative notions of blackness associated with racial hierarchization and structural oppression—in other parts of the world. This is not to deny the historical particularities of trans-Atlantic slavery nor to belittle its exceptional brutality. However, anti-B/black racism does not originate from capitalism nor does the West monopolize its production. Among Muslims, for instance, anti-Blackness reaches back to the days of Prophet Muhammad—and to pre-Islamic times. A Nubian poet by the name of Suḥaym (d. mid-seventh century), whose extraordinary talent earned him a place in the tenth-century Arabic book of songs, *Kitāb al-Aghānī*, in attempting to redeem his fate, also revealed the pervasive anti-Blackness in the society where he was but a Black slave:

> *My clothes harm my blackness not, for I am like musk—those who have tasted its scent forget it not.*
> *I am made to wear a gown of black, yet underneath is a shirt white round the neck.*[12]

وما ضرَّ أثوابي سوادي وإنَّني      لكالمسك لا يسلو عن المسكِ ذائقُه

كُسيتُ قَميصاً ذا سواد وتحته      قميصٌ من القُوهيّ بيض بنائقُه

It reads almost as though Suḥaym could accomplish partial vindication only by distancing himself from Blackness, whose presumably repulsive earthiness has to be sublimated—though not without remainder—through a cleansing act of burning and thus converted into colorless fragrance. The black gown is only for laymen's gaze, while those in the know are to spot the ring of white that remains uncontainable under a cloak of black.

There is no doubt that Islam has a complicated relationship with slavery; and the Muslim trade in slaves, spanning Europe, the Americas, Africa, and Asia, was as transregional if not as brutal as the trans-Atlantic slave trade. Early Muslim slaves to the Americas were either direct victims of kidnapping by white European colonizers or war captives sold to the latter by local parties locked in blood feuds in the Senegambian river valley of West Africa.[13] The Europeans did not invent slavery in Africa; they were the latecomers to a wider and historically more diverse and wide-ranging system, which they later developed into a qualitatively different form of exploitation and oppression. While sub-Saharan Black Africans constituted for Muslims a major source for slaves, to the point where the word ʿabīd ("slave") is still associated with Blackness in colloquial Arabic, slavery in Islam never quite followed the color line strictly. Ibn Battuta was known to rank his white Greek maidservant higher than others, and white slaves, Slavs in particular, were readily imported into the Muslim world in the Ottoman period.[14] Manumitted slaves were known to rise in the military rank and file and eventually reign over eminent Islamic dynasties (such as among the Mamlūks in medieval Egypt). Their successful careers demonstrated the extent to which "slavery," as a generalizing term, may not be able to cover the range of configurations that define how human beings were turned into property in Muslim societies.[15]

If the concept of slavery is in need of a historically informed and anthropologically sophisticated revision, the same can be said of Blackness. Just as slavery in Islam never quite traced the color line, the term "black," or its cognate Kunlun 崑崙 in Chinese historical records, too did not always refer exclusively to men and women—whether enslaved or not—of African origins brought to China via the maritime trade of Arab and Persian merchants. While the earliest appearance of the term Kunlun in Chinese writing by no means indicated an association with blackness—it seemed to be a rhetorical description of the extraordinary heights of some mountains—by the fourth century or so, the term for the first time began to acquire a meaning that referred to the color black.[16] Its obscure origin, for instance, is apparent in the following account given of Li Lingrong (351–400 AD; thus two centuries earlier than Suḥaym), concubine to the Jianwen Emperor of the eastern Jin 東晉 dynasty:

> Her name is Lingrong and her birth was humble. While the Jianwen Emperor was still the Lord of Kuaiji, he had had three sons. Daosheng, the crown prince and heir apparent, had his status abolished, and another son, the Lord Xian, died young. All of his concubines could not birth a son for ten years (諸姬絕孕 十年無子). The emperor thus consulted a sorcerer by the name of Hu Qian, who said, "a woman in the servants' quarter will give birth to two precious sons, one of whom will carry on the royal blood of Jin." . . . For a few years, the emperor recruited a specialist

in physiognomy and showed him all his favourite concubines. Alas, none of them exhibited the right features. At the time in the weaving workshop there was a woman, who was tall and black, and all the servants in the palace called her [a] Kunlun (形長而色黑 宮人謂之崑崙). When she arrived, the physiognomist went "Here is she!" The emperor that night demanded her companionship. Thereafter she dreamed of two dragons encircling her knees and the sun and the moon falling into her embrace. These were indeed auspicious omens. Upon learning of this the emperor was amazed, and went into her. Thus were born Emperor Liezong and Lord Wenxiao of Kuaiji. She died at the age of fifty.[17]

The source here compels us to acknowledge the significant fact that one of the earliest appearances of *Kunlun* as associated with the color black was in the biography of a woman servant turned concubine. Nonetheless, the text affords no definite explanation as to the genealogy of the term. What further complicates the matter is the possibility that the word itself, while appearing to be native to the Chinese language, could have been a loan word. In the massive eighth-century dictionary *Yi Qie Jing Yin Yi* 一切經音義, the eminent Buddhist monk Shi Huilin 釋慧琳 explained thus:

> the sound is *kun lun*, and colloquially *gulun* 骨論. Refers to the aliens on islands of the South Sea. Quite black, mostly naked. They can tame wild beasts—rhinoceros and elephants and such. There are multiple types [of Kunlun]: some are Sengqi, others are Tumi, still others are Gutang, Gemie, and others. Regardless, they are all base and lowly (種類數般 即有僧祇 突彌 骨堂 閣蔑等 皆卑賤人也). They have no manners, and they live by robbing and kidnapping. They are cannibals—like the evil Rakasa. Their language is odd and different from all the other aliens'. Good at swimming. They can dive and spend a whole day under water without dying (善入水 竟日不死).[18]

Gemie likely refers to the ancient Khmer people in contemporary Cambodia, while Sengqi is often considered a Chinese transliteration of Zanj, the term medieval Muslims used to refer to sub-Saharan East Africans along the Swahili coast. We cannot take the entry at its word: there is no reason for us to believe that Shi Huilin, or the popular usage wherefrom he drew his source, knew how to distinguish among the diverse populations who seemed to share the same skin color, nor can we be sure that a Bantu slave, purchased by medieval Muslim merchants on their voyage, would not have first ended up somewhere in Southeast Asia before they were mixed up with other equally "base and lowly" peoples of dark complexion and sent off to China.

While Ronald Segal's estimation that, among the Black slaves traded in Islam, the gender ratio is roughly one male to every two females (in contrast to two males to every female in trans-Atlantic slavery) may be less than accurate, it is still true that slavery among Muslims laid more stress on domestic service than on hard field labor.[19] For a Muslim merchant involved in transregional trade, the service may well include navigating a ship, thus the reason for Shi Huilin's inclusion of impressive diving skills in his entry on *Kunlun/Gulun*. The eighth-century poet luminary Zhang Ji once composed a poem with the very title *Kunlun er* 崑崙兒 (while *er* means "son," here, the word is a diminutive indicating contempt):

Home to the *Kunlun* are the islands amidst the sea;
Yet, led forth by barbarian visitors, they have come to roam Han lands.
Grasping language, they are the mythical Mynah birds,
Crossing billowing waves, they first set foot on Yulin Island.
Gold rings once dangled luridly from their ears;
With conch-spiralled hair, long and coiling, they still refuse to bind their heads.
Black as lacquer is the flesh and skin they cherish;
They stride about half-stripped of tree-cotton garments.[20]

崑崙家住海中州　蠻客將來漢地遊
言語解教秦吉了　波濤初過郁林洲
金環欲落曾穿耳　螺髮長卷不裹頭
自愛肌膚黑如漆　行時半脫木綿裘

While dynasties rose and fell, there seems to be a certain continuity in the transregional circulation of *Kunlun* insofar as the Chinese records are concerned. In 976 AD, it is said that three *dashi* diplomats—the "barbarian visitors" in Zhang Ji's poem—visited the Song court, and they brought with them a *Kunlun* slave with "deep-set eyes and black skin" (目深體黑).[21] The *dashi* envoy were likely Arabs (*dashi* is a Chinese transliteration of *tāzh*, the latter being the name medieval Persians gave to Arabs), though they could equally have been Persians.[22] Neither can we be certain that they were official envoys instead of intrepid merchants, for official duty and private profiteering were never quite separate in both the Abbāsid and the Chinese imperial court. Zhang Ji's poem locates the origin of *Kunlun* in an oceanic world but offers no clue as to its whereabouts. Shi Huilin, whose dictionary was compiled in the same period, mentioned that the *Kunlun* language is "odd and different from all the other aliens," which means that the crew on the ships might well have been multilingual as much as multiracial and multireligious, with Muslims playing the dominant role as the shipmasters and owners of the goods as well as the people in transit.

We have rare visual cues to help us imagine the composition of the crew of these seagoing vessels. An exquisite thirteenth-century illustrated manuscript of *Maqāmāt al-Ḥarīrī* includes a miniature that depicts a cross-Indian Ocean voyage of medieval Muslim merchants (figure 3.2). The ship is an Arab dhow, its design wonderfully echoing the restored model of the ninth-century shipwreck near Belitung in contemporary Indonesia.[23] In the hull, gazing expectantly at the horizon, are impeccably groomed merchants in luscious turbans. On the deck, however, are black sailors steering the ship atop immense swells. *Maqāmāt al-Ḥarīrī* was composed in the eleventh century and quickly became a popular collection of stories among Arabs of the high Abbāsid period, and Yaḥya ibn

Figure 3.2. *Maqāmāt al-Ḥarīrī*, Paris Arabe 5847, folio 119 verso.
Source: Courtesy of Bibliothèque Nationale de France.

Maḥmūd al-Wāsiṭī, the painter and calligrapher who produced the illustrated manuscript in question, obviously wished to ride this tide of popularity in his own favor.

The story that figure 3.2 is supposed to serve as an illustration to is titled "The Omani Maqāma," Oman being a key site in the medieval Perso-Arab maritime trade. Abu Ḥārith, the narrator, at the beckoning of some affair of importance, was called upon to visit Oman. While the ship was about to set sail, a mysterious figure appeared on the shore and requested to tag along; he was soon enough outed to be the very same trickster friend of Abu Ḥārith's, Abu Zayd, who was often the true protagonist of the stories. Blackness figures only obliquely in the story: Abu Ḥārith states that in preparation for the trip he moved to the ship his "blacks." The word used in the text is asāwidī ("my blacks"). Instead of translating the word literally, however, Steingrass's translation only has "chattels." And where slaves and servants are involved, the words used are either ʿabīd or ghilma ("boys"), though in al-Wāsiṭī's rich pictorial representation, all appear as black, with no evident association with Africa or the African diaspora.[24] One important detail in the original text, which is again lost in Steingrass's English rendition, thus describes the slave boys when the latter were speechless concerning their master's grief: "They spoke neither of white nor of black" (lā fāhū bi-baydāʾ wa lā sawdāʾ), which appears in Steingrass's translation as "[they] spoke not either fair or foul."[25] The moralistic association of white/black with fair/foul is in line with the prevailing ideology of the high Abbāsid Arab-Muslim society, and the idiomatic Arabic expression is thus done great justice in spirit if not in word by Steingrass's carefully calibrated translation. The moralized opposition between fair and foul mirrors the binary mindset that pits white self against black other. Incidentally, the master king was also painted black, which is by no means implied by the original text (figure 3.3).

It must be noted at this point that the sources I have drawn on so far, while bilingual, exhibit a clear homogeneity in that most are drawn from literature or historical records with a strong fantastical flavor. Maqāmāt al-Ḥarīrī is a collection of popular anecdotes that may reflect some level of historical truth, while the biography of Li Lingrong and the dictionary entry for Kunlun both purport to be based on veritable history but display a mix of fact and fiction: the involvement of a physiognomist in one case, and cannibalism in another, certainly does not render them reassuring evidence on which reliable arguments can be built. Yet in many cases, evidence of this sort is the only material we have available to us, and one can make the argument that the fine line between fact and fiction, truth and fantasy, itself constitutes a local manifestation of a global literary convention that continues to obliterate B/black presences in the history of the transregional Muslim maritime trade. It seems as though conventional historical writings, in both Arabic and Chinese, could not but render those that fascinate and frighten

Figure 3.3. *Maqāmāt al-Ḥarīri*, Paris Arabe 5847, folio 122 verso.
Source: Courtesy of Bibliothèque Nationale de France.

them in fantastical language—that B/black sailors and B/black slaves employed on the seafaring journeys beyond Arabia and Persia could not but appear as ghosts and phantasmagorical beings in these writings. What intertextual resonances in the bilingual archive can help us give this speculation some evidentiary credibility?

## From Intertextual to Transregional

Another common name given to *Kunlun* is *Mohe* 摩訶, of no less obscure linguistic origins. The term was popularized by a report in *Taiping Guangji* 太平廣記 (completed ca. 978 AD), or *Extensive Records of the Taiping Era*. It is said that on a family visit to Canton, Tao Xian 陶峴, a descendent of the literary luminary Tao Yuanming 陶淵明 (ca. 365–427 AD), had the unusually good fortune to procure three exquisite treasures: an ancient sword, a jade ring, and a seafaring *Kunlun* slave (*Kunlun nu*) by the name of Mohe who "is an extraordinary swimmer— brave and agile" (善遊水而勇捷). "Every time he travelled on beautiful waters Tao Xian would drop the sword and the ring and order Mohe to retrieve both, simply for the fun of it all." Such "fun" lasted for a couple of years, in the course of which Mohe lost a finger to a poisonous water snake—until at last, when they were undertaking a trip to Xisai Mountain in Hubei and Tao Xian did the same since the water "was dark and stagnant" and he thought "there must be some monster therein," Mohe finally met his end:

> [Tao Xian] dropped the sword and the ring in water and commanded Mohe to jump in and retrieve both. So he did. The water turned and swelled and after a while Mohe returned, empty-handed and consumed. "The sword and the ring can no more be retrieved," he lamented. "Therein is a dragon of more than two *jang* long (i.e., over six metres), and the sword and the ring have fallen in his path. Every time I extended my hands to reach for both, the dragon burst into a daunting rage." Thereupon Tao Xian replied, "The sword, the ring, and you are my three treasures. Now that the other two are lost, what use do I have of you? Return and retrieve both [or die doing it]." Knowing that his end had arrived, a great thunderous roar was heard from Mohe and his hair broke loose; blood of scarlet red flowed from his bulging eyes. And lo and behold, in the slave went and never did he return. Hours passed, and members of his body rose to the surface. There they lay foul and exposed.[26]

Tao Xian's fascination with and brutal exploitation of Mohe represents only one such instance where black slaves known to be "good at swimming" became the plaything of Chinese aristocrats. Keeping *Kunlun* slaves as entertaining natators for recreational purposes or more serious seagoing activities was apparently a popular status-marker that affluent Chinese adopted from the "barbarian visitors."[27] Whether from Southeast Asia or coastal East Africa, we still know depressingly little about who these *Kunlun* slaves were, what languages they spoke, and whether they had been kidnapped or sold as war captives into slavery. They were not as "fortunate"—for want of a better word—as Omar ibn Said, the Muslim scholar who was kidnapped in West Africa in the early nineteenth century and sent off to South Carolina and who left behind a small archive of manuscripts that included a short yet significant autobiography.[28] However, how can we make tangential records resonate across languages and spaces so these *Kunlun nu* can begin to acquire a presence, if not an incidentally assertive one, as we have seen in al-Wāsiṭī's illustration?

The tenth-century Arabic geographical work ʿAjāʾib al-Hind (Marvels of India) may be of use in this respect. Compiled reputedly by Buzurg ibn Shahryār al-Rām Hormuzī around 953 AD—exactly the same period when Taiping Guangji was completed—the work is a collection of sailors' tales related to the author by globetrotting captains and adventurous merchants. Just as in medieval Arabic writing, the term jāfā is often used to refer to the wider Malay Archipelago instead of Java in particular; so too does India in this context cover a broad geographical area that ranges as wide as from East Africa to Sumatra, with China located in between. The stress is invariably on the coastal regions, and many of the related stories—from massive fish or turtles mistaken by credulous captains as islands in the middle of nowhere to colossal birds used as aerial carriers by shipwrecked sailors for daring escapes—find strong echos, both in plotlines and in the Arabic vocabulary employed, with early manuscripts of the popular One Thousand and One Nights.

One of the tales in ʿAjāʾib al-Hind was narrated by Abu al-Zahr al-Barkhatī, a notable of the port of Sirāf (in contemporary Iran) who converted to Islam after being a fire-worshipping Magian following the religion of India (majūsiyyan ʿalā dīn al-Hind). The story states that al-Barkhatī's paternal grandfather traveled in a ship he owned, seeking to reach the island of Fanṣūr, and yet—as often happens in these stories—a violent gale blew them off course and threw them into the embrace of some unknown bay. Once the gale had passed, the sea was dead silent, with no wind to carry them where they needed to go. Unable to dock the ship, they drifted among the islands and were finally brought by the wave to one of them, on the shore of which they saw people resting and playing. Once the local people's trepidation was put to rest, the stranded merchants began what they were best at: trade. The following, worth quoting at length, describes the scene at this particular moment:

> We motioned to them and asked, "Do you have any merchandise we can buy?" "We have nothing but slaves (raqīq)," thus they replied. So we said unto them, "Good. Bring the slaves then." So they brought them. Never had we seen finer slaves. They were cheerful in nature (ḍuḥūk al-sann), they sang and played and bantered and took delight in funny tales. Their bodies were soft like cream, and they appeared so agile and brisk it seems as though they were ready to take flight at any moment. Except that their heads were small and below their flanks were wings like those wings that sea turtles have. We said unto them, "What the heck is this?" Laugh they did, and so they said, "all of the people of these islands are like this, so this is all you can have." They motioned to the sky, "Indeed God created us thus so we saw nothing awry in this [shape of ours]." "This is an opportunity!" We said [amongst ourselves], as we saw this as a chance for

some good catch. Every one of us bought to the extent he could afford. We emptied our ship of goods and loaded it full with slaves and provisions. No sooner had we bought some slaves from them did they bring us even more beautiful ones, and before long our ship was freighted with creatures finer than which no one had ever laid eyes upon. Alas if we had been allowed to bring this business to fruition we would have enriched generations of our progenies. . . . When the moment of departure arrived, a strong gust began to blow to us from these islands and towards our land. We bid farewell, and they said unto us, "Come again, God willing!" We did wish to return, and so did the captain, who, however, desired to come back with his ship alone, sans the merchants. For the whole night he and his men studied the stars and the constellations and the horizons and the pathways for departure and return. All of us were over the moon. At the break of dawn off we went from the island, riding the wind [that blew toward our land]. Once the island had vanished from view some of the slaves began to weep. Our hearts tightened from such wailing. Then some of them said unto others, "Why are you crying? Come, let us dance and sing and find merriment!" Then all the slaves stood, and dance they did, and they sang and laughed. We found this quite marvellous. We said to ourselves, "Well, at least this is better than weeping!" So we left them to it and each minded his own business. Little did we know that they were playing fools on us! By God [I swear that I saw them] fly into the sea like locusts and the ship rode immense swells as high as mountains and as terrifying as lightning. We did not again gain a clear sight of them until the ship had overtaken them for about one league. We heard them sing and laugh and flap their wings. Then we knew that they would not have done this had they possessed no might to conquer the terror of the high sea, and now it was impossible for us to bring them back.[29]

While we may not have space to discuss this episode in detail, it includes a number of significant elements that animate an informed historical imagination: similar to the trans-Atlantic slave trade, locals—in particular those who held power—also sold slaves to incoming merchant slavers. An accidental encounter, like the one described in this anecdote, could convert into a long-term enterprise. The text is wonderfully ambiguous concerning the identity of the slaves: for if the sellers belonged to the same group as the sold—that is, they too had wings attached to their flanks—then the moment of astonishment would seem oddly deferred for the Arab merchants. They showed no sign of being astounded when they first saw the natives lulling about on the seashore. Were the statements proclaiming the identity between the two groups thus a later Arab interjection because, in the eyes of the Arab narrator, they were after all fantastical creatures of the same island? No mention is made of whether the slaves being sold were black. Yet the conflation of various indigenous peoples resonates strongly with the equally sweeping claim made by Shi Huilin that all *Kunlun*, whether from East Africa or Southeast Asia, were invariably black and equally "base and lowly." Given the prevalent association of B/blackness with slavery in the high Abbāsid Arab-Islamic society, the possibility of them having been black cannot be ruled out.[30]

By a stroke of serendipity, al-Wāsiṭī's illustrated *Maqāmāt al-Ḥarīrī* once again comes to our aid. For one of the illustrations he made for "The Omani Maqāma" depicts a ship, whereupon we find the rare copresence of both black sailors and half-human, half-animal creatures with wings sprouting out from their flanks (figure 3.4). Oman appears frequently in *ʿAjāʾib al-Hind*, for the simple reason that both it and Yemen—the port of Aden specifically—were crucial entrepôts of trade for seafaring medieval Arab, Persian, and Jewish merchants. While some scholars

Figure 3.4. *Maqāmāt al-Ḥarīrī*, Paris Arabe 5847, folio 121 recto.
Source: Courtesy of Bibliothèque Nationale de France

have argued that this rich portrayal has largely been a figment of al-Wāsiṭī's painterly imagination, when the French Orientalist L. Marcel Devic used the same illustration as the frontispiece to his translation of ʿAjāʾib al-Hind, he obviously perceived more than an incidental correspondence.[31] For an illustrator whose knowledge of Arab folklore would have been essential to his professional success, it would surprise no one if al-Wāsiṭī had consulted the popular pool of tales of which ʿAjāʾib al-Hind was but one representative; he might well have consulted the book itself. Shi Huilin's cavalier racism (that all Kunlun are "equally base and lowly") seems but a common reaction, his sanctioned ignorance colluding with the equally insouciant attitude of the Arabs to obliterate the diverse histories gathered in even just one hold of human cargo.

## Conclusion: Race and the Prospect of a Subaltern Transregionalism

How are we to read these intertextual resonances and work through a puzzle of silences to restore some clarity to the often obscured figures of black sailors and slaves—the essential human infrastructure that underpins the connectivity of the medieval Islamicate world? Every so often, the sources present themselves like a hall of mirrors, and we are left with an amalgamation of skewed sights. It feels as though every observer was an onlooker, every writer an eavesdropper, every geographer an easy prey to marvelous illusions. Anecdotes abound, fantasies proliferate, yet history in the conventional sense seems in woefully short supply. We are thus compelled to look from behind, over the shoulders of those who saw but did not recognize, and by so doing wish for the best in reconstructing what is mostly missing.

In a recent article, Tom Hoogervorst insists on retaining the crucial distinction between maritime and mainland Southeast Asia in historical research. His remark on Srivijaya (三佛齊 San Fo Qi in medieval Chinese records), the Malay Buddhist thalassocratic empire that ruled much of Southeast Asia from the seventh to the twelfth century AD (the period that produced all the sources we have used in this article), is particularly pertinent to the present discussion:

> Srivijaya infused unparalleled quantities of spices . . . gold, tin, precious stones, ivory, rhinoceros horns, exotic birds, rainforest products, commodities from the sea, and slaves into trans-Asiatic trade networks. This range of poorly accessible resources reached the ports of Srivijaya through the hands of semi-sedentary foragers with specialized expertise to obtain them. The relations of these groups with Srivijaya and later polities were constantly renegotiated and often leveraged between mutual dependence and political subordination, reflecting a wider pattern throughout Southeast Asian history.[32]

Laying stress on the distinctiveness of coastal indigenous peoples in Southeast Asia thus skirts multiple boundaries of numerous empires and religions. If we are to consider the fact that the mighty Srivijaya systematically exploited the labor of Sama-Bajau—a coastal Austronesian indigenous group—and exported slaves to the trans-Asiatic trade networks, then the scenario we earlier encountered in ʿAjāʾib al-Hind could be deemed, sans a small amount of charming fantasy, a rather faithful reflection of what must have been a common reality in medieval maritime trade across the Indian Ocean and the South China Sea.

Neither Buddhism nor Islam, nor empires purportedly built on their spiritual appeal—whether Chinese, Perso-Arab, or Malay—acknowledged the often racialized exploitations they had imposed on the indigenous populations of maritime Southeast Asia and coastal East Africa. These groups were often described as being black or associated with black slaves in historical writings across languages. However, whether their origins could be traced to Africa is often unclear in the text, and this lack of attention to their origins is in stark contrast to the stress laid on the apparent features of their skin color. More recent projects, keen on reanimating medieval connectivities to feed contemporary imperialist ambitions—such as China's Belt and Road Initiative—will likely replicate, if not exacerbate, analogous patterns of exploitation and inequity. Focusing on the fleeting yet insistent eruptions of B/black presence in the multilingual archive can help us reimagine an alternative Global Asia of the subaltern that unfolds as much along bustling coastlines as on billow-braving ships. When Black people are no longer one; when Africa is but one node in a vast network of local yet globally linked hubs where B/black sailors and slaves are recruited; and when current regimes of global imperialism bring ever more forcefully to the surface the extent of connectivity among apparently disparate structures of racial and economic inequity, are we thus on the cusp of excavating the long-buried histories of a subaltern transregionalism that could be drawn upon as inspiration to resist contemporary iterations of global empire? The challenge is daunting, and Asian Studies as a field will likely have much to reckon with.

## Acknowledgements

Eric Schluessel read an earlier draft of this essay and provided valuable suggestions. Jia Hui Lee's wisdom and erudition lead me to ask more questions than can be included in this preliminary paper. I thank Benjamin Ridgway for his contribution in significantly improving the translation of Zhang Ji's poem. Naomi Koltun-Fromm, in addition to offering helpful comments, organized an intimate workshop around this paper in December 2021. I thank Maud McInerney and Luis Rodriguez-Ricon for their participation and recommendations. This paper has also been presented at a Faculty Research Seminar at Haverford College organized by Gustavus Stadler and Lindsay Reckson. I thank Christina Knight, Emily Hong, and Ava Shirazi for their generous readings and criticisms. This essay has benifited greatly from the scrutiny of the editors of this volume, Nitasha Tamar Sharma, Marvin Dale Sterling, and William Bridges, for which I am eternally grateful.

## Notes

[1] While it is true that in medieval Persian works, the word *chīn* often refers to Central Asia and East Turkestan, while *mā chīn* (the greater China) is mostly used for what is now known as China, perhaps as in most such cases where historical toponyms are involved, it is not always clear which place is referred to by which term. For *chīn* and *mā chīn* as used by Ferdawsī in his *Shāhnāmeh*, see Ja'afari and Pashazanus 1392.

[2] Ho 2017; 2006; Vink 2007; Worden 2017; Lambourn 2018; Jacob 2019; Prange 2018; Sood 2016; Schottenhammer 2008; 2019.

[3] For example, Li 2019.

[4] A few notable exceptions are worth mentioning here. The work of Don Waytt (2009) remains an essential reference, and Frank Dikötter's foundational survey (1994), while not always accurate, is still extremely useful and informative. For a general overview of recent works published on China-Africa relations—some of these works treat race more squarely than others—see Siu and McGovern 2017.

[5] Cf. Burton 2012; Menon 2014; Schueller 2003.

[6] Schine 2021.

[7] Ghosh and Chakrabarty 2002, 149.

[8] Ibid., 149.

[9] Erie 2016; Stroup 2022. Some examples to the contrary may be found in Chen 2014 and Hammond 2020.

[10] Gilroy 1993.

[11] Two groundbreaking books in this direction are worth mentioning. Robbie Shilliam's extraordinary *The Black Pacific* (2015)Pasifika and Pakeha activists incorporated the ideologies of the African diaspora into their struggle against colonial rule and racism, and their pursuit of social justice? This book challenges predominant understandings of the historical linkages that make up the (post- explores the Oceanic connections and the Indigenous-Black alliances in anti-colonial struggles; and Nitasha Tamar Sharma's recently published *Hawai'i Is My Haven: Race and Indigeneity in the Black Pacific* (2021) offers another much-needed vision for linking the Pacific to the Atlantic in the study of both Blackness and blackness and for examining their complex historical interactions.

[12] The original text of the poem can be found in Al-Isfahani 2008, 22:213.

[13] Diouf 1998, 4–48; Turner 2003, 11–46; GhaneaBassiri 2010, 9–58.

[14] Tolmacheva 2017; Webb 2020.

[15] Cf. Brown 2020.

[16] A line from Nine Songs 九歌 contained in *Chuci* 楚辭, for instance, has 登崑崙兮四望 心飛揚兮浩蕩. It is clear that the 崑崙 in later historical records, where it is associated almost exclusively with the color black, is derived from a completely different source— likely of a non-Chinese origin.

[17] Translated from Xu 1985, 1:311. Unless otherwise noted, all translations from Chinese, Arabic, and Persian texts in this article are my own.

[18] Translated from Shi 1988, 81:1325.

[19] Segal 2001, 4; Brown 2020, 128.

[20] Translation adapted from Chin 2004, with essential contribution from Benjamin Ridgway and Eric Schluessel.

[21] *Songshi* 宋史, *liezhuan* 列傳 249, *waiguo* 外國 6. Accessed on Dec. 20, 2021, at https://ctext.org/wiki.pl?if=gb&chapter=989027&remap=gb.

[22] See the last entry on *tāz* in the encyclopaedic Persian dictionary *Dehkhodā*. An online version is accessible at https://dehkhoda.ut.ac.ir/fa/dictionary/81202/%D8%AA%D8%A7 %D8%B2.

[23] Chong and Murphy 2017; Krahl 2010.

[24] al-Ḥarīrī 1978, 318.

[25] Al-Hariri 1898, 97.

[26] Original text where this excerpt is extracted is accessible at https://ctext.org/taiping-guangji/420/taoxian/zh.

[27] See, for instance, Zhu Yu's *Ping Zhou Ke Tan* 萍洲可談 (completed ca. 1119), vol. 2, no. 8. Accessed on Dec. 20, 2021, at https://ctext.org/wiki.pl?if=gb&chapter=57805.

[28] See Said 2011. Additional materials about Omar ibn Said is also available in the Omar ibn Said Collection held by the Library of Congress. For detail see https://www.loc.gov/ collections/omar-ibn-said-collection/about-this-collection/.

[29] al-Rām Hormuzī 1908, 24–25.

[30] Here the terminological ambiguity indicates exactly where the proposed project may break new ground. While I draw attention to the conceptual distinction between Blackness and blackness in the introduction to this article, the boundary between the two is necessarily a fuzzy one: Blackness as associated with Africa and black as a color attributed to all people considered as darker than oneself cross into each other when, for instance, both African slaves and Oceanic sailors work on the same ship and serve the same masters. To what extent is Blackness in upper case useful here, or does it at times run into some conceptual gridlock that demonstrates precisely its limit in helping us explore the interconnection between the Black Atlantic and the Black Pacific?

[31] O'Kane 2012, 49; Ettinghausen 1977, 123.

[32] Hoogervorst 2017, 754.

## Bibliography

Al-Hariri. *The Assemblies of Al-Hariri, Vol. II, Containing the Last 24 Assemblies.* Translated by F. Steingass. London: Royal Asiatic Society of Great Britain and Ireland, 1898.

Al-Isfahani, Abu Al-Faraj. *Kitāb Al-Aghāni.* 3rd ed. Vol. 22. 25 vols. Beirut: Dar Sadir, 2008.

Brown, Jonathan A. C. *Slavery and Islam.* New York: Simon and Schuster, 2020.

Burton, Antoinette M. *Brown over Black : Race and the Politics of Postcolonial Citation.* Gurgaon: Three Essays Collective, 2012.

Chen, J. T. "Re-Orientation: The Chinese Azharites between Umma and Third World, 1938–55." *Comparative Studies of South Asia, Africa and the Middle East* 34, no. 1 (2014): 24–51.

Chin, J. K. "Ports, Merchants, Chieftains and Eunuchs: Reading Maritime Commerce of Early Guangdong." In *Guangdong: Archaeology and Early Texts (Zhou-Tang).* Wiesbaden, Germany: Harrassowitz Verlag, 2004: 217–239.

Chong, Alan, and Stephen A. Murphy. *The Tang Shipwreck: Art and Exchange in the 9th Century.* Asian Civilisations Museum, 2017.

Dikötter, Frank. *The Discourse of Race in Modern China.* London: Hurst, 1994.

Diouf, Sylviane A. *Servants of Allah: African Muslims Enslaved in the Americas.* New York: NYU Press, 1998.

Erie, Matthew S. *China and Islam : The Prophet, the Party, and Law.* New York: Cambridge University Press, 2016.

Ettinghausen, Richard. *Arab Painting.* New York: Rizzoli, 1977.

GhaneaBassiri, Kambiz. *A History of Islam in America: From the New World to the New World Order.* Cambridge: Cambridge University Press, 2010.

Ghosh, Amitav, and Dipesh Chakrabarty. "A Correspondence on Provincializing Europe." *Radical History Review* 83, no. 1 (2002): 146–72.

Gilroy, Paul. *The Black Atlantic: Modernity and Double Consciousness.* Cambridge: Harvard University Press, 1993.

Hammond, Kelly A. *China's Muslims and Japan's Empire: Centering Islam in World War.* Chapel Hill: UNC Press Books, 2020.

Ḥarīrī, Abū Muḥammad al-Qāsim al-. *Maqāmat Al-Ḥarīrī.* Beirūt: Dār Bayrūt lil-Ṭibāʿa wa-l-Nashr, 1978.

Ho, Engseng. *The Graves of Tarim: Genealogy and Mobility across the Indian Ocean.* Berkeley: University of California Press, 2006.

———. "Inter-Asian Concepts for Mobile Societies." *The Journal of Asian Studies* 76, no. 4 (2017): 907–928.

Hoogervorst, Tom. "Tracing Maritime Connections between Island Southeast Asia and the Indian Ocean World." In *The Routledge Handbook of Archaeology and Globalization,* edited by Tamar Hodos. London: Routledge, 2017.

Hormuzī, Buzrug bn Sharyār al-Rām. *Kitāb 'Ajā'b al-Hind.* Based on the 1883 Leiden manuscript. Cairo: Muṣṭafā Fahmī al-Katabī, 1908.

Ja'afari, Aliakbar, and Hamidreza Pashazanus. "Chīn Dar Shāhnāme-Ye Ferdowsī." *Matnshenāsī-Ye Adab-e Fārsī* 20, no. 4 (1392): 59–72.

Jacob, Wilson Chacko. *For God or Empire: Sayyid Fadl and the Indian Ocean World.* Stanford: Stanford University Press, 2019.

Krahl, Regina. *Shipwrecked: Tang Treasures and Monsoon Winds.* Smithsonian Institution, 2010.

Lambourn, Elizabeth A. *Abraham's Luggage: A Social Life of Things in the Medieval Indian Ocean World.* Asian Connections. Cambridge: Cambridge University Press, 2018.

Li, Darryl. *The Universal Enemy: Jihad, Empire, and the Challenge of Solidarity.* Stanford: Stanford University Press, 2019.

Menon, Dilip M. "Bandung Is Back: Afro-Asian Affinities." *Radical History Review* 119 (2014): 241–45.

O'Kane, Bernard. "Text and Paintings in the Al-Wāsiṭī 'Maqāmāt.'" *Ars Orientalis* 42 (2012): 41–55.

Prange, Sebastian R. *Monsoon Islam: Trade and Faith on the Medieval Malabar Coast.* Cambridge Oceanic Histories. Cambridge: Cambridge University Press, 2018.

Said, Omar Ibn. *A Muslim American Slave: The Life of Omar Ibn Said.* Edited by Ala Alryyes. University of Wisconsin Press, 2011.

Schine, Rachel. "Race and Blackness in Premodern Arabic Literature." Oxford Research Encyclopedia of Literature. October 29, 2021.

Schottenhammer, Angela. *The East Asian Mediterranean: Maritime Crossroads of Culture, Commerce and Human Migration.* Wiesbaden: Otto Harrassowitz Verlag, 2008.

———. *Early Global Interconnectivity across the Indian Ocean World, Volume I: Commercial Structures and Exchanges.* New York: Springer, 2019.

Schueller, Malini Johar. "Articulations of African-Americanism in South Asian Postcolonial Theory: Globalism, Localism, and the Question of Race." *Cultural Critique* 55, no. 55 (2003): 35–62.

Segal, Ronald. *Islam's Black Slaves: The Other Black Diaspora*. New York: Macmillan, 2001.

Sharma, Nitasha Tamar. *Hawai'i Is My Haven: Race and Indigeneity in the Black Pacific*. Durham: Duke University Press, 2021.

Shi, Huilin. *Yiqie Jing Yinyi*. Taishō Tripiṭaka. Vol. 81. 100 vols. Tokyo: Daizo Shuppansha, 1988. http://tripitaka.cbeta.org/T54n2128.

Shilliam, Robbie. *The Black Pacific: Anti-Colonial Struggles and Oceanic Connections*. London: Bloomsbury Publishing, 2015.

Siu, Helen F., and Mike McGovern. "China–Africa Encounters: Historical Legacies and Contemporary Realities." *Annual Review of Anthropology* 46, no. 1 (2017): 337–355.

Sood, Gagan D. S. *India and the Islamic Heartlands: An Eighteenth-Century World of Circulation and Exchange*. Cambridge: Cambridge University Press, 2016.

Stroup, David R. *Pure and True: The Everyday Politics of Ethnicity of China's Hui Muslims*. Studies on Ethnic Groups in China. Seattle: University of Washington Press, 2022.

Tolmacheva, Marina A. "Concubines on the Road: Ibn Battuta's Slave Women." In *Concubines and Courtesans: Women and Slavery in Islamic History*, edited by Matthew S. Gordon and Kathryn A. Hain. New York: Oxford University Press, 2017: 164–189.

Turner, Richard Brent. *Islam in the African-American Experience*. Bloomington: Indiana University Press, 2003.

Vink, Markus P. M. "Indian Ocean Studies and the 'New Thalassology.'" *Journal of Global History* 2, no. 1 (2007): 41–62.

Webb, Simon. *The Forgotten Slave Trade: The White European Slaves of Islam*. Barnsley: Pen & Sword Books Limited, 2020.

Worden, Nigel. "Writing the Global Indian Ocean." *Journal of Global History* 12, no. 1 (2017): 145–154.

Wyatt, Don J. *The Blacks of Premodern China*. Illustrated edition. Philadelphia: University of Pennsylvania Press, 2009.

Xu, Song. *Jiankang Shilu*. Edited by Chenshi Zhang. Vol. 1. 2 vols. Beijing: Zhonghua Publishing House, 1985.

# 4

# THE ASIANIST IS MUSLIM

## THINKING THROUGH ANTI-MUSLIM
## RACISM WITH THE MUSLIM LEFT

### Soham Patel and M. Bilal Nasir

In the days following September 11, 2001, Edward Said penned an article in the *Guardian*, pointing out that the United States was far from an innocent "sleeping giant" attacked by "Muslims" and "Islam," as it had presented itself in the wake of the strikes on New York and Washington.[1] Rather, Said argued that the United States was the primary aggressor and an imperial "superpower almost constantly at war, or in some kind of conflict, all over the Islamic domains."[2] In reminding the public of the status of the United States as a global empire, the postcolonial scholar called attention to how the "age-old religious hostility to (and ignorance of) 'Islam'" overwhelmingly shaped American foreign policy in West, South, and Central Asia.[3] In remarkable foresight, Said warned of a "long war"—since deemed the "Forever War" or the "Global War on Terror"—to come if the United States and its public intellectuals did not radically transform the imperial culture that "made imaginable, even natural, imperial vision(s) of the Arab-Muslim East as a space demanding intervention."[4]

In this account of rising anti-Muslim sentiment and its consequences for US empire in the wake of 9/11 just over twenty years ago, Said merely extended many of the main arguments of his text *Orientalism*. In it, Said offered a trenchant critique of racialized distinction Orientalists, and therefore also colonial powers, historically made between the "Orient" and the "Occident" to claim authority over and to politically dominate the former. In other words, for Said, the problem of representing the Orient was not merely one of cultural essentialism but, more importantly, of governing the "Oriental" subject of Western Empire.

This critique approached Orientalism as a discourse or, more specifically, a discursive tradition that pervades domains as distinct as journalism, state bureaucracy, and academic scholarship.[5] It is for this reason that the publication of *Orientalism* and the advent of postcolonial studies rattled the discipline of "Oriental studies," leading to its breakup into Asian Studies and Middle East and Near Eastern studies departments. It also immensely shaped the epistemological and pedagogical approaches to questions of race, politics, and imperialism in emergent ethnic studies departments. While Said's critical interventions have clearly reverberated throughout the academy, his central concern with the othering of Muslims and Islam remain marginal to debates in area studies, such as Asian Studies, and in the humanities and the humanistic social sciences more broadly. This is especially curious because Said stated in interviews and popular articles that the "anti-Islamic" attitude of self-described "experts" involved with projects of European empire motivated him to write *Orientalism*, as did public discourses of the so-called Muslim World as the primary threat to Western morality, reason, and power.[6]

In this essay, we take Said's poignant interventions as a point of departure to address the limitations of Asian Studies regarding the question and representation of Muslims and Islam.[7] In many ways, our inquiry emerges from the erasure of Muslims from the category of Asian, as well as more recently from the category of Asian American, especially given the public discourse around anti-Asian racism. However, our chapter's intervention rests in offering Asian Studies a reflection upon European Orientalist discourse as a way to return to the centrality of Muslims and Islam in bridging Asian and Asian American histories and politics. To do this, we argue that the figure of the Muslim unsettles not only diaspora studies but also area studies.

While scholarship on diaspora has traditionally explored transnational movements and national circuits of power, area studies has been fixated upon region. The racial figure of the Muslim is neither national, transnational, nor regional, but global, whereby being everywhere and nowhere at the same time. For this reason, the figure of the Muslim reveals the limitations of Asian Studies and offers the field the possibility to reevaluate its thought and politics beyond "Asia." We thus consider how centering anti-Muslim rhetoric—or more specifically, anti-Muslim racism—and global Muslim politics can bring about a *critical* Asian Studies that connects the region, broadly conceived, and its diasporas in solidarity with the Global South and its ongoing political struggles against imperial racism, empire, and the violent conditions brought on by coloniality.

## Anti-Muslim Racism

Our suggestion that the "Asianist is Muslim" invites scholars within the field of Asian Studies to critically revise their position on Muslims and Islam. While academics and public commentators have mostly explored the discourse around the supposed predisposition of Muslims toward terror in the post-9/11 period, critical Muslim studies scholars have drawn on thinkers like Edward Said to argue that the racialization of Muslims and Islam extends back to the advent of colonial modernity. While colonialism effectively "[secularized] human existence" and initiated the rise of race as a master category, the concept of religion has received less consideration.[8] In other words, many scholars in the field of Asian and Asian American Studies who study race begin their inquiry into modern racism without accounting for the role of religion in the historical formation of coloniality. The discussion of religion is not only necessary but critical to understanding how Muslims and Islam are central to modern racial formation.

The racialization of non-Europeans, such as Muslims, constitutes a world-system dominated by coloniality, a matrix that orders our global and local economies, politics, and knowledges, and shapes the sensibilities and perceptions of people who have come under its sway in the Global South and its diasporas. According to decolonial scholars, coloniality denotes the *longue durée* of colonialism and its persistent structural effects on racial, religious, class, gendered, and sexual dimensions of social life.[9] We aruge that the figure of the Muslim, which served as Christendom's primary other in the late medieval era, brought this structure into being and that Muslims and Islam continue to importantly shape modern projects of race—including anti-Black racism, anti-Indigenous racism, and anti-Asian racism, among others—that demarcate humans from subhumans and non-humans.[10]

The Muslim has become a fungible taxonomy that US empire deploys to classify a broad range of intersectional identities embodying a political position other than secular liberal humanism.[11] While Muslims have historically been a faith-based community (*ummat al-Islam*), we are interested in foregrounding the concept of anti-Muslim racism within the field of Asian Studies. We make this move to reveal how anti-Muslim racism shapes the lives of not only Asians but many other groups that have been racialized as Muslim as a result of the US-led Global War on Terror. Simply put, foregrounding the Muslim within the field opens a new horizon of possibilities and solidarities for Asians and the Asian diaspora. Doing so, however, requires an examination of how anti-Muslim racism is constituted between the domains of religion and race.

As has been well-documented in the anthropology of Islam, the concept of "religion" is not universal but is instead a product of modern secular power. In his groundbreaking scholarship in postcolonial anthropology, Talal Asad suggests that the "secular" is not equivalent to the "non-religious," nor is secularism the de facto separation between "religion" and "politics."[12] Instead, the secular is a concept with an indeterminate relationship to its other—religion—that brings together certain attitudes, behaviors, sensibilities, and knowledges deemed indispensable for living a modern life. In this formulation, secularism must be understood as an administrative project of government that depends on the secular or secularity to manage everyday rational and moral life and cultivate properly modern selves. It is through secularism that modern states have historically established the social conditions to secularize populations and bring them under the care of the sovereign. Asad maintains that the secular is conceptually prior to secularism and, therefore, that the rationalities and moralities internal to secularity authorize modern power and its interventionist impulse.

However, secularity is not only conceptually prior to secularism, as Asad suggests, but also race. In her important work on race and colonialism, Sylvia Wynter argues that Columbus's voyage across the Atlantic set the stage for the Protestant Reformation and the "secularizing intellectual revolution of Renaissance humanism," which subsequently prompted the rise of the secular modern state.[13] Wynter adds that the colonial West and its secular epistemologies replaced premodern distinctions, such as mortal/immortal, natural/supernatural, and human/ancestors, with an overarching human/nonhuman distinction through contact with the New World and the enslavement of Africans. The West, as an imperial entity, thus produced a secular slot of otherness dominated by emerging notions of modern race.[14]

While Wynter importantly probes the relationship between secularism and race, she does not consider how the race concept emerged prior to European imperial intervention in the New World. Anthropologist Junaid Rana argues, "the story of the race concept emerges out of the religious exclusions practiced in the fourteenth and fifteenth century" as part of the centuries-long imperial project of the *Reconquista*.[15] Prior to Columbus's arrival in the New World, the processes that led to the genocide and forced conversion of Indigenous peoples in the Americas developed through the Castilian crown's subjugation of Muslims and Jews. Following the fall of Muslim rule in Granada, the conquistadors killed and expelled many Muslims and Jews in the Iberian Peninsula, allowing only those that converted to Christianity to stay in their homes. In analyzing conversion in relation to the emerging concept of race, Rana argues:

The prospect of conversion or death for Jews and Muslims was itself the act of shifting the religious into racial conceptions. For the explorers, it is important to note that Muslims and Jews constituted an early category of religious-racial other to transpose onto indigenous groups of the New World in the form of racial thought.[16]

In short, though conversion did not entail a physical death, it involved a type of social death, replacing Islamic, Judaic, or other forms of indigenous, theological, ethical selves and ways of life with those privileged by European empire. As the forerunner to the rise of the matrix of coloniality, the *Reconquista* produced pseudoracial knowledges based on notions of theological difference to distinguish the civilized Christian from the savage Muslim. Even those that converted to Christianity (*moros* and *marannos*) were never deemed properly "human" as they were unable to fully rid themselves of their allegiances to Islam and Judaism. While the West employed religion to categorize differences amongst the non-Christian populations of Europe and beyond, the birth of the secular sciences and the European man enshrined race as the primary system of classification in the modern world. Based on this history of the *Reconquista* and how it informs the political, epistemological, and ontological foundations of the modern West, it is our argument that the figure of the Muslim is central to the emergence of coloniality. It thus occupies an important racialized position as a theological and political "other" that the West continues to draw upon to shape and organize modern systems of capital accumulation, land dispossession, warfare, policing, and modern state sovereignty.[17] The post-9/11 era continued, if not intensified, this system of racial violence. The crisis mobilized an arsenal of modern state power—lethal and nonlethal—upon those suspected of being the source of terror: Muslims and Islam. Through biopolitical and ontopolitical technologies, the modern nation-state subjects Muslims to regimes of detention, deportation, and genocide. However, for Muslims, the process of racialization is not tied to a racial being but a racial becoming.[18]

> It is the corporeal features that may mark Muslim racialized being, but it is the coupling of the corporeal with the cultural that shifts the figure of the Muslim from a racial being to a racial becoming: Buried not too deep in this conversation of disparate philosophy is often the idea of biological difference—for example, the arguments that religious people are hardwired to think a certain way, "that their culture is different from ours" or that "they hate our way of life and will destroy us." Embedded in these rationales is a combination of biological and cultural reasoning that is central to racialization and a versatile and flexible process in fixating on a racial object. This is to say that the racialized Muslim is not a fixed racial object but becomes one and is profiled as a *racialized threat as potentiality*. Anti-Muslim racism, then, is about a kind of racialized becoming that is always in flux and is different from other forms of racism that have become part of a racial common sense. Anti-Muslim racism is the incarnation of a shifting conceptual apparatus that comprises racism as a technique and white supremacy as a systemic end.[19] (emphasis added)

This process of racialization does not simply involve identifying what a Muslim looks like but, more importantly, what a Muslim may become in the future. This is a distinct feature of the racial infrastructure of the counterterror state—a future-oriented state project that targets Muslims in the present as a preemptive measure against the potential or possibility that Muslims may become terrorists in the future. It is the logic of preemption and the emerging modalities of biopower, or more specifically, ontopower, that anchor Muslim racial becoming in the context of the US-led Global War on Terror.[20]

In this regard, the racial infrastructure that is created to police and contain Muslimness is shaped by the imperial racism of the US-led Global War on Terror that renders Muslims a global threat.[21] The everyday forms of racialized violence, such as surveillance, policing, deportation, and warfare, in the US and beyond depends on and is generative of anti-Muslim racism as Muslim racial becoming. In doing so, the West places Muslims within what Frantz Fanon called the "zone of nonbeing," or a "a zone for the subhuman," rendering them into legitimate targets of state-sanctioned racial violence and warfare. In containing Muslims and Islam within this zone, US empire casts them outside the domains of the political and juridical and subjects them to a world where anti-terror technologies, such as drones, and counterinsurgency strategies are omnipresent.[22]

While race casts Muslims out of the category of the political, in many ways, Muslims and Islam have also come to unsettle and disrupt modern understandings of *homo politicus*. For many, the nation-state dominates modern political imaginaries. The nation-state is where law and capital come to be regulated, and where democracy and freedom come to manifest—ultimately, where sovereignty is expressed. But the figure of the Muslim exists outside of secular liberal formations because they are neither in the nation-state nor of it. As a result of this, the modern world's positioning of Muslims in a zone of nonbeing should be read as a diasporic subject position where, regardless of geography, the Muslim is always out of place. In this sense, Muslims in a Muslim-majority nation, such as Arab Muslims in Egypt, are thus equally as displaced as Muslims in a minoritarian community, such as Black American Muslims in the United States, because of how the modern state intervenes in and dominates all aspects of Muslim ethical and political life.[23] The globality of anti-Muslim racism therefore collapses the distinction between the so-called Muslim world and its diasporas, and in many cases, between Muslims and non-Muslims. The modern state and its racialized technologies of death and dispossession at once target and dominate Kashmiris, Palestinians, Uyghurs, Black diasporas, Muslim and non-Muslim Arabs, and Sikhs, among other groups.

The rise of coloniality and modern race cannot be understood without considering the modern formation of anti-Muslim racism. While the Castilian crown laid the ground for modern race and anti-Muslim racism to emerge during the *Reconquista* and the Spanish Inquisition, these formations have historically shifted with changes to geopolitics and Western empire. Anti-Muslim racism has come to overwhelmingly inform the grammar of race in the twenty-first century with the onset of the US-led Global War on Terror and the globality of counterinsurgency-as-governance. Such conditions of race have immensely shaped everyday Muslim and Islamic life and the specter of physical and social death across Asia and the Asian diasporas. However, Muslims and those racialized as Muslims have not taken the US-led Global War on Terror and anti-Muslim racism lying down. They have forged robust movements of protest and critique across the lines of Muslim and non-Muslim, local and global, and religious and secular.

## On Muslim Decoloniality

Under conditions of coloniality, the question arises: What constitutes decolonization, or more specifically, decoloniality? Given the centrality of the modern state in upholding the racialized conditions of coloniality, decolonial thinkers have argued that the aim of decoloniality must not be to form sovereign nation states but to "offer horizons of liberation . . . beyond state designs, and corporate and financial desires."[24] In thinking beyond the sovereign state as a redemptive territorial imaginary, Sohail Daulatzai offers the concept of the "Muslim International," which connects "geographies of violence and shared territories of struggle against racial terror, global capital, and war" and where "ideas about community, resistance, and belonging can be engaged" in an anti-Muslim world.[25] While this political formation encompasses the Global South or the "Third World," it also includes minoritarian Muslim and non-Muslim communities that oppose the architecture of governing paradigms brought about by policing and militarism and their strategies of anti-terrorism and counterinsurgency. This is because, as mentioned in the previous section, the nation-state has made Muslims and the global ummah, as well as those racialized as Muslim, diasporic. Thus, the Muslim International intervenes to offer a political imaginary where these overlapping Black and Brown diasporas may root themselves in an alternative site for world-making. While the racial figure of the Muslim includes Desi and Arab communities, or what Asian American Studies scholar Nitasha Sharma coins as "Post-9/11 Brown," the figure also encompasses Black, Indigenous, Latinx, and other Asian American communities.[26] As such, it is important for us to name this site the "Muslim International" precisely due to the globality of the racializing logics that dominate, if not seek to eliminate, all aspects of Muslim ethical and political life. The name forces us to think beyond the racial paradigms of the coloniality that imagines the elimination of the Muslim from the secular world. It forces us to reckon with the possibility that Muslims could struggle and contest the global political order on their own terms. It is in response to such conditions of coloniality that an emergent scholarly and activist "Muslim Left" in the US has come to see themselves as part of the Muslim International and its ethical agenda of "[imagining] another world in line with struggles for social justice, decolonial liberation, and global solidarity."[27]

An important aspect of Muslim Internationalism as a conceptual tool and political formation in critical Muslim studies involves addressing the tensions between secularists and religionists. In the US and beyond, leftist politics often presupposes the attitudes, sensibilities, and notions of progressive history internal to secularity. As we have argued, secularity remains intimately entangled with coloniality, upholding the conceptual grammar of modern race and racialization. It is for this reason that those on the so-called left often racialize religion and approach religious practitioners as victims of "false consciousness." Such a position considers religion a hindrance to liberation, foreclosing the possibility of a radical politics against anti-Muslim racism that draws on religious traditions, such as Islam.

To remedy such tensions, scholars of the Muslim Left have turned to figures like El Hajj Malik El-Shabazz, or Malcolm X, who sought to forge global antiracist solidarities between both religious and secular Black Americans, Asians, and Africans in the Global South and in the diaspora. Malcolm X, for example, saw himself as part of the ummah *and* part of the four-fifths of the "Darker World" and worked until the end of his life to connect the struggles of Muslims and non-Muslims alike against white supremacy and empire. Figures like Malcolm, and the tradition of Muslim Internationalism that he inaugurated, therefore offer a model for building global networks of solidarity against anti-Muslim racism and other iterations of racism (e.g. anti-Black, anti-Indigenous, anti-Latinx, anti-East Asian, anti-South Asian, etc.) that move beyond the secular and religious divide. In the context of the United States, Muslim Americans across racial groups have drawn on Malcolm, or El Hajj Malik El-Shabazz, as both a secular and religious figure to build pan-racial coalitions of solidarity that address white supremacy and anti-Muslim racism, as well as racial hierarchies that pit West and South Asian American Muslims against Black American Muslims.[28] Accounting for Malcolm as at once a theologian and radical political thinker, we argue that a decolonial ethics—an ethics "oppositional in nature in contexts defined by modernity/coloniality" that involves reorienting "the self in conditions of systematic dehumanization"—forged in response to anti-Muslim racism must not only consider secularist traditions but also religious ones, such as Islam.[29]

A critical Asian Studies must account for such formations of radical Muslim politics and Muslim decoloniality. In the last two decades, the US-led Global War on Terror has systemized a global infrastructure of anti-Muslim racism, as well as given rise to Muslim political movements against policing, militarism, and other forms of state-sanctioned anti-terror violence from Srinigar to Los Angeles, Xinjiang to Lagos, Palestine to Peshawar, and London to Damascus. These sites of protest and radical Muslim politics reorient the relationship between Asian and Asian American Studies, effectively unsettling the idea of "Asia" as a region politically closed off from its diasporas. Probing global anti-Muslim racism and the US-led Global War on Terror further brings the political movements of Asia in conversation with those in Asian America. Engaging with the Muslim International and the Muslim Left links area studies and critical ethnic studies, establishing a space for a critical Asian Studies that attends to insurgent, transnational intellectual and political projects rooted in traditions of Muslim decoloniality.

## Conclusion

This essay probed the question of what constitutes "the Asianist" by reimagining Asian Studies through the racial figure of the Muslim and the presumed problem of Islam. We began with an exploration of how Edward Said and his incisive critique of Orientalism informed the epistemological and disciplinary foundations of Asian Studies in the US. While Asian Studies received and incorporated *Orientalism*'s concern for Western essentialisms of the "East," the discipline disregarded Said's primary concern with how representations of Muslims and Islam recursively shapes Western imperial interventions across the Asian continent. With the onset of the US-led Global War on Terror, Asian American Studies scholars started analyzing how the long-standing logics of anti-Muslim racism under conditions of coloniality had come to structure global Muslim and non-Muslim life. These debates not only connected the plight of Asians to Asian Americans but also gave rise to conceptual tools to describe emergent forms of oppositional politics.

We argue that a shift from Asian Studies to *critical* Asian Studies demands taking account of Muslim Internationalism and the Muslim Left. In other words, if Asian Studies hopes to speak to issues of race, empire, and coloniality, it must attend to the forms of anti-Muslim racism that US empire has globalized in the twenty-first century, as well as the various secular and religious movements that have emerged in critique of such a world. This certainly requires returning to Edward Said and his important texts that reconfigured the field more than half a century ago but also engaging with traditions of politics and scholarship from the Muslim Left.

## Notes

[1] Said, "Islam and the West are Inadequate Banners."

[2] Ibid.

[3] Ibid.

[4] El Haj, "Edward Said and the Political Present," 538.

[5] El Haj draws on the work of Talal Asad and his conception of tradition to argue that "Orientalist discourse is an archive of systematic statements and bodies of knowledge, continuously drawn on and reformulated, that converges with broader prevailing philosophical tendencies at different moments in time (e.g., race theory in the 19th century), all the while retaining a powerful trace of itself as Europe reexperiences the Orient but never as something wholly new or alien" (Ibid., 545).

[6] Said, "Islam through Western Eyes."

[7] Anthropologists in Asian Studies and Middle East studies have produced several important ethnographies probing Islam as an embodied and discursive tradition. While these texts address the asymmetries of empire and anthropological representations of Muslim and Islam, they have paid less attention to how global anti-Muslim racism shapes and informs everyday Islamic practice. See Mahmood, *Politics of Piety*; Hirschkind, *The Ethical Soundscape*; Agrama, *Questioning Secularism*.

[8] Sylvia Wynter, "Beyond the Word of Man: Glissant and the New Discourse of the Antilles," 639.

[9] Walter Mignolo, *Local Histories/Global Designs*; Nelson Maldonado-Torres, *Against War*.

[10] For more on the centrality of the figure of the Muslim in late medieval, and therefore also early modern, European formations of race, see Arjana, *Muslims in the Western Imagination*.

[11] Daulatzai, *Black Star, Crescent Moon*; Jamal and Naber, *Race and Arab Americans Before and After 9/11*; Junaid Rana, *Terrifying Muslims*; Razack, *Casting Out*.

[12] Asad, *Formations of the Secular*.

[13] Wynter, "Unsettling the Coloniality of Being/Power/Truth/Freedom: Towards the Human, After Man, Its Overrepresentation—An Argument."

[14] For a more detailed discussion on the intimacies between race, religion, and secularism, see Fernando, *The Republic Unsettled: Muslim French and the Contradictions of Secularism*; Lloyd, "Introduction: Managing Race, Managing Religion" in *Race and Secularism in America*; Nasir, "Mad Kids, Good City: Counterterrorism, Mental Health, and the Resilient Muslim Subject."

[15] Junaid Rana. "The Story of Islamophobia."

[16] Ibid.

[17] We make this argument based on the work of several scholars of religion and the anthropology of religion. Gil Anidjar argues that while Europe constructed the Jew as the internal theological enemy, it deemed the Muslim its external political enemy. Since Jews have increasingly been folded into the political position of whiteness, particularly after WWII, the figure of the Muslim has come to occupy both positions as at once an internal (theological) and external (political) enemy, particularly in the context of the US-led Global War on Terror. In this regard, the figure of the Muslim is foundational to the development of discourses and practices of colonial difference-making that created the conditions for racial domination, including the transatlantic slave trade and settler colonialism in the Americas. Furthermore, given that the figure of the Muslim is at the

center of the more recent US-led Global War on Terror, we make this argument to show that scholarship on race and empire must critically think about how the specter of Islam informs and sustains the ontological and epistemological foundations of the so-called West. For more, see Hussein Ali Agrama, 2016, "Thinking with Saba Mahmood," *The Immanent Frame*; Gil Anidjar, *The Jew, the Arab: A History of the Enemy*; Sylvester A. Johnson, *African American Religions, 1500–2000: Colonialism, Democracy, and Freedom*; Tomaž Mastnak, *Crusading Peace: Christendom, the Muslim World, and Western Political Order*; Leerom Medovoi, "Dogma-Line Racism: Islamophobia and the Second Axis of Race"; Junaid Rana, "The Story of Islamophobia."

[18] Rana, "The Racial Infrastructure of the Terror-Industrial Complex."

[19] Daulatzai and Rana, "Introduction" in *With Stones in Our Hands*, xv–xvi.

[20] The theory of Muslim racial becoming depends on the interrelated concepts of preemption and ontopower. Preemption operates on the basis of a "threat-matrix" that deems potential threats not only imminent to the present but more importantly to the future. The epistemology of preemption rests on complete uncertainty, for present-future threats are always "in potential" or in a state of "becoming." For this reason, preemptive power returns to "life's unlivable conditions of emergence in order to bring life back, redirecting its incipience to alter-emergent effect" (Massumi 41). Brian Massumi terms this security formation "ontopower" because its point of application is at the level of nature and ontology rather than territory and population—as is the case with biopower. For a more detailed discussion of preemption and ontopower, see Masco, *Theater of Operations*; Massumi, *Ontopower: War, Powers, and the State of Perception*.

[21] Soham Patel, "Policing Insurgents: Race and Security in the Forever War" (unpublished manuscript, May 2021), typescript.

[22] Daulatzai, "Introduction" in *Fifty Years of the Battle of Algiers*, xvii.

[23] For a discussion of the Muslim ummah as a diasporic formation, see S. Sayyid, *Recalling the Caliphate: Decolonization and World Order*, 114–116.

[24] Mignolo and Walsh, "On Decoloniality: Concepts, Analytics, Praxis," 125.

[25] Daulatzai, *Black Star, Crescent Moon*, xxii–xxiii.

[26] Sharma, "Rap, Race, Revolution," in *Audible Empire*.

[27] Daulatzai and Rana, "Introduction" in *With Stones in Our Hands*, x.

[28] For more on this, see Abdul Khabeer, *Muslim Cool*; Grewal, *Islam is a Foreign Country*; Kashani, "The Audience is Still Present."

[29] Maldonado-Torres, "Race, Religion, and Ethics in the Modern/Colonial World," 7, 16.

## Bibliography

Abu El-Haj, Nadia. "Edward Said and the Political Present." *American Ethnologist*. 32 (2005): 538–555.

Abdul Khabeer, Su'ad. *Muslim Cool: Race, Religion, and Hip Hop in the United States*. New York: NYU Press, 2016.

Agrama Hussein Ali, "Thinking with Saba Mahmood." *The Immanent Frame,* February 25, 2016. https://tif.ssrc.org/2016/02/25/thinking-with-saba-mahmood/.

Amaney, Jamal and Nadine Christine Naber. *Race and Arab Americans Before and After 9/11: From Invisible Citizens to Visible Subjects.* Syracuse: Syracuse University Press, 2008.

Anidjar, Gil. *The Jew, the Arab: A History of the Enemy.* Palo Alto: Stanford University Press, 2003.

———. *Semites: Race, Religion, Literature.* Palo Alto: Stanford University Press, 2007.

Asad, Talal. *The Idea of an Anthropology of Islam.* Center for Contemporary Arab Studies 1 (1986): 1–30.

———. *Genealogies of Religion: Discipline and Reasons of Power in Christianity and Islam.* Baltimore: Johns Hopkins University Press, 1993.

———. *Formations of the Secular.* Palo Alto: Stanford University Press, 2003.

———. *On Suicide Bombing.* New York: Columbia University Press, 2007.

Aydin, Cemil. *The Idea of the Muslim World.* Cambridge: Harvard University Press, 2017.

Bouteldja, Houria. *Whites, Jews, and Us: Toward a Politics of Revolutionary Love.* Pasadena: Semiotext(e), 2017.

Daulatzai, Sohail. *Black Star, Crescent Moon: The Muslim International and Black Freedom Beyond America.* Minneapolis: University of Minnesota Press, 2012.

———. *Fifty Years of the Battle of Algiers: Past as Prologue.* Minneapolis: University of Minnesota Press, 2016.

Daulatzai, Sohail and Junaid Rana. *With Stones in Our Hands: Writings on Muslims, Racism, and Empire.* Minneapolis: University of Minnesota Press, 2018.

Deeb, Lara. *An Enchanted Modern.* Princeton: Princeton University Press, 2006.

Fanon, Frantz. *The Wretched of the Earth.* New York: Grove Press, 2005.

———. *Black Skin, White Masks.* New York: Grove Press, 2008.

Felber, Garret. *Those Who Know Don't Say: The Nation of Islam, the Black Freedom Movement, and the Carceral State.* Raleigh: University of North Carolina Press, 2020.

Fernando, Mayanthi. *The Republic Unsettled: Muslim French and the Contradictions of Secularism.* Durham: Duke University Press, 2014.

Gomez, Michael. *Black Crescent: The Experience and Legacy of African American Muslims in the Americas*. Cambridge: Cambridge University Press, 2005.

Grewal, Zareena. *Islam is a Foreign Country*. New York: NYU Press, 2014.

Hesse, Barnor. "Racialized Modernity: An Analytics of White Mythologies." *Ethnic and Racial Studies* 30, no. 4 (2007): 643–663.

Hirschkind, Charles. *The Ethical Soundscape: Cassette Sermons and Islamic Counterpublics*. New York: Columbia University Press, 2006.

Johnson, Sylvester A. *African American Religions, 1500–2000: Colonialism, Democracy, and Freedom*. New York: Cambridge University Press, 2015.

Kashani, Maryam. "The Audience is Present: Invocations of El-Hajj Malik El-Shabazz by Muslims in the United States." In Sohail Daulatzai and Junaid Rana eds., *With Stones in Our Hands: Writings on Muslims, Racism, and Empire*. Minneapolis: University of Minnesota Press, 2018.

Kahn, Jonathon Samuel. *Race and Secularism in America*. New York: Columbia University Press, 2016.

Kundnani, Arun. *The Muslims Are Coming!* London: Verso Books, 2014.

Mahmood, Saba. *The Politics of Piety: The Islamic Revival and the Feminist Subject*. Princeton: Princeton University Press, 2005.

Maldonado-Torres, Nelson. *Against War: Views from the Underside of Modernity*. Durham: Duke University Press, 2008.

———. "Race, Religion, and Ethics in the Modern/Colonial World." *Journal of Religious Ethics*. 42, no. 4 (2014): 691–711.

Mamdani, Mahmood. *Good Muslim, Bad Muslim: America, the Cold War, and the Roots of Terror*. New York: Pantheon Books, 2004.

Masco, Joseph. *The Theater of Operations: National Security Affect from the Cold War to the War on Terror*. Durham: Duke University Press, 2014.

Massumi, Brian. *Ontopower: Wars, Powers, and the State of Exception*. Durham: Duke University Press, 2015.

Mastnak Tomaž. *Crusading Peace: Christendom, the Muslim World, and Western Political Order*. Berkeley: University of California Press, 2002.

Medovoi, Leerom. "Dogma-Line Racism Islamophobia and the Second Axis of Race." *Social Text*. 30, no. 2 (2012): 43–74.

Mignolo, Walter. *Local Histories/Global Designs: Coloniality, Subaltern Knowledges, and Border Thinking*. Princeton: Princeton University Press, 2012.

Mignolo, Walter and Catherine E. Walsh. *On Decoloniality: Concepts, Analytics, Praxis.* Durham: Duke University Press, 2018.

Nadine, Naber. *Arab America: Gender, Cultural Politics, and Activism.* New York: NYU Press, 2012.

Nasir, M. Bilal. "Mad Kids, Good City: Counterterrorism, Mental Health, and the Resilient Muslim Subject." *Anthropological Quarterly* 92, no. 3 (2019): 817–844.

Patel, Soham. "Policing Insurgents: Race and Security in the Forever War." Unpublished manuscript, May 2021, typescript.

Rana, Junaid. *Terrifying Muslims: Race and Labor in the South Asian Diaspora.* Durham: Duke University Press, 2011.

———. "The Story of Islamophobia." *Souls.* 9, no. 2 (2007): 148–161.

———. "The Racial Infrastructure of the Terror-Industrial Complex." *Social Text* 34 4, no. 129 (2016): 111–138.

Razack, Sherene. *Casting Out: Race and the Eviction of Muslims from Western Law and Politics.* Toronto: University of Toronto Press, 2008.

Said, Edward. *Orientalism.* New York: Pantheon Books, 1978.

———. "Islam through Western Eyes." *The Nation*, April 26, 1980. https://www.thenation.com/article/archive/islam-through-western-eyes/.

———. "Islam and the West are Inadequate Banners." *The Guardian*, September 16, 2001. https://www.theguardian.com/world/2001/sep/16/september11. terrorism3

———. *Culture and Imperialism.* New York: Vintage Books, 1994.

———. *Covering Islam: How the Media and the Experts See the Rest of the World.* New York: Vintage Books, 1997.

Sayyid, Salman. *Recalling the Caliphate: Decolonization and World Order.* London: C. Hurst & Co., 2014

Sharma, Nitasha, "Rap, Race, Revolution: Post-9/11 Brown and a Hip Hop Critique of Empire." In *Audible Empire: Music, Global Politics, Critique,* eds. Ronald Radano and Tejumola Olaniyan, 292–313. Durham: Duke University Press, 2016.

Wynter, Sylvia. "Beyond the Word of Man: Glissant and the New Discourse of the Antilles." *World Literature Today.* 63, no. 4 (1989): 637–648.

———. "Unsettling the Coloniality of Being/Power/Truth/Freedom: Towards the Human, After Man, Its Overrepresentation—An Argument." *CR: The New Centennial Review* 3, no. 3 (2003): 257–337.

# 5

# RACIAL CAPITALISM AND THE NATIONAL QUESTION IN THE EARLY PEOPLE'S REPUBLIC OF CHINA

## Jeremy Tai

Recent diplomatic, economic, and military tensions between the United States and the People's Republic of China have compelled quite a few scholars and observers to debate whether we are witnessing a new Cold War. The comparison often loses sight of the uneven quality of the Cold War and the ideological departures of reform-era China, but one commonality between the past and present is the spotlight on racial and ethnic conflict. The early PRC participated in a global critique of US imperialism and Jim Crow while Americans countered with their own evidence of abuses and dissent in the socialist world. Similarly, nationalists in each country now point to various forms of injustice in the other, whether it is white supremacy, xenophobia, racist violence, and systemic racism in the US, or the mass surveillance, detention, and assimilation of non-Han peoples in the PRC. In our present political conjuncture, how can China scholars productively bring together these transnational discussions of race and ethnicity in a way that troubles such instrumentalization that only reinforces geographical and conceptual divisions inherited from Cold War knowledge production?

Scholars of East Asia have long interrogated the origins of area studies in the postwar period, namely, how these interdisciplinary programs were meant to not only remedy the shortage of reliable information about non-European nations but also support American strategic interests during the Cold War. The empirical premises of area studies were undermined when area specialists applied modernization theory to different societies and evaluated them according to an American ideal type that was far from realized domestically.[1] During the Vietnam War, the Committee of Concerned Asia Scholars anticipated Edward Said's later critique of Orientalism and criticized the field's complicity with US foreign policy. They departed from earlier representations by reflecting on the history of imperialism and presenting radical political subjects.[2] At the same time, student demands for greater inclusion and representation at US universities led to the formation of ethnic studies in the late 1960s.

Despite this shared moment of counterhegemonic protest, scholars have noted a deep-seated disciplinary divide between the study of geopolitics in area studies and that of race in ethnic studies that reflects foundational orientations to power, visible in both methodology and positionality.[3] Critical race scholar David Theo Goldberg has pointed out how comparative accounts in area studies can be problematic for the study of race because the juxtaposition of discrete national examples can miss how race and racism are both "globally circulating, interacting, relational conditions" and "locally indexed, resonant, impacting."[4] For literary critic Shu-mei Shih, scholars working in Asian Studies can appear to escape the realities of US racial politics by producing civilizational and culturalist scholarship, which recasts racialization as cultural difference and disavows the global connections constituting racial formation. In fact, area specialists can be quite dismissive of colleagues working in the vein of ethnic studies—an unease symptomatic of the premise of separation from one's object of study in area studies.[5] Studies of Afro-Asian solidarity, Asian diasporas, and other trans-Pacific connections have worked to bridge these fields, but critical approaches to race remain limited in Asian Studies, especially when compared to the popularity of critical theory and postcolonial studies.[6]

I build on these discussions focusing on divisions within the US academy by turning to the ways that certain conventions in the PRC can also foreclose considerations of race in the China field, even as it is home to a significant body of scholarship on nationalism and ethnicity. In The Intimacies of Four Continents, Asian American Studies scholar Lisa Lowe considers how liberal narratives of freedom were articulated within a context marked by settler colonialism, slavery, indenture, and empire and served to disavow their constitutive violence. For Lowe, reading across areas in the archive of liberalism can reveal imbricated processes and unspoken intimacies of colonized and dispossessed peoples.[7] Chinese socialism articulated its own understandings of liberation, and its archive reveals categorical distinctions that can be productively brought together to illustrate the relations, tensions, and contradictions between different political projects. My discussion below considers how the archive of actually existing socialism separated race (*zhongzu*) and nation/ethnicity (*minzu*) within a discursive field shaped not only by historical materialism but also by the geopolitical necessity to differentiate racialization in capitalist countries from ethnopolitics in socialist countries. This essay extends the insights of previous scholarship that has problematized the conceptual distinction between race and nation/ethnicity in other contexts by illustrating how its reification in China has functioned to externalize questions of racialization and the geography of racial capitalism.[8]

The discussion below first brings Cedric Robinson's concept of racial capitalism to bear on existing scholarship that has attended to Chinese experiences and criticisms of the global color line. Next, I examine the trajectory of the terms "race" and "nation" after their moment of translation, particularly the ways in which leftist intellectuals differentiated them in response to right-wing conflations, often with reference to orthodox Marxist definitions of race as precapitalist. Lastly, I show how socialist intellectuals in the early PRC moved beyond orthodox understandings of race amidst solidarity forged with anti-racist and anti-colonial movements, but how the Cold War context also meant that their internationalist critiques of racial capitalism were separated from discussions of domestic ethnopolitics.

## Racial Capitalism and Chinese Understandings of the Global Color Line

In *Black Marxism*, Cedric Robinson argued against conventional Marxist understandings of capitalism as a force of historical progress that negated feudalism and introduced the proletariat as the universal subject of history. Capitalism instead maintained premodern and early modern modes of violence and subjugation based on regional, cultural, and linguistic differences and further articulated them to include the categories of biological racism, reflecting its tendency to differentiate, not homogenize.[9] Building on the Black radical tradition, Robinson's concept of racial capitalism has inspired much scholarship on how the human, less-than-human, and nonhuman have been defined through capitalist world-making processes of settlement, slavery, imperialism, and migration.[10] Scholars have long argued the analytic category of abstract labor can obscure racial divisions central to the production of surplus value.[11] Recent attention to indigenous, racialized, and gendered forms of expropriation reveal the limits of analyses centered on the exploitation of the "free" waged worker by illustrating the often violent and coercive conditions necessary for the establishment of private property regimes, debt and extractive economies, labor-intensive industries, and social reproduction.[12]

Robinson's concept of racial capitalism has been conspicuously absent in the China field, but existing scholarship would suggest that it is far from foreign to Chinese society and culture. Since the nineteenth century, political authorities and intellectuals in China have been highly conscious of how the global color line structured the country's standing vis-à-vis imperialist powers in the modern capitalist world. Early on, imperialist wars against China sought to demonstrate its racial inferiority and its need to cast off supposedly barbaric practices for its own universal principles, including free trade.[13] Nineteenth-century liberal thinkers heralded the introduction of Chinese coolies to British and Spanish colonies as a transition from unfree to free labor, but despite the presence of contacts, conditions likened to slavery led some to argue that indentured workers were far from harbingers of freedom.[14] In the Americas and Southeast Asia, anti-Chinese violence and exclusion also occurred through the identification of the "Asiatic racial form" with the seemingly abstract and destructive dimensions of capitalism, such as mercantile capital, mechanical efficiency, and less-than-human labor exempt from the needs of normative social reproduction.[15] As a founding moment in the modern immigration system, Chinese exclusion allowed settlers to appropriate native identity and assimilate indigenous and racialized communities, all while spurring protests in China and compelling diasporic populations to return to an imagined homeland.[16]

The late Qing translation of race and nation overlayed existing understandings of social difference in China (e.g., Han versus Manchu) and shaped understandings of a new capitalist world materializing in imperialist competition, war, colonization, concessions, and debt. The meaning of these neologisms remained fluid, and ambiguities shared with European discourses made them available for various projects across the political spectrum.[17] When intellectuals embraced the modern concept of the nation (*minzu*), their search for an imagined community also identified a shared predicament (*tongzhong*, "same race/kind") with other societies undergoing dispossession and the loss of sovereignty around the world.[18] Alongside references to Red, Brown, and Jewish nations, the figure of the Black slave (*Heinu*) became a popular metaphor in modern Chinese literature for considering various forms of subjugation and possibilities for redemption.[19] Even though race (*renzhong/zhongzu*) could be construed through historical configurations of power rather than phenotype or culture, many elites reproduced the logics, hierarchies, and exclusions of racialist thinking, even when they were accused of being provincial.[20] Han nationalists defined the nation as a primordial community based in blood relations to first distinguish themselves from the Manchus and later claim common ancestry with non-Han peoples amidst debates over the nature and limits of the body politic.[21] Some attempted to cross the global color line by claiming the superiority of the yellow race and possibilities for pan-Asianism or its proximity to whiteness and the need for intermarriage and racial amalgamation.[22] By the 1930s, ethnologists rejected notions of consanguinity that led to the conflation of nation and race, differentiating them with reference to culture and phenotype or arguing the latter was irrelevant because of racial mixing over the years.[23]

## Distinguishing Race and Nation as Anti-Fascism

The Chinese Communist Party (CCP) too distinguished the concepts of race and nation when organizing on different political fronts, which became articulated in relation to the perils of fascism. Communist internationalism and class-based organizing had long rejected liberal and fascist conceptualizations of race, but the Holocaust led socialist intellectuals to further disavow problematic theories that seemed commensurable with fascism. Biologist Zhou Jianren had introduced eugenic principles for racial improvement in the 1920s, but after the Second World War, he warned that the ruling class of capitalist countries deployed eugenics to serve as the basis for false claims of an innate lack of intelligence and morality among the oppressed, which supposedly led to criminality.[24] Pseudoscientific abstractions about the inherited qualities of populations not only occluded the analyses of social conditions, but they also served as a justification for racism, class discrimination, war, and colonialism, with the Holocaust as its gravest example. Even though fascism had been defeated, Zhou argued it was important to remain vigilant, as its remnants could spread. He pointed to acts of violence being committed by GIs stationed in China after the war, and he argued that they were extensions of racism and injustice experienced by African Americans in the US.[25]

Socialist intellectuals also distanced themselves from the Guomindang (GMD), who they deemed "fascist Han chauvinists," a Chinese counterpart to Great Russian chauvinism. In the 1920s and 1930s, Marxist philosophers Li Da and Qu Qiubai introduced the national question using Soviet sources, but the implications of Stalin's claims that the nation was a social formation particular to the capitalist epoch were unclear for semicolonial China, where intellectuals debated the periodization of feudalism and capitalism in Chinese history.[26] When organizing in the hinterland, the CCP tried to win the support of non-Han peoples by recognizing a multiethnic polity, espousing the right to self-determination, incorporating ethnic oppression into social analysis, and banning ethnic slurs and insults.[27] Its intellectuals lambasted the GMD for arguing that Han and non-Han peoples were the main and branch stocks of the same race and blood, differentiated only by religion and region.[28] Marxist historian Lü Zhenyu argued that such arguments about racial stocks followed the wishful thinking of German and Japanese fascists. In contrast to GMD assimilationist accounts and lack of recognition, he also reminded readers how Han and non-Han peoples had been mutually constituted over time.[29]

In the early PRC, some social scientists responded to the remnants of fascist ideology by reproducing an orthodox Marxist designation of race as a precapitalist social formation, or situating it outside of history altogether. Historian Huang Yuanqi attributed the conflation between nation and race to the right-wing emphasis on blood relations and the lack of standardization in Soviet translations. He explained Chinese society comprised different races until the Warring States period, after which racial amalgamation occurred and clans emerged as the primary unit of social organization. The Qing conquest, the feudal system, and imperialism arrested national formation for Han and non-Han, but once the CCP liberated them from imperialists, bureaucratic capitalists, Han landlords, and non-Han elites, they had become a new democratic *minzu*.[30] Sociologist Rong Guanxiong also criticized early PRC intellectuals for misuses of race, particularly in references to non-Han peoples that led to a barrage of new terms, such as "racial wars," "racial contradictions," "racial oppression," and "racial struggles." According to Rong, race was an effect of environmental factors on outward appearance that had no bearing on economic production, social development, or cultural formation—it was a biological phenomenon subject to anthropological research, not a social one like nation, which was subject to ethnological research.[31] For these social scientists, race could not be a determining factor for historical analysis or a category for modern political organizing.

## Internationalist Solidarity and Cold War Orientations

Earlier worlding practices combined with a global moment of decolonization, and a new socialist state served as the grounds for internationalist solidarity with anti-colonial and anti-racist struggles that moved discussions of race beyond orthodox positions. The official journal *World Affairs* (*Shijie zhishi*) became an important forum for critiques of racial capitalism, with coverage of apartheid in South Africa and Jim Crow in the US often presented to Chinese audiences as continuous with wartime fascism. Editor Chen Zanwei reported how under Prime Minister D. F. Malan, the passage of legislation, such as the Prohibition of Mixed Marriages, Group Areas Act, Suppression of Communism Act, and Pass Laws in South Africa subjected indigenous Africans, Indians, Malays, and Chinese to forced removal, separate settlements, political disenfranchisement, low-wage and dangerous work in mines, unhealthy environments, and counterinsurgency campaigns. By contrast, white South Africans held over 88 percent of land, and US investment in copper, magnesium, and uranium mines; motor vehicle and rubber production; and shipbuilding grew during and after the war. As Zhou Enlai and Mao Zedong issued statements of solidarity, the journal publicized the work of anti-apartheid activists in organizing the general strike of June 26, 1950, and the historic Defiance Campaign of 1952.[32]

Writing after the UN denunciation of racist policies in South Africa, scholar of international law Chen Tiqiang reminded readers in the lead-up to the Bandung

Conference that racism and colonialism were the common experience of African and Asian peoples. Racism facilitated the oppression of national minorities and colonized and semi-colonized nations, and it also facilitated labor exploitation and false consciousness that displaced class-based politics. The clearest example of racism was found in Aryanism and the genocide of six million Jews, the most shameful page in human history. In the postwar period, the racial divisions produced in apartheid South Africa were mirrored in European landholdings in Tunisia, the Gold Coast, and the Belgian Congo and the hyperexploitation of indigenous labor in Nigeria, Kenya, and French North Africa. For Chen, the center of racism was not Africa but the United States, where the ruling classes also manipulated the rule of law to perpetuate white supremacy (*bairen youyue lun*) and indoctrinate contempt for the colored races whose labor reaped great profits for American capitalists. Following the end of slavery, the police, the courts, and white supremacists colluded with one another to commit gross injustices against Black people, including political disenfranchisement, segregation, voter intimidation, and lynching. The conceits of so-called "American democracy" were only further challenged by racist violence and exclusion against Chinese and other Asian communities, later reproduced in Australia and New Zealand. The state of emergency in British Malaya also witnessed the deportation of Chinese and the establishment of fortified new villages for Chinese supporters of insurgents. From these examples meant to foster Afro-Asian solidarity, Chen Tiqiang concluded that racism could not be considered a domestic issue, particularly after the Universal Declaration of Human Rights and its definition of crimes against humanity.[33]

The PRC was very much in dialogue with the Black radical tradition that inspired Cedric Robinson's concept of racial capitalism. W. E. B. Du Bois had long been invested in linking African and Asian liberation movements, from his early discussions of the global color line to later calls for African countries to build closer relations with China during the Cold War.[34] For Black radicals such as Du Bois, China challenged a white and Western vision of class struggle, and its revolution represented an extension of their anti-capitalist and anti-racist politics on the world stage.[35] Besides critical coverage of US policies and racist violence, the editors of *World Affairs* demonstrated solidarity by publishing firsthand accounts in translation. An op-ed written by a nineteen-year-old Black resident of Buffalo sought to dispel any illusions about northern states with a description of the dire poverty in her city and the need for socialism. A 1959 essay by James E. Jackson, southern director for the Communist Party, discussed the Black freedom struggle for economic opportunities, political rights, and social welfare as well as its intersections with worker, anti-imperialist, and communist organizing. A 1963 interview conducted with Robert and Mabel Williams in Beijing described their work with the NAACP, armed self-defense against white supremacists, and their exile to Cuba.[36]

Official visits by W. E. B. and Shirley Graham Du Bois, William Worthy, Vicki Garvin, and Robert and Mabel Williams produced sympathetic accounts of the PRC for American audiences while also contributing to increased representations of Black agency in Chinese state media.[37] Furthermore, representations of their visits, the student sit-ins in 1960, the Freedom Rides, desegregation in Little Rock and the University of Mississippi, the March on Washington, and the ongoing armed struggle in South Africa inspired some Chinese intellectuals to attend to race as a social question by revisiting Marx's discussion of primitive accumulation in *Capital* and then extending its insights on expropriation to an era of US imperialism and monopoly capitalism. Social scientists Zhang Chunhan and Shi Zhemin challenged orthodox periodization by considering how the capitalist class inherited existing forms of racism, introduced new notions of physiological and mental differences, and popularized them on a global scale for the purposes of exploitation and colonization. They argued that US policies obscured the material effects of racism, including hyperexploitation (*ewai boxue*) through wage gaps, by not recognizing how racial oppression was animated by class struggle as identified by Williams.[38] As Black activists and organizations took the media to be a site of anti-racist struggle and held race relations in the US up to global scrutiny during the Cold War, American policymakers began to turn to multiculturalism and to challenge white supremacist beliefs in the face of Southern elites that argued against racial integration precisely because of its socialist support.[39]

At a time of geopolitical competition, the PRC pitted racial capitalism against its own vision of socialist ethnopolitics, with the effect that racism could only exist elsewhere. According to Chen Tiqiang and others, the Soviet Union and China had eliminated racial oppression domestically to become "a big loving and united family of different nationalities."[40] Like the Soviet Union, the CCP departed from its earlier position regarding self-determination following Japanese overtures to non-Han peoples and the establishment of puppet states during the Second World War. Nationality eventually became a category of territorial governance when the constitution promulgated the right to autonomy and self-government for non-Han peoples, ethnologists surveyed newly consolidated territory and designated official classifications for political representation, and CCP leaders pursued a United Front with local elites while training minority cadres drawn from the lower classes.[41] While race could not be considered a domestic issue, nationality became one in China. Publications on the national question emphasized how the historical relationships between different tribes, tribal federations, and nations in China, including their contradictions and wars, were domestic in nature (*guonei xingzhi*).[42] The CCP also maintained the separation of race and ethnicity by carefully orchestrating itineraries for foreign visitors that kept politically sensitive subjects out of sight, including the Tibetan uprising in 1959.[43]

In spite of the political lines drawn between racial capitalism and socialist ethnopolitics, China scholars have documented problematic representations, assimilationist policies, and political violence targeting ethnic and religious minorities as "backward" and "feudal."[44] Political elites in the PRC did not completely abandon notions of blood lineage either, eventually drawing on them to articulate the idea that revolutionary credentials could be determined by personal background rather than political consciousness.[45] At the same time, Mao-era solidarity with foreign entities was betrayed by nationalism, such as the 1962 border war with India, and developmentalist hierarchies, especially in relations with African countries.[46] Not unlike the ways in which class-based politics subsumed the political subjects of woman and nation, state media also followed Mao's 1963 declaration that "the racial question is in essence a class question" and the universalist frame of world proletarian revolution flattened differences, including distinct experiences of expropriation.[47]

## Conclusion

This essay seeks to move beyond the comparativist methods and disciplinary divisions of the Cold War by reading across areas in the archive of Chinese socialism. I attend to the relational construction of race and nation in the early PRC though their historical conceptualization in relation to one another, global events and transnational connections that shaped their definitions, their mobilization for different emancipatory projects—namely, solidarity against racial capitalism and Han chauvinism—and contradictions that blurred political boundaries. Emptied of their former political content, the disarticulated concepts of race and ethnicity have often been reduced to foreign and domestic modes of social differentiation in the reform era, which can allow nationalists to claim that there is no racism in their country and can allow China scholars to deny the relevance of race to the field. Yet, the externalization of race and racism is particularly dubious these days as China's participation in global capitalism has been accompanied by prominent examples of Islamophobia and anti-Blackness. Not only has the Chinese state taken cues from the US, Israel, and Europe for its rhetoric of terrorism and programs of counterinsurgency.[48] Policy advisors have also proposed casting off socialist understandings of ethnicity tied to territory for a depoliticized model of American multiculturalism, which has been criticized for enabling neoliberal restructuring and governance, introducing new forms of privilege and stigma, and obscuring ongoing dispossession.[49] While some scholars and observers have looked to the imperial past for understanding present-day geopolitics, transhistorical gestures to a Chinese world order can miss capitalism's history of exploiting various axes of difference, including race, to produce surplus value as well as the anti-racist and socialist worldmaking projects of its critics. This essay suggests it may be useful to instead consider China's evolving relationship to racial capitalism, including the legacies and limitations of earlier critiques.

## Notes

[1] Harry Harootunian, *History's Disquiet: Modernity, Cultural Practice, and the Question of Everyday Life*. New York: Columbia University Press, 2000, 29–30, 33–34; Masao Miyoshi and H. D. Harootunian, eds., *Learning Places: The Afterlives of Area Studies*. Durham: Duke University Press, 2002, 2, 8; Bruce Cumings, "Boundary Displacement: The State, the Foundations, and Area Studies during and after the Cold War," in Miyoshi and Harootunian, *Learning Places*, 268.

[2] Fabio Lanza, *The End of Concern: Maoist China, Activism, and Asian Studies*. Durham: Duke University Press, 2017.

[3] Evelyn Hu-DeHart, "From Area Studies to Ethnic Studies: The Study of the Chinese Diaspora in Latin America," in Shirley Hune, ed., *Asian Americans: Comparative and Global Perspectives*. Pullman: Washington State University Press, 1991.

[4] David Theo Goldberg, "Racial Comparisons, Relational Racisms: Some Thoughts on Method," *Ethnic and Racial Studies* 32, no. 7 (September 2009): 1271–1282.

[5] Shu-mei Shih, "Comparative Racialization: An Introduction," *PMLA* 123, no. 5 (October 2008): 1347–1348; Shu-mei Shih, "Racializing Area Studies, Defetishizing China," *positions* 27, no. 1 (2019): 35, 41, 43–44; Gavin Walker and Naoki Sakai, "Guest Editors' Introduction: The End of Area," *positions* 27, no. 1 (2019): 7.

[6] Andrew F. Jones and Nikhil Pal Singh, "Guest Editors' Introduction," *positions: east asia cultures critique* 11, no. 1 (2003): 4–5; Naoki Sakai, "From Area Studies toward Transnational Studies," *Inter-Asia Cultural Studies* 11, no. 2 (2010): 267.

[7] Lisa Lowe, *The Intimacies of Four Continents*. Durham: Duke University Press, 2015, 2–5, 20–21.

[8] See, for example, Michael Omi and Howard Winant, *Racial Formation in the United States: From the 1960s to the 1990s*. New York: Routledge, 1994; Alexander Weheliye, *Habeas Viscus: Racializing Assemblages, Biopolitics, and Black Feminist Theories of the Human*. Durham: Duke University Press, 2014, Chapter 3.

[9] Cedric J. Robinson, *Black Marxism: The Making of the Black Radical Tradition*. Chapel Hill: University of North Carolina Press, 2000, 10, 26.

[10] Here, I am drawing from Weheliye's concept of "racializing assemblages" that discipline humanity into full humans, non-quite-humans, and nonhumans in Weheliye, *Habeas Viscus*.

[11] Lisa Lowe, *Immigrant Acts: On Asian American Cultural Politics*. Durham: Duke University Press, 1996; David R. Roediger, *The Wages of Whiteness: Race and the Making of the American Working Class*. New York: Verso, 1999.

[12] See, for example, Glen Sean Coulthard, *Red Skin, White Masks: Rejecting the Colonial Politics of Recognition*. Minneapolis: University of Minnesota Press, 2014; Manu Karuka, *Empire's Tracks: Indigenous Nations, Chinese Workers, and the Transcontinental Railroad*.

Oakland: University of California Press, 2019; Edward Baptist, *The Half Has Never Been Told: Slavery and the Making of American Capitalism*. New York: Basic Books, 2014; Evelyn N. Glenn, *Unequal Freedom: How Race and Gender Shaped American Citizenship and Labor*. Cambridge: Harvard University Press, 2002; Alys E. Weinbaum, *The Afterlife of Reproductive Slavery: Biocapitalism and Black Feminism's Philosophy of History*. Durham: Duke University Press, 2019.

[13] See, for example, James Hevia, *English Lessons: The Pedagogy of Imperialism in Nineteenth-Century China*. Durham: Duke University Press, 2003; Lowe, *The Intimacies of Four Continents*, Chapter 4.

[14] Moon-Ho Jung, *Coolies and Cane: Race, Labor, and Sugar in the Age of Emancipation*. Baltimore: Johns Hopkins University Press, 2006; Lisa Yun, *The Coolie Speaks: Chinese Indentured Laborers and African Slaves of Cuba*. Philadelphia: Temple University Press, 2008.

[15] Colleen Lye, *America's Asia: Racial Form and American Literature, 1893–1945*. Princeton: Princeton University Press, 2005; Pheng Cheah, *Inhuman Conditions: On Cosmopolitanism and Human Rights*. Cambridge: Harvard University Press, 2006; Iyko Day, *Alien Capital: Asian Racialization and the Logic of Settler Colonial Capitalism*. Durham: Duke University Press, 2016.

[16] J. Kēhaulani Kauanui, *Hawaiian Blood: Colonialism and the Politics of Sovereignty and Indigeneity*. Durham: Duke University Press, 2008; Adam McKeown, *Melancholy Order: Asian Migration and the Globalization of Borders*. New York: Columbia University Press, 2008; Jason Oliver Chang, *Chino: Anti Chinese Racism in Mexico, 1880–1940*. Urbana: University of Illinois Press, 2017; Shelly Chan, *Diaspora's Homeland: Modern China in the Age of Global Migration*. Durham: Duke University Press, 2018; Mae Ngai, *The Chinese Question: The Gold Rushes and Global Politics*. New York: W. W. Norton & Company, 2021.

[17] See, for example, Ann Stoler: *Carnal Knowledge and Imperial Power: Race and the Intimate in Colonial Rule*. Berkeley: University of California Press 2010; Tolz, "Race, Ethnicity, and Nationhood in Imperial Russia," in David Rainbow, ed., *Ideologies of Race: Imperial Russia and the Soviet Union in Global Context*. Montreal: McGill-Queen's University Press, 2019, 33.

[18] Rebecca E. Karl, *Staging the World: Chinese Nationalism at the Turn of the Twentieth Century*. Durham: Duke University Press, 2002, 38–44.

[19] Michael Gibbs Hill, *Lin Shu, Inc.: Translation and the Making of Modern Chinese Culture*. New York: Oxford University Press, 2012, Chapter 3; Jing Tsu, *Failure, Nationalism, and Literature: The Making of Modern Chinese Identity, 1895–1937*, Stanford: Stanford University Press, 2005, 77.

[20] Karl, *Staging the World*, 38; Frank Dikotter, *The Discourse of Race in Modern China*, Hong Kong: Hong Kong University Press, 1992, 80–82, 107–115; Benjamin Schwartz, *In Search of Wealth and Power: Yen Fu and the West*, Cambridge: The Belnap Press, 1964, 182–184.

[21] Kai-wing Chow, "Imagining Boundaries of Blood: Zhang Binglin and the Invention of the Han 'Race' in Modern China," in Frank Dikotter, ed., *The Construction of Racial*

*Identities in China and Japan*, Hong Kong: Hong Kong University Press, 1997; James Leibold, *Reconfiguring Chinese Nationalism: How the Qing Frontier and Its Indigenes Became Chinese*, New York: Palgrave Macmillan, 2007.

[22] Emma Teng, *Eurasian: Mixed Identities in the United States, China, and Hong Kong, 1842-1943*, Berkeley: University of California Press, 2013, Chapter 4; Tsu, *Failure, Nationalism, and Literature*, 81.

[23] James Leibold, "Competing Narratives of Racial Unity in Republican China: From the Yellow Emperor to Peking Man," *Modern China* 32, no. 2 (2006): 207-208.

[24] Dikotter, *Discourse of Race in Modern China*, 171-172; Tsu, *Failure, Nationalism, and Literature*, 104-105.

[25] Zhou Jianren, "Zhongzu qishi yu zhongzu zhuyi," *Daxue* 6, nos. 3-4 (1947): 50-51; Zhou Jianren, *Lun youshengxue yu zhongzu qishi*. Shanghai: Sanlian shudian, 1950, 4-6, 8-9, 50-61.

[26] Leibold, *Reconfiguring Chinese Nationalism*, 150-151; Arif Dirlik, *Revolution and History: Origins of Marxist Historiography in China, 1919-1937*. Berkeley: University of California Press, 1978.

[27] Uradyn E. Bulag, "Good Han, Bad Han: the Moral Parameters of Ethnopolitics in China," in Thomas Mullaney, James Leibold, Stéphane Gros, and Eric Vanden Bussche, eds., *Critical Han Studies: The History, Representation, and Identity of China's Majority*. Berkeley: University of California, 2012.

[28] Leibold, *Reconfiguring Chinese Nationalism*, 161, 164.

[29] Lü Zhenyu, *Zhongguo minzu jianzhi*. Harbin: Guanghua shudian, 1948, 161-162.

[30] Huang Yuanqi, "Zhongguo lishishang de zhongzu yu minzu," *Xin shixue tongxun* (1952): 3-5.

[31] Rong Guanxiong, "Renmen gongtongti buneng tong zhongzu hun wei yi tan," *Shixue yuekan* 21-23.

[32] Chen Zanwei, "Nanfei lianbang de zhongzu qishi he minzu yapo," *Shijie zhishi* no. 6 (1952): 17-18; Zanwei, "Nanfei renmin de fan zhongzu yapo yundong," *Shijie zhishi* no. 47 (1952): 18.

[33] Chen Tiqiang, "Ya Fei renmin fandui zhongzu zhuyi," *Shijie zhishi* no. 8 (1955), 14-16.

[34] Bill Mullen and Cathryn Watson, eds., *W. E. B. Du Bois on Asia: Crossing the World Color Line*. Jackson: University Press of Mississippi, 2005.

[35] Robin D. G. Kelley, *Freedom Dreams: The Black Radical Imagination*. Boston: Beacon Press, 2002; Robeson Taj Frazier, *The East is Black: Cold War China in the Black Radical Imagination*. Durham: Duke University Press, 2015, 40.

[36] Ma`erkana Sinai'er Jiemu, "Meiguo de Zhongzu pingdeng," *Shijie zhishi* no. 14 (1950): 19; Jin Xing, "Buru huxue, yan de huzi: jieshao san K dang neimu," *Shijie zhishi* no. 16 (1956): 31; Zhanmushi Jiekesun, "Meiguo heiren zhengqu ziyou douzheng de daolu," *Shijie zhishi* no. 23 (1959): 10-12; Yu Mu, "Shengli de shi women: Luobote Weilian fufu fangwenji," *Shijie zhishi* no. 19 (1963).

[37] Frazier, *The East is Black*, 30, 54–55, 58–59; Keisha Brown, "Blackness in Exile: W. E. B. Du Bois' Role in the Formation of Representations of Blackness as Conceptualized by the Chinese Communist Party," *Phylon* 53, no. 2 (Winter 2016): 20–33.

[38] Zhang Chunhan and Shi Zhemin, "Zhongzu qishi he jieji douzheng," *Jianghuai xuekan* (1963): 1–7; Zhang Dimao, "Zhongzu wenti shizhi shang shi jieji wenti," *Zhongshan daxue xuebao* (1963): 1–19; Chang Gong, "Meiguo de Heiren wenti," *Shijie zhishi* no. 16 (1963): 11–14.

[39] Frazier, *The East is Black*, 8–9; Thomas Borstelmann, *The Cold War and the Color Line: American Race Relations in the Global Arena*. Cambridge: Harvard University Press, 2003, 65; Jodi Melamed, "The Spirit of Neoliberalism: From Racial Liberalism to Neoliberal Multiculturalism," *Social Text 24*, 4, no. 89 (1 December 2006): 1–24.

[40] Chen, "Ya Fei renmin fandui zhongzu zhuyi," 16; Zhang and Shi, "Zhongzu qishi he jieji douzheng," 7.

[41] See, for example, Thomas Mullaney, *Coming to Terms with the Nation: Ethnic Classification in Modern China*. Berkeley: University of California Press, 2011; Benno Weiner, *The Chinese Revolution on the Tibetan Frontier*. Ithaca: Cornell University Press, 2020.

[42] Lü Zhenyu and Jiang Ming, "Zhongguo minzu guanxi fazhan de lishi tedian," *Minzu tuanjie* no. 4 (1958): 10–11.

[43] Frazier, *The East is Black*, 57–61. By contrast, the US State Department attempted to shield visiting diplomats from experiencing white supremacy and prejudice themselves. See Renee Romano, "No Diplomatic Immunity: African Diplomats, the State Department, and Civil Rights, 1961–1964," *Journal of American History* 87, no. 2 (September 2000): 546–579.

[44] Morris Rossabi, ed. *Governing China's Multiethnic Frontiers*. Seattle: University of Washington Press, 2004; Melvyn C. Goldstein, Ben Jiao, and Lhundrup Tanzen, *On the Cultural Revolution in Tibet: The Nyemo Incident of 1969*. Berkeley: University of California Press, 2009; Ben Hillman and Gray Tuttle, eds. *Ethnic Conflict and Protest in Tibet and Xinjiang: Unrest in China's West*. New York: Columbia University Press, 2016; James A. Millward, *Eurasian Crossroads: A History of Xinjiang*. New York: Columbia University Press, 2007.

[45] See, for example, the discussion of the bloodline theory in Yiching Wu, *The Cultural Revolution at the Margins: Chinese Socialism in Crisis*. Cambridge: Harvard University Press, 2014.

[46] See, for example, Lin Chun, "China's Lost World of Internationalism," in Ban Wang, ed., *Chinese Visions of World Order: Tianxia, Culture, and World Politics*. Durham: Duke University Press, 2017, 190-191; Jamie Monson, *Africa's Freedom Railway: How a Chinese Development Project Changed Lives and Livelihoods in Tanzania*. Bloomington: Indiana University Press, 2009.

[47] Brown, "Blackness in Exile," 26; Frazier, *The East is Black*, 18.

[48] Adam Hunerven, "Spirit Breaking: Capitalism and Terror in Northwest China," *Chuang* no. 2 (2019): 485–523; David Brophy, "Good and Bad Muslims in Xinjiang," *Made in China Journal* 4, no. 2 (April–June 2019): 44–53; Darren Byler, "Preventative Policing as Community Detention in Northwest China," *Made in China Journal* 4, no. 3 (July–September 2019): 88–94.

[49] Christopher Atwood, "Bilingual Education in Inner Mongolia: An Explainer," *Made in China Journal*, August 30, 2020, madeinchinajournal.com/2020/08/30/bilingual-education-in-inner-mongolia-an-explainer; Christian Sorace, "Undoing Lenin: On the Recent Changes to China's Ethnic Policy," *Made in China Journal* 5, no. 2 (May–August 2020): 36–45; Melamed, "The Spirit of Neoliberalism," 15-18; Roxanne Dunbar-Ortiz, *An Indigenous People's History of the United States*. Boston: Beacon Press, 2014, 5.

## Bibliography

Atwood, Christopher. "Bilingual Education in Inner Mongolia: An Explainer." *Made in China Journal*, August 30, 2020. madeinchinajournal. com/2020/08/30/bilingual-education-in-inner-mongolia-an-explainer.

Baptist, Edward. *The Half Has Never Been Told: Slavery and the Making of American Capitalism*. New York: Basic Books, 2014.

Borstelmann, Thomas. *The Cold War and the Color Line: American Race Relations in the Global Arena*. Cambridge: Harvard University Press, 2003.

Brophy, David. "Good and Bad Muslims in Xinjiang," *Made in China Journal* 4, no. 2 (April–June 2019): 44–53.

Brown, Keisha. "Blackness in Exile: W. E. B. Du Bois' Role in the Formation of Representations of Blackness as Conceptualized by the Chinese Communist Party." *Phylon* 53, no. 2 (Winter 2016): 20–33.

Bulag, Uradyn E. "Good Han, Bad Han: the Moral Parameters of Ethnopolitics in China." In Thomas Mullaney, James Leibold, Stéphane Gros, and Eric Vanden Bussche, eds. *Critical Han Studies: The History, Representation, and Identity of China's Majority*. Berkeley: University of California, 2012.

Byler, Darren. "Preventative Policing as Community Detention in Northwest China," *Made in China Journal* 4, no. 3 (July–September 2019): 88–94.

Chan, Shelly. *Diaspora's Homeland: Modern China in the Age of Global Migration*. Durham: Duke University Press, 2018.

Chang Gong. "Meiguo de Heiren wenti." *Shijie zhishi* no. 16 (1963): 11–14.

Chang, Jason Oliver. *Chino: Anti-Chinese Racism in Mexico, 1880–1940*. Urbana: University of Illinois Press, 2017.

Cheah, Pheng. *Inhuman conditions: On Cosmopolitanism and Human Rights* Cambridge: Harvard University Press, 2006.

Chen Tiqiang. "Ya Fei renmin fandui zhongzu zhuyi." *Shijie zhishi* no. 8 (1955): 14–16.

Chen Zanwei. "Nanfei lianbang de zhongzu qishi he minzu yapo." *Shijie zhishi* no. 6 (1952): 17–18.

Chen Zanwei, "Nanfei renmin de fan zhongzu yapo yundong." *Shijie zhishi* no. 47 (1952): 18.

Chow, Kai-wing. "Imagining Boundaries of Blood: Zhang Binglin and the Invention of the Han 'Race' in Modern China." In Frank Dikotter, ed., *The Construction of Racial Identities in China and Japan*. Hong Kong: Hong Kong University Press, 1997.

Coulthard, Glen Sean. *Red Skin, White Masks: Rejecting the Colonial Politics of Recognition*. Minneapolis: University of Minnesota Press, 2014.

Cumings, Bruce. "Boundary Displacement: The State, the Foundations, and Area Studies during and after the Cold War." In Masao Miyoshi and H. D. Harootunian, eds., *Learning Places: The Afterlives of Area Studies*. Durham: Duke University Press, 2002.

Day, Iyko. *Alien Capital: Asian Racialization and the Logic of Settler Colonial Capitalism*. Durham: Duke University Press, 2016.

Dikotter, Frank. *The Discourse of Race in Modern China*. Hong Kong: Hong Kong University Press, 1992.

Dirlik, Arif. *Revolution and History: Origins of Marxist Historiography in China, 1919–1937*. Berkeley: University of California Press, 1978.

Dunbar-Ortiz, Roxanne. *An Indigenous People's History of the United States*. Boston: Beacon Press, 2014.

Frazier, Robeson Taj. *The East is Black: Cold War China in the Black Radical Imagination*. Durham: Duke University Press, 2015.

Glenn, Evelyn N. *Unequal Freedom: How Race and Gender Shaped American Citizenship and Labor*. Cambridge: Harvard University Press, 2002.

Goldberg, David Theo. "Racial Comparisons, Relational Racisms: Some Thoughts on Method." *Ethnic and Racial Studies* 32, no. 7 (September 2009): 1271–1282.

Goldstein, Melvyn C., Ben Jiao, and Lhundrup Tanzen. *On the Cultural Revolution in Tibet: The Nyemo Incident of 1969*. Berkeley: University of California Press, 2009.

Harootunian, Harry. *History's Disquiet: Modernity, Cultural Practice, and the Question of Everyday Life*. New York: Columbia University Press, 2000.

Hevia, James. *English Lessons: The Pedagogy of Imperialism in Nineteenth-Century China*. Durham: Duke University Press, 2003.

Hill, Michael Gibbs. *Lin Shu, Inc.: Translation and the Making of Modern Chinese Culture*. New York: Oxford University Press, 2012.

Hillman, Ben and Gray Tuttle, eds. *Ethnic Conflict and Protest in Tibet and Xinjiang: Unrest in China's West*. New York: Columbia University Press, 2016.

Hu-DeHart, Evelyn. "From Area Studies to Ethnic Studies: The Study of the Chinese Diaspora in Latin America." In Shirley Hune, ed., *Asian Americans: Comparative and Global Perspectives*. Pullman: Washington State University Press, 1991.

Huang Yuanqi. "Zhongguo lishishang de zhongzu yu minzu." *Xin shixue tongxun* (1952): 3–5.

Hunerven, Adam. "Spirit Breaking: Capitalism and Terror in Northwest China." *Chuang* no. 2 (2019): 485–523.

Jin Xing. "Buru huxue, yan de huzi: jieshao san K dang neimu." *Shijie zhishi* no. 16 (1956): 31.

Jones, Andrew F. and Nikhil Pal Singh. "Guest Editors' Introduction." *positions* 11, no. 1 (2003): 1–9.

Jung, Moon-Ho. *Coolies and Cane: Race, Labor, and Sugar in the Age of Emancipation*. Baltimore: Johns Hopkins University Press, 2006.

Karl, Rebecca E. *Staging the World: Chinese Nationalism at the Turn of the Twentieth Century*. Durham: Duke University Press, 2002.

Karuka, Manu. *Empire's Tracks: Indigenous Nations, Chinese Workers, and the Transcontinental Railroad*. Oakland: University of California Press, 2019.

Kauanui, J. Kēhaulani. *Hawaiian Blood: Colonialism and the Politics of Sovereignty and Indigeneity*. Durham: Duke University Press, 2008.

Kelley, Robin D. G. *Freedom Dreams: The Black Radical Imagination*. Boston: Beacon Press, 2002.

Lanza, Fabio. *The End of Concern: Maoist China, Activism, and Asian Studies*. Durham: Duke University Press, 2017.

Leibold, James. "Competing Narratives of Racial Unity in Republican China: From the Yellow Emperor to Peking Man." *Modern China* 32, no. 2 (2006): 181–220.

Leibold, James. *Reconfiguring Chinese Nationalism: How the Qing Frontier and Its Indigenes Became Chinese*. New York: Palgrave Macmillan, 2007.

Lin Chun. "China's Lost World of Internationalism." In Ban Wang, ed., *Chinese Visions of World Order: Tianxia, Culture, and World Politics*. Durham: Duke University Press, 2017.

Lowe, Lisa. *Immigrant Acts: On Asian American Cultural Politics*. Durham: Duke University Press, 1996.

Lowe, Lisa. *The Intimacies of Four Continents*. Durham: Duke University Press, 2015.

Lü Zhenyu and Jiang Ming. "Zhongguo minzu guanxi fazhan de lishi tedian." *Minzu tuanjie* no. 4 (1958): 10–11.

Lü Zhenyu. *Zhongguo minzu jianzhi*. Harbin: Guanghua shudian, 1948.

Lye, Colleen. *America's Asia: Racial Form and American Literature, 1893–1945*. Princeton: Princeton University Press, 2005.

Ma'erkana Sinai'er Jiemu. "Meiguo de Zhongzu pingdeng." *Shijie zhishi* no. 14 (1950): 19.

McKeown, Adam. *Melancholy Order: Asian Migration and the Globalization of Borders*. New York: Columbia University Press, 2008.

Melamed, Jodi. "The Spirit of Neoliberalism: From Racial Liberalism to Neoliberal Multiculturalism." *Social Text 24*, 4, no. 89 (1 December 2006): 1–24.

Millward, James A. *Eurasian Crossroads: A History of Xinjiang* (New York: Columbia University Press, 2007.

Miyoshi, Masao and H. D. Harootunian, eds. *Learning Places: The Afterlives of Area Studies*. Durham: Duke University Press, 2002.

Monson, Jamie. *Africa's Freedom Railway: How a Chinese Development Project Changed Lives and Livelihoods in Tanzania*. Bloomington: Indiana University Press, 2009.

Mullaney, Thomas. *Coming to Terms with the Nation: Ethnic Classification in Modern China*. Berkeley: University of California Press, 2011.

Mullen, Bill and Cathryn Watson, eds. *W. E. B. Du Bois on Asia: Crossing the World Color Line*. Jackson: University Press of Mississippi, 2005.

Ngai, Mae. *The Chinese Question: The Gold Rushes and Global Politics*. New York: W. W. Norton & Company, 2021.

Omi, Michael and Howard Winant. *Racial Formation in the United States: From the 1960s to the 1990s*. New York: Routledge, 1994.

Robinson, Cedric J. *Black Marxism: The Making of the Black Radical Tradition.* Chapel Hill: University of North Carolina Press, 2000.

Roediger, David R. *The Wages of Whiteness: Race and the Making of the American Working Class.* New York: Verso, 1999.

Romano, Renee. "No diplomatic immunity: African Diplomats, the State Department, and Civil Rights, 1961–1964." *Journal of American History* 87, no. 2 (September 2000): 546–579.

Rong Guanxiong. "Renmen gongtongti buneng tong zhongzu hun wei yi tan." *Shixue yuekan* 21–23.

Rossabi, Morris, ed. *Governing China's Multiethnic Frontiers.* Seattle: University of Washington Press, 2004.

Sakai, Naoki. "From Area Studies toward Transnational Studies." *Inter-Asia Cultural Studies* 11, no. 2 (2010): 265–274.

Schwartz, Benjamin. *In Search of Wealth and Power: Yen Fu and the West.* Cambridge: The Belnap Press, 1964.

Shih, Shu-mei. "Comparative Racialization: An Introduction." *PMLA* 123, no. 5 (October 2008): 1347–1362.

Shih, Shu-mei. "Racializing Area Studies, Defetishizing China." *positions* 27, no. 1 (2019): 33–65.

Sorace, Christian. "Undoing Lenin: On the Recent Changes to China's Ethnic Policy." *Made in China Journal* 5, no. 2 (May–August 2020): 36–45.

Stoler, Ann. *Carnal Knowledge and Imperial Power: Race and the Intimate in Colonial Rule.* Berkeley: University of California Press, 2010.

Teng, Emma. *Eurasian: Mixed Identities in the United States, China, and Hong Kong, 1842–1943.* Berkeley: University of California Press, 2013.

Tolz, Vera. "Race, Ethnicity, and Nationhood in Imperial Russia." In David Rainbow, ed., *Ideologies of Race: Imperial Russia and the Soviet Union in Global Context.* Montreal: McGill-Queen's University Press, 2019.

Tsu, Jing. *Failure, Nationalism, and Literature: The Making of Modern Chinese Identity, 1895–1937.* Stanford: Stanford University Press, 2005.

Walker, Gavin and Naoki Sakai. "Guest Editors' Introduction: The End of Area." *positions* 27, no. 1 (2019): 1–32.

Weheliye, Alexander. *Habeas Viscus: Racializing Assemblages, Biopolitics, and Black Feminist Theories of the Human.* Durham: Duke University Press, 2014.

Weinbaum, Alys E. *The Afterlife of Reproductive Slavery: Biocapitalism and Black Feminism's Philosophy of History*. Durham: Duke University Press, 2019.

Weiner, Benno. *The Chinese Revolution on the Tibetan Frontier*. Ithaca: Cornell University Press, 2020.

Wu, Yiching. *The Cultural Revolution at the Margins: Chinese Socialism in Crisis*. Cambridge: Harvard University Press, 2014.

Yu Mu. "Shengli de shi women: Luobote Weilian fufu fangwenji." *Shijie zhishi* no. 19 (1963).

Yun, Lisa. *The Coolie Speaks: Chinese Indentured Laborers and African Slaves of Cuba*. Philadelphia: Temple University Press, 2008.

Zhang Chunhan and Shi Zhemin. "Zhongzu qishi he jieji douzheng." *Jianghuai xuekan* (1963): 1–7.

Zhang Dimao. "Zhongzu wenti shizhi shang shi jieji wenti." *Zhongshan daxue xuebao* (1963): 1–19.

Zhanmushi Jiekesun. "Meiguo heiren zhengqu ziyou douzheng de daolu." *Shijie zhishi* no. 23 (1959): 10–12.

Zhou Jianren. "Zhongzu qishi yu zhongzu zhuyi." *Daxue* 6, nos. 3–4 (1947): 50–51.

Zhou Jianren. *Lun youshengxue yu zhongzu qishi*. Shanghai: Sanlian shudian, 1950.

# 6

# SCIENCE WITHOUT BORDERS?

## THE CONTESTED SCIENCE OF "RACE MIXING" CIRCA WORLD WAR II IN JAPAN, EAST ASIA, AND THE WEST

### Kristin Roebuck

In 1967, Mamiya Hiroshi of the Department of Internal Medicine at Tōhō University in Japan published a study of abnormal hemoglobin in the leading *Journal of the Japanese Society of Internal Medicine*. Since the discovery of hemoglobin—the molecule that transports oxygen in red blood cells—in 1949, scientists worldwide had identified over 120 forms of "abnormal" hemoglobin. Most of these varieties were harmless products of allelic variation in human gene pools, but some variants of hemoglobin, such as sickle cell, were potentially deadly. Mamiya devoted much of his paper to explicating methodologies for identifying serological abnormalities, with photographs, diagrams, and descriptions detailing electrophoresis tanks, spectrophotometers, globin fingerprints, and peptide maps. The most arresting aspect of Mamiya's methodology, however, was not so much the technology as the philosophy he used to target, sort, and label human populations. In one group, Mamiya agglomerated people he described as "mixed-blood children" (*konketsuji*) with Japanese mothers and fathers who were "largely black Americans and white Americans; other than that, American Indian, Filipino, Russian, Indian and Korean are included." In the opposing group, Mamiya gathered "our countrymen"—the Japanese—defined not in terms of citizenship but rather in terms of racial purity, which Japanese children with foreign fathers lacked.[1]

Mamiya announced that he had discovered dangerous serological and genetic differences between "mixed-blood" and "pure" Japanese. "The author was not able to confirm even a single case of abnormal hemoglobin among our 3000 countrymen, but two cases of abnormal hemoglobin were confirmed among 179 konketsuji." This amounted to a startlingly high rate of abnormality: 1.1 percent among konketsuji, in contrast to a mere 0.02 percent among "proper Japanese" (honrai no Nihonjin). For Mamiya, his findings were "proof that at this moment, genes that factor in abnormal hemoglobin are being introduced by konketsuji on an ongoing basis. On the grounds of our science of race hygiene [eugenics], this is a problem we cannot take lightly." Neither of the konketsuji whose blood and genes Mamiya labeled "abnormal" suffered from any disease.[2] Regardless, Mamiya marked them as vessels of hereditary foreign contagion. In contrast, Mamiya concluded with pride that "with regard to hemoglobin, our country is truly pure."[3]

In thus reifying "pure blood" and the biopolitical threat posed by "race mixing" in an otherwise "pure" nation, Mamiya was neither a scientific renegade nor relic of an ancien régime of race hygiene. On the contrary, the preference for "pure blood" was firmly established after World War II amid public and political uproar over konketsuji born to Japanese mothers and foreign soldiers and civilians stationed in Japan during the Allied occupation (1945–1952).[4]

Japan had embraced racial assimilation, mixing, and universalism at an earlier historical moment—the high imperial era of the 1910s through the early 1940s—when the United States was pursuing isolationism, segregation, and, much like Germany, white supremacy. The balance of scientific and political opinion shifted in both East and West circa the 1940s and 1950s, as the United States turned outward during World War II and the Cold War, while Japan turned inward and shed its universal aspirations. In parallel, postcolonial Korea asserted its biological and political uniqueness. After defeat in 1945, a shrunken Japan and liberated Korea embraced biopolitical particularism and "pure-blood" nationalism while the enlarged United States reimagined itself as the standard-bearer of universal values in a nominally color-blind but deeply color-ranked world empire.[5] Had World War II ended differently, so too might the prevailing scientific stance on "race mixing" in the US, Japan, Germany, and Korea.

In researching and publicizing the scientific construct called konketsuji, scientific and medical professionals played a key but underappreciated role in constructing postimperial Japanese as a homogenous race and "pure-blood" nation. Mamiya was thus working well within local postwar scientific norms and desires when he claimed to have proved a genetic link between "blood mixing," bodily pathology, and biopolitical menace. Yet this is not the impression one would get from otherwise illuminating studies by leading historians of Japan, who proclaim that doctrines of racial purity and the practice of race science receded in postwar Japan amidst what Miriam Kingsberg Kadia terms "worldwide" reaction to "horrors . . . committed by Nazi Germany."[6] Similarly, Japan historian Laura Hein asserts that the "post-fascist generation" repudiated "the discredited fascist fantasy" of Japanese purity.[7] Scholars who make such claims generally offer little or no evidence to substantiate them.[8] In the absence of evidence, what explains scholarly consensus on this point?

Historians of Japan appear to have imported as fact an assumption made by Western historians of science that scientific norms of racial "purity" peaked worldwide circa the 1930s, only to be repudiated worldwide in light of Nazi atrocities. Trauma, horror, and what historians of science Diane Paul and William Provine term "revulsion" provide the motive for mid-twentieth-century scientific actors to become anti-racist activists in this master narrative of moral and scientific progress.[9] For example, Elazar Barkan's classic study of "the retreat of scientific racism" opens by declaring that the "Nazi regime has compelled us all to recognize the lethal potential of the concept of race and . . . led to the decline and repudiation of scientific racism."[10] Similarly, Saul Dubow asserts that "the Nazi Holocaust . . . alerted humanity as a whole to the terrifying consequences of politicized racism."[11] But who is this "humanity as a whole," this "all of us"? Western scholars have too quickly elided the constituency of their universal human "we." In these studies, evidence for the bold proposition of a global revolution against scientific racism is in fact drawn from the activities of scientists working predominantly in English in a small corner of the world known as "the West." Étienne Balibar affirms that French scholars, too, redefined themselves as enlightened adversaries of the racism of their German rivals.[12] On examination, then, this apparently borderless narrative turns out to be a provincial narrative about US, British, and French victors in World War II, who took it upon themselves not only to destroy the Nazi regime but also to dismantle the scientific basis for that rival regime's legitimacy as an instance and architect of racial purity. Implicit in many such studies is the assumption that non-Western actors, such as Asians, were not studying and defining "race" on their own terms.

In fact, in most of the world, scientists had concerns that differed from debunking or distancing themselves from Nazis. Pioneering historians of science Jaehwan Hyun, Hoi-eun Kim, and Projit Bihari Mukharji have recently explored how physical anthropologists, serologists, and geneticists in Korea and India have practiced race science in ways that both co-opt and contradict the presumed Euro-American hegemony over the sciences. The Asian history of science confounds established narratives of a mid-twentieth-century scientific revolution against racial purity centered on the Nazi eruption into history and the French-Anglo-American suppression of that eruption on behalf of a world assumed to be cheering from the sidelines. In India, scientific investigations of racialized castes and Aryan supremacy showed no sign of abating after World War II.[13] Meanwhile, in East Asia, the rise and fall of the Japanese empire proved more salient than that of the Third Reich in setting scientific, political, and moral agendas.

In Japan and Korea, doctrines of racial purity and the conviction that "mixed-race" populations were inferior or even dangerous were marginalized in the early twentieth century. After Japan annexed Korea in 1910, the weight of scholarly and journalistic opinion in Japan swung decisively toward the notion that the Japanese were a constitutionally "mixed-blood" people with a world-historical gift for assimilating diverse "races" into a harmonious imperial whole.[14] During World War II, even proud Koreans such as Yi Kwang-su and Yi Yŏng-gŭn took Japanese names—Kayama Mitsurō and Ueda Tatsuo, respectively—and collaborated with Japan's government-general to promote "mixed-blood" identity and "mixed-blood" imperialism. Kayama and Ueda celebrated the "mixed" bloodlines of Japanese and Koreans as the organic basis for a heterogeneous but unified empire. And like many wartime Japanese, they promoted further "blood mixing" to fuse freshly conquered or conquerable peoples into the imperial family-state.[15]

It was only *after* World War II that doctrines of "pure blood" emerged as the scientific mainstream in Japan and Korea. Upon defeat, Japan suddenly lost diverse territories ranging from Korea to New Guinea, Taiwan to Sakhalin. The imperial orthodoxy that the Japanese were a "mixed-blood" people with a world-historical gift for fusing heterogenous "races" into a harmonious whole abruptly lost most of the geopolitical evidence in its favor. In Korea, thirty-five years of Japanese occupation (1910–1945) were followed by division between North and South and internationalized civil war (1950–1953). In this context, nationalist scientists and politicians in both North and South promoted Korean "pure blood" to stake a biological claim to the unity and independence that proved out of reach geopolitically.[16] Just as Korean nationalists reacted against Japan's "mixed-blood" empire with appeals to "pure blood," so too did many Japanese after their empire collapsed and new sources of unity, identity, and pride were sorely needed. Although some Japanese scholars in the wake of defeat stuck to their old pro-"mixing" position, they swiftly lost influence to proponents of a "pure-blood" Japan which had never assimilated foreign elements and probably never should.[17]

In the postwar era, Japanese scientists energetically produced new evidence in favor of racial "purity" by chronicling the alleged abnormalities of *konketsuji* and making them a foil against which to construct "pure" Japanese. The term *konketsuji* could denote any offspring born of interracial or international sex, concepts that overlapped or fused given that race and nation were captured by the single term *minzoku*. However, in postwar Japan, the *konketsuji* of primary interest were those born to Japanese mothers by fathers in Western, primarily American, military uniforms. These "mixed-blood" children were identified racially with the foreign father rather than the native mother, fusing "pure blood" with patrilineal ideology. Thus *konketsuji* were routinely labeled either white or Black, but not Japanese. In other words, "mixed-blood" children were defined in popular and scientific discourse as *foreign* children rather than as Japanese children with diverse ancestry. Even the diversity of their fathers' ancestry was oversimplified to fit a black-white dichotomy, as if there were no other races or mixes of races overseas. The notion that "mixed" children did not belong in Japan was most literally expressed in the 1950s in frequent calls by politicians and pundits on both the right and left that *konketsuji* be deported *en masse* to live with people of "their own race." Generally, this meant sending *konketsuji* to the United States, but in an ambiguous triumph of "racial" over national thinking, Black *konketsuji* were also dispatched to Brazil.[18] Less crucial to Japanese activists than what happened overseas was what happened in Japan, the bodies displaced and ideologies ingrained as the "mixed" child's bonds with his Japanese mother and motherland were denied, along with the child's potential racial bond with other Japanese.[19] The postwar era saw the rise of a belief system that its Japanese critics dub a "myth of racial homogeneity."[20] Japanese scientists played a prominent but little acknowledged role in constructing pure blood "Japaneseness" and the innate "foreignness" of racialized minorities, including *konketsuji*, as nonpartisan, immutable, natural facts.

Chief among these scientists was Koya Yoshio (1890–1974), wartime bureaucrat in the Ministry of Welfare and postwar director of Japan's National Institute of Public Health. In the high imperial era of expansion and assimilation, Koya was among an embattled minority who had decried "blood mixing."[21] In the postimperial era, he found peers and the public more receptive to his argument. At the Allied occupation's end in 1952, Japanese presses and politicians fulminated that two hundred thousand *konketsuji* had been sired and abandoned by foreign soldiers in Japan. In reality, government surveys turned up only three to five thousand "occupation babies," few of them orphans.[22] Nonetheless, outrage over "blood mixing" gave Koya an opportunity to bring eugenic arguments against "blood mixing" to a broad audience.

*Ladies' Review* (*Fujin kōron*) was a leading magazine catering to Japanese women with an interest in international affairs, fashion, and culture. For Koya, there was no audience more in need of counseling about the perils of planting Western seeds in Japanese soil. At occupation's end, *Ladies' Review* printed a stream of articles about the undesirable consequences of sex with foreign, particularly American, men. One cautioned that *konketsuji* were inclined to criminality.[23] Several warned that *konketsuji* were fated to misery in Japan and should be transported overseas to live among "members of their race."[24] By the time Koya published his article in 1953, readers of *Ladies' Review* were thus accustomed to being lectured about the inherently risky nature of interracial sex and family formation. Even so, Koya stands out for extreme fearmongering. Koya warned that if adequate countermeasures were not soon taken, "mixed-blood" children would someday unite into a revolutionary caste that would rise up to slaughter the Japanese "race." If this threat of genocide were not enough, Koya offered additional warnings against "blood mixing," particularly with Black foreigners. For even if the "sociological" problems leading to race war could somehow be solved, such konketusji would remain, according to Koya, genetically unfit by natural law.[25]

To ensure his anti-"blood mixing" message reached a wide audience, Koya delivered it not only in Ladies' Review but also in speeches delivered across Japan. In this peregrinating public health crusade, Koya was joined by public intellectual and professor of medicine Nagai Hisomu (1876–1957), cofounder in 1930 of the Japan Race Hygiene Association (RHA), of which Koya was vice president.[26] The RHA, in addition to placing members and followers in government posts, hospitals, universities, and eugenic marriage counseling centers throughout Japan, also functioned as a lobbyist and hub for research and the popularization of race hygiene. Scholars have explored the RHA and the careers of Nagai and Koya in some detail.[27] Yet there has been virtually no mention of their postwar crusade to forestall "blood mixing."[28]

It was precisely to address this threat that Nagai and Koya took to innumerable stages in their nationwide tour at the end of the Allied occupation.[29] Nagai had long been a proponent of eugenic marriage, collaborating with leading feminists like Ichikawa Fusae and Katō Shizue in the Japan Society for the Promotion of Eugenic Marriage, founded in 1935.[30] In 1934, Nagai had published a Handbook on Marriage replete with eugenic instruction on mate selection and hygienic reproduction. So popular was his handbook that it went through seven editions, the last published posthumously in 1960, and Nagai spun off additional handbooks as well.[31] Yet despite his leading role, in the 1930s, in promoting an explicitly German and Hitlerian model of race hygiene for Japan, Nagai's eugenic texts and marital handbooks in that era made little to no mention of "blood mixing" or racial "purity."[32] Not until defeat and occupation would Nagai begin to emphasize the innate inferiority of konketsuji and the threat they posed to the Japanese "race." For Nagai, as for many of his contemporaries, this newly awoken horror of konketsuji was entangled with humiliation and resentment at defeat and governance by foreign men. Of particular salience for Nagai, Koya, and many others was their disgust at the postwar sexual liberation—or debasement—of Japanese women, and their parallel disgust at the widespread, weak-kneed embrace of liberal, American values and American men that millions of Japanese had so recently fought to the death to resist.

In his 1949 New Handbook on Marriage, Nagai foretold that if "blood mixing" continued without regard for race hygiene, "there will be no alternative but for the entire *minzoku* to fall into the fate of ruin."[33] Lest anyone doubt, in *The Fate of the Race: I Appeal to the People of Japan*, Nagai explained that *minzoku* "carries a biological meaning, namely, a group of people bound by blood . . . who bear the genetic stock of the same ancestors."[34] From start to finish, this book emphasized the postwar threat of racial extinction and hope of racial revival. "Beloved 70 million countrymen of Japan! Fellow countrymen who endlessly love Japan, who love the Japanese race, who wish from their hearts for the rebirth of New Japan. The poisoned cup overhangs our lips!"[35] Such were the book's final words, driving home the urgency of its lengthy call to enforce race hygiene. Only thus could "the *minzoku* gain ultimate victory" in an international battle for survival, which, the text made clear, however severe Japan's setback in 1945, had not been lost altogether.[36] In short, "we keenly feel that race hygiene simply must be the foundation of long-term plans for rebuilding the nation."[37] From his position of scientific authority as former dean of the medical faculty at Tokyo University, Nagai endorsed the political principle, radical in its rejection of recent imperial projects yet increasingly mainstream in postwar Japan, that of all possible forms of government, "the most suitable situation is one *minzoku* to one state."[38] Obviously "blood mixing" imperiled this ideal.

Historian Aiko Takeuchi-Demirci argues that after the catastrophe of World War II, many experts and laymen in Japan considered eugenic marriage to be imperative to "save the Japanese from racial extinction." Thus, periodicals like *Iden* (*Heredity*), *Seikatsu kagaku* (*Science of Living*), and *Shufu to seikatsu* (*Housewife and Lifestyle*) published prolifically on the topic of eugenic marriage in the late 1940s and 1950s.[39] In 1949, amidst this mass-mediated eugenic-marriage boom, Nagai Hisomu published a *New Handbook on Marriage* that counseled readers to "gladly sacrifice the small self for the sake of a great ideal," namely, "the eternal flourishing of the *minzoku* [race]." In an extended discussion of "Marriage with a Different Race (Blood-Mixing)," Nagai advanced many reasons to eschew such unions, including "disturbing social problems that will occur due to blood-mixing," "national self-respect," and genetics. "We must be aware that numerous undesirable sorts may proliferate as a result of blood-mixing." Thirteen years prior in the imperial era, Nagai had described *konketsuji* as intermediate types, noting of "race mixing" in the United States that "the intelligence of black *konketsuji* is on the whole superior to pure black people and inferior to pure white people."[40] Needless to say, this estimate endorsed anti-Black racism, but Nagai did not intend it as an argument against race-mixing. By contrast, in the postwar era, Nagai recanted his view of *konketsuji* as intermediate types, informing readers instead that "the abilities of mixed-blood children of white and black people . . . are by and large inferior even to pure blacks."[41] In short, there was no upside to "blood mixing." *Konketsuji* were generally the worst of the worst, undesirable and inassimilable. Whether of white or Black paternity, Korean or Filipino, *konketsuji* born in Japan would tend toward genetic inferiority. Contrary to the false promises of the now dismantled and discredited Japanese empire, no amount of assimilation and intermarriage could overcome inborn divisions of blood between *minzoku*. On the contrary, Nagai warned, intermarriage debased all "races."

Chief among those who sought out and published empirical evidence of genetic inferiority among *konketsuji* in the early postwar era was Ishiwara Fusao (1883–1974), vice-director of the Microbial Institute at Nihon University. At the end of the Allied occupation in 1952 and for almost twenty years thereafter, Ishiwara published numerous studies demonstrating and explaining "mixed-blood" inferiority in leading scholarly journals including *Heredity*, the *Journal of Anthropology*, and *Race Hygiene*.[42] Ishiwara and his colleagues frequently cited Western scholars—above all, American and German geneticists and eugenicists Charles Davenport and Eugen Fischer—in discussions of "blood mixing," but no expert was more often cited in Japan than Ishiwara himself. However, the research that secured Ishiwara's postwar prominence was not his first foray into studying *konketsuji*. In 1941, his first paper on the topic expressed effusive praise for the positive effects of racial hybridization. The "hybrids" in Ishiwara's 1941 study were products of Japanese and Chinese "mixture" growing up in Tokyo. As Japan struggled to conquer and absorb China, Ishiwara found Japanese-Chinese *konketsuji* to be healthier, fatter, and taller than other children growing up in the same Japanese environment. Ideal physical specimens, these *konketsuji* also excelled at schoolwork and possessed appealing personalities.[43] In short, Ishiwara raised no alarms about "blood mixing" in the heyday of empire. However, upon defeat in 1945, Ishiwara lost interest in Japanese-Chinese hybrids and began instead decades of research on white-Japanese and Black-Japanese hybrids, about whom he rarely found anything positive to say.

As a microbial expert, Ishiwara expressed deep interest in physical maladies among postwar *konketsuji*, diagnosing them with high rates of hemophilia, abdominal hernia, and skin diseases, as well as impaired intelligence and sociability and outright idiocy. He summed up his conclusions in the journal *Heredity* as follows. "In consanguineous marriages, genetic ties are too close, and in *konketsuji* genetic ties are too distant. In these cases, the skin and mucous membrane lose their powers of resistance [to disease]." Ishiwara concluded his analysis by expounding on Hitler's philosophy of "Land and Blut." In the wake of six years of occupation by sexually active foreign soldiers, Ishiwara mused, "There is a subtle psychological order to national territory and national blood. Blood mixing shakes this order."[44] Ishiwara's attempts to prove and protect this blood-based "order" went on for decades. His opinions are of particular import because Ishiwara led a team of researchers investigating *konketsuji* under the auspices of the Ministry of Welfare's Institute for Research on Population Problems. In 1954, his team published a one-hundred-page report entitled *Anthropometric Influences of Emigration and Blood Mixture on Japanese Race* [sic], in which the notion of genetic disorders caused by "blood mixing" feature prominently.[45]

Ishiwara's conversion from pro- to anti-"mixing" corresponds to a general *tenkō* ("ideological reversal") in Japan. During the war, *konketsuji* were born of imperial expansion and celebrated as such; after the war, they were rejected as the illegitimate offspring of defeat and postwar decadence. Postwar animus toward *konketsuji* targeted those sired by enemy forces above all, but all *konketsuji* were polluted by association. Banished from speech and even memory was the positive valence once attached to "mixtures" such as Japanese-Chinese or Japanese-Korean. At the occupation's end, Koreans in Japan were stripped of their citizenship and were removed from Japan *en masse*, along with mixed Korean-Japanese families, to dark and uncertain fates in North Korea.[46] The early postwar era was an era of low-violence ethnic cleansing. From this era's deliberate and coercive sorting of populations by "blood" and "race," the nonoverlapping and "homogenous" nations of Japan and Korea were born.

How can we situate Japanese and East Asian race hygiene in the transnational history of science? In the last ten to fifteen years, a new wave of scholars has challenged the once canonical narrative of race science's mid-century decline in the West, chronicling the ways in which it continued to be practiced in fields like genetics and biomedicine into the twenty-first century. Yet for all the critical insights they offer, such revisionists in some respects replicate the master narrative they set out to critique, leaning heavily on Nazi impacts and Anglophone protagonists to explicate trends in "science" *tout court*. Michael Yudell, for example, asserts that mid-twentieth-century population geneticists preserved "race" for science by divorcing it from "the fallacy of the eugenic proposition" amidst "a worldwide reaction to Nazi eugenical horrors."[47] Yet despite repeatedly invoking "worldwide" trends, Yudell does not pause his Anglocentric tale to evidence worldwide reaction. Nor is this skipped step unusual in a field that *sotto voce* asks us to embrace an implicitly diffusionist model whereby "the rest" cannot help but follow where the Anglophone "West" and its scientists lead.

Michelle Brattain is among the few to account for the general omission of non-Western scientists from the mid-century history of race science. In her article on the 1950s UNESCO Statements on Race—often brandished as evidence of global scientific thought, despite their overwhelmingly Western European and American authorship—Brattain asserts that there were no scientific experts outside the West capable of weighing in on race at the time.[48] The claim has the distinct virtue of being easily falsified. More difficult to refute are abstract, agentless arguments verging on teleology, as when sociologist Jenny Reardon asserts that "theories of race that underwrote Nazi racial hygiene declined in science once the legitimacy of the Nazi regime had been undermined."[49] The fact that the "scientists" and "science" under study are distinctly Anglophone is rhetorically smoothed away in favor of science without borders.

Redefining the mid-century decline of race hygiene as local rather than global, Anglophone and French rather than absolute, is more faithful to the evidence. Language communities, contingent identities, national and imperial histories, and what historian Hiromi Mizuno terms "scientific nationalism" matter a good deal more to the history and future of science than is allowed by accounts of science without borders.[50] Ironically, given their anti-racist ethos, dominant scholarly narratives of the mid-century decline of race hygiene and scientific endorsements of racial "purity" have come to function as yet another installment in the epic march of progress and modernity in which the West takes center stage and plays the leading role. In reality, neither before nor after the mid-century turning point identified with Nazism and its suppression did German, Japanese, Korean, or Anglophone sciences represent "worldwide" or "real" science because science is a diverse human practice embedded in particular human worlds and worldviews.

Postwar Japanese and Korean uses of "race hygiene" fit the European pattern only if we abandon presumptions of globally synchronous scientific "progress" and look instead for common ground in an asynchronous time: the wasteland of Europe after World War I, where eugenicists offered their scientific expertise "as a solution to the crises facing their countries after the war."[51] Europeans and East Asians who lost their political and emotional maps of the world after the fall, respectively, of the Austro-Hungarian and Russian empires in 1917 and 1918 and the Japanese empire in 1945, equally turned to the modern sciences of race to map their identities and that of their neighbors anew: who they were and where they belonged, to which government, nation, history, and future.

Suffice it to say, then, that sciences are not univocal. Their findings are not foretold but decided by human actors in human time. That human agency and identity are central to the practice of science may seem so obvious as to not merit stating. Yet false universals continue to obscure our view of science and its practitioners. This essay proposes an anti-racist methodological turn toward a global study of science that seeks not only to decenter the West but also to notice and explain variations across time and space without recourse to hierarchy, teleology, elision, or aporia. We must attend to how diverse scientists are unevenly situated in a global field of knowledge production by relating science to power and the local to the global, and by recognizing that the local is everywhere.

In a global field, it may be entirely coherent for scientists on opposite ends of the earth—or opposite ends of war and occupation—to move in opposing directions at the same moment, amassing evidence and authority for competing scientific paradigms. This parting of scientific ways is exactly what happened with the sciences of identity and heredity—race science, genetics, eugenics, and anthropology—in the mid-twentieth century. Further research, including that done in Asian Studies, will no doubt yield further examples of this nonlinear, contested, global development of the sciences.

## Notes

[1] Mamiya, "Ijō kesshokuso," 29.

[2] Mamiya, "Ijō kesshokuso," 29, 35–37.

[3] Mamiya, "Ijō kesshokuso," 36.

[4] Kanō, "'Konketsuji' mondai"; Roebuck, "Orphans"; and Shimoji, *Konketsu*, 61–133.

[5] Sakai, "Imperial Nationalism."

[6] Hein, "Art of Persuasion," 748; Morris-Suzuki, "Ethnic Engineering," 523–524; Kowner, "Race," 92, 100; and Kadia, *Into the Field*, 94.

[7] Hein, *Post-Fascist Japan*, 181.

[8] Of these historians, only Kingsberg adduces evidence to support her claim, but that evidence is perfunctory.

[9] Paul, "Eugenics," 589; and Provine, "Geneticists," 796. See also Stepan, *Idea of Race*, 172–173; Farber, *Mixing Races*; and Kühl, *For the Betterment*, 105–106.

[10] Barkan, *Retreat*, 1. See also Barkan, "Race," 693–707; and Proctor, "Three Roots," 221.

[11] Dubow, *Scientific Racism*, 1.

[12] Balibar, "Racism," 1632–1634.

[13] Mukharji, "Serosocial to Sanguinary" and "Bengali Pharaoh."

[14] Oguma, *Genealogy*.

[15] See e.g., Ueda, *Sumera Chōsen*; Oguma, *Self-Images*, 213; Park, "Yi Kwang-su," 179; Ijichi, "Kōateki konketsuron"; and Nanba, "Minzokuteki yūgō."

[16] Hyun, "Blood Purity" and "Racializing *Chōsenjin*"; Kim, "Reauthenticating Race"; and Shin, *Ethnic Nationalism*.

[17] Nanta, "Physical Anthropology," 38; and Oguma, *Genealogy*.

[18] Roebuck, "Orphans."

[19] Postwar Japanese discourse on *konketsuji* rigidly linked race/gender roles, such that the possibility, for example, that an American woman might bear a Japanese man's baby was rarely acknowledged.

[20] Kanō, "'Konketsuji' mondai"; and Oguma, *Genealogy*.

[21] See e.g., Koya, *Kokudo*, 120–32.

[22] Roebuck, "Orphans," 1, 8.

[23] Sawada et al, "Keredomo konketsuji," 50.

[24] Nishi, "Konketsuji," 53; see also Matsushita, "Konketsuji," 78; and Uemura, "Ridgeway," 38.

[25] Koya, "Konketsu."

[26] "Kiken," 5.

[27] See e.g., Chung, *Struggle for National Survival,* 88–96, 143–156; Katō, *"Ren'ai kekkon,"* 179–188, 206–210; Oguma, *Genealogy,* 216–233; Suzuki, *Nihon,* 93–97, 144–168; and Yokoyama, *Nihon,* 153–271.

[28] Sakano discusses Koya's opposition to "blood mixing" but does not mention Nagai or the RHA in "Konketsu to tekiō," 188–215.

[29] "Kiken."

[30] Katō, *"Ren'ai kekkon"*; and Otsubo, "Engendering Eugenics," 244.

[31] Nagai, *Daini kekkon*; *Kekkon dokuhon*; and *Shin kekkon.*

[32] See Nagai, *Kekkon dokuhon* (1939); and *Yūseigaku gairon.*

[33] Nagai, *Shin kekkon,* 320.

[34] Nagai, *Minzoku,* 13.

[35] Ibid., 101.

[36] Ibid., 82.

[37] Ibid., 5.

[38] Ibid., 13.

[39] Takeuchi-Demirci, *Contraceptive Diplomacy,* 164–67.

[40] Nagai, *Yūseigaku gairon,* 209.

[41] Nagai, *Shin kekkon,* 263, 317–323.

[42] See e.g. Ishiwara, "Konketsuji no kenkyū"; "Konketsuji no kenkyū (I)"; and "Konketsuji no chinō."

[43] Ishiwara, "Nikka konketsu," 162–65.

[44] Ishiwara, "Konketsuji no kenkyū (I)," 28–29.

[45] Ministry of Welfare, *Konketsu.*

[46] Morris-Suzuki, *Exodus.*

[47] Yudell, *Race,* 8.

[48] Brattain, "Race."

[49] Reardon, *Race,* 18; and Roberts, *Fatal Invention,* 47.

[50] Mizuno, *Science for the Empire.*

[51] Turda, *Modernism,* 122; and Turda and Weindling, eds., *"Blood and Homeland."*

## Bibliography

Balibar, Étienne. "Racism Revisited: Sources, Relevance, and Aporias of a Modern Concept." *PMLA* 123, no. 5 (Oct. 2008): 1630–1639.

Barkan, Elazar. "Race and the Social Sciences." In Theodore Porter and Dorothy Ross, eds., *The Cambridge History of Science* Vol. 7 (New York: Cambridge University Press, 2008), 693–707.

———. *The Retreat of Scientific Racism: Changing Concepts of Race in Britain and the United States between the World Wars.* New York: Cambridge University Press, 1996.

Brattain, Michelle. "Race, Racism, and Antiracism: UNESCO and the Politics of Presenting Science to the Postwar Public," *American Historical Review* 112, no. 5 (Dec. 2007): 1386–1413.

Chung, Juliette. *Struggle for National Survival: Chinese Eugenics in a Transnational Context, 1896–1945.* New York: Routledge, 2002.

Dubow, Saul. *Scientific Racism in Modern South Africa.* New York: Cambridge University Press, 1995.

Farber, Paul Lawrence. *Mixing Races: From Scientific Racism to Modern Evolutionary Ideas.* Baltimore: Johns Hopkins University Press, 2010.

Hein, Laura. "The Art of Persuasion: Audiences and Philosophies of History." *Positions: East Asia Cultures Critique* 16, no. 3 (Winter 2008): 743–751.

———. *Post-Fascist Japan: Political Culture in Kamakura after the Second World War.* London: Bloomsbury, 2018.

Hyun, Jaehwan. "Blood Purity and Scientific Independence: Blood Science and Postcolonial Struggles in Korea, 1926–1975." *Science in Context* 32 (2019): 239–260.

———. "Racializing *Chōsenjin*: Science and Biological Speculations in Colonial Korea." *East Asian Science, Technology, and Society: An International Journal* 13, no. 4 (Dec. 2019): 489–510.

Ijichi Susumu. "Kōateki konketsuron." *Kaizō* 21 (March 1939): 82–88.

Ishiwara Fusao. "Konketsuji no chinō oyobi gakuryoku tesuto no seiseki ni tsuite (II)." *Jinruigaku zasshi* 77, no. 4 (Aug. 1969): 1–7.

———. "Konketsuji no kenkyū wa dō natte iru ka?" *Iden* 6, no. 11 (1952): 45–48.

———. "Konketsuji no kenkyū wa dō natte iru ka (I)." *Iden* 7, no. 1 (1953): 25–29.

———. "Nikka konketsu jidō no igakuteki chōsa." *Minzoku eisei* 9, no. 3 (1941): 162–65.

Kadia, Miriam Kingsberg. *Into the Field: Human Scientists of Transwar Japan.* Stanford: Stanford University Press, 2020.

Kanō Mikiyo. "'Konketsuji' mondai to tan'itsu minzoku shinwa no seisei." In Okuda Akiko et al., *Senryō to sei: seisaku, jittai, hyōshō*. Tokyo: Inpakuto shuppankai, 2007.

Katō Shūichi. *"Ren'ai kekkon" wa nani o motarashita ka: sei dōtoku to yūsei shisō no hyakunenkan*. Tokyo: Chikuma shinsho, 2004.

"Kiken na kyōiku no waku: sodachiyuku konketsuji." *Yomiuri shinbun* morning edition (Nov. 26, 1952): 5.

Kim, Hoi-eun. "Reauthenticating Race: Na Sejin and the Recycling of Colonial Physical Anthropology in Postcolonial Korea." *Journal of Korean Studies* 21, no. 2 (2016): 449–483.

Kowner, Rotem. "Race and Racism." In Sven Saaler ed., *Routledge Handbook of Modern Japanese History*. London: Taylor and Francis, 2017, 92–102.

Koya Yoshio. *Kokudo • jinkō • ketsueki*. Tokyo: Asahi shinbunsha, 1941.

———. "Konketsu monogatari: sekaiteki ni mita konketsuji mondai." *Fujin kōron* 39, no. 4 (1953): 164–169.

Kühl, Stefan. *For the Betterment of the Race: The Rise and Fall of the International Movement for Eugenics and Racial Hygiene*, trans. Lawrence Schofer. New York: Palgrave Macmillan, 2013.

Mamiya Hiroshi. "Ijō kesshokuso ni kansuru kenkyū," *Nihon naika gakkai zasshi* 56, no. 6 (June 1967): 28–37.

Matsushita Shizuko. "Konketsuji o sodatete." *Fujin kōron* 37, no. 12 (1951): 76–79.

Ministry of Welfare. *Konketsu oyobi imin ni yoru Nihon minzoku tai'i no eikyō ni tsuite*. Tokyo: Kōseishō jinkō mondai kenkyūjo, 1954.

Mizuno, Hiromi. *Science for the Empire: Scientific Nationalism in Modern Japan*. Stanford: Stanford University Press, 2008.

Morris-Suzuki, Tessa. "Ethnic Engineering: Scientific Racism and Public Opinion Surveys in Midcentury Japan." *Positions: East Asia Cultures Critique* 8, no. 2 (Fall 2000): 499–529.

———. *Exodus to North Korea: Shadows from Japan's Cold War*. Lanham: Rowman & Littlefield, 2007.

Mukharji, Projit Bihari. "The Bengali Pharaoh: Upper-Caste Aryanism, Pan-Egyptianism, and the Contested History of Biometric Nationalism in Twentieth-Century Bengal." *Comparative Studies in Society and History* 59, no. 2 (2017): 446–476.

————. "From Serosocial to Sanguinary Identities: Caste, Transnational Race Science and the Shifting Metonymies of Blood Group B, India c. 1918–1960." *The Indian Economic and Social History Review* 51, no. 2 (2014): 143–176.

Nagai Hisomu. *Daini kekkon dokuhon: dokushinsha no tame ni.* Tokyo: Shunjūsha, 1950.

————. *Kekkon dokuhon.* Tokyo: Shunjūsha, 1934, 1939, 1960.

————. *Minzoku no unmei: Nihon kokumin ni uttau.* Tokyo: Muramatsu shoten, 1948.

————. *Yūseigaku gairon* Vol. 1. Tokyo: Yūzankaku, 1936.

Nanba Monkichi. "Minzokuteki yūgō no kihon mondai: gengo, konketsu, ijū." *Gaikō jihō* No. 800 (April 1, 1938): 70–87.

Nanta, Arnaud. "Physical Anthropology and the Reconstruction of Japanese Identity in Postcolonial Japan." *Social Science Japan Journal* 11, no. 1 (2008): 29–47.

Nishi Kiyoko. "Konketsuji no mondai ni kansuru Amerika tokyoku no iken." *Fujin kōron* 38, no. 7 (1952): 53.

Oguma Eiji. *Genealogy of "Japanese" Self-Images,* trans. David Askew. Melbourne: Trans Pacific Press, 2002.

Otsubo, Sumiko. "Engendering Eugenics: Feminists and Marriage Restriction Legislation in the 1920s." In Barbara Molony and Kathleen Uno, eds., *Gendering Modern Japanese History.* Cambridge: Harvard University Press, 2005, 226–256.

Park, Chan-seung. "Yi Kwang-su and the Endorsement of State Power." *Seoul Journal of Korean Studies* 19, no. 1 (Dec. 2006): 161–189.

Paul, Diane. "Eugenics and the Left." *Journal of the History of Ideas* 45, no. 4 (1984): 567–590.

Proctor, Robert. "Three Roots of Human Recency: Molecular Anthropology, the Refigured Acheulean, and the UNESCO Response to Auschwitz." *Current Anthropology* 44, no. 2 (April 2003): 213–239.

Provine, William. "Geneticists and the Biology of Race Crossing." *Science* new series 182, no. 4114 (Nov. 1973): 790–796.

Reardon, Jenny. *Race to the Finish: Identity and Governance in an Age of Genomics.* Princeton: Princeton University Press, 2005.

Roberts, Dorothy. *Fatal Invention: How Science, Politics, and Big Business Re-Create Race in the Twenty-First Century.* New York: The New Press, 2011.

Roebuck, Kristin. "Orphans by Design: "Mixed-Blood" Children, Child Welfare, and Racial Nationalism in Postwar Japan," *Japanese Studies* 36 (2016): 191–212.

Sakai, Naoki. "Imperial Nationalism and the Comparative Perspective," *Positions: East Asia Cultures Critique* 17, no. 1 (Spring 2009): 159–205.

Sakano Tōru. "Konketsu to tekiō nōryoku: Nihon ni okeru jinshu kenkyū 1930–1970 nendai." In Takezawa Yasuko ed., *Jinshu no hyōshō to shakaiteki riariti*. Tokyo: Iwanami shoten, 2009, 188–215.

Sawada Miki et al. "Keredomo konketsuji wa . . . sodatte yuku: zadankai." *Fujin kōron* 38, no. 7 (1952): 50–57.

Shimoji Rōrensu Yoshitaka. *"Konketsu" to "Nihonjin": Haafu, daburu, mikkusu no shakaishi*. Tokyo: Seidosha, 2018.

Shin, Gi-Wook. *Ethnic Nationalism in Korea: Genealogy, Politics, and Legacy*. Stanford: Stanford University Press, 2006.

Stepan, Nancy. *The Idea of Race in Science*. London: Macmillan, 1982.

Suzuki Zenji. *Nihon no yūseigaku: sono shisō to undō no kiseki*. Tokyo: Sankyō shuppan, 1983.

Takeuchi-Demirci, Aiko. *Contraceptive Diplomacy: Reproductive Politics and Imperial Ambitions in the United States and Japan*. Stanford: Stanford University Press, 2018.

Turda, Marius. *Modernism and Eugenics*. New York: Palgrave Macmillan, 2010.

Turda, Marius Paul J. Weindling, eds., *"Blood and Homeland": Eugenics and Racial Nationalism in Central and Southeast Europe, 1900–1940*. Budapest: Central European University Press, 2007.

Ueda Tatsuo [Yi Yŏng-gŭn]. *Sumera Chōsen*. Tokyo: Nihon seinen bunka kyōkai, 1943.

Uemura Tamaki. "Ridgeway fujin e: panpan ni atarashii michi o hiraku tame niwa." *Fujin kōron* Vol. 38, no. 5 (1952): 36–40.

Yokoyama Takashi. *Nihon ga yūsei shakai ni naru made: kagaku keimō, media, seishoku no seiji*. Tokyo: Keisō shobō, 2015.

Yudell, Michael. *Race Unmasked: Biology and Race in the Twentieth Century*. New York: Columbia University Press, 2014.

# 7

# Toward an Afro-Japanese and Afro-Ainu Feminist Practice

## Reading Fujimoto Kazuko and Chikappu Mieko

**Felicity Stone-Richards**

Ayumu Kaneko, in chronicling the history of Black Studies as an academic discipline in Japan, presents us with a generative question: "What can black history in Japan do for critical interventions in contemporary issues of Japanese politics, society and culture?"[1] A new body of academic scholarship has recently been flourishing in examining the space where Japanese people engage with and adopt aspects of Afro-diasporic culture and political practice, a practice that is coming to be defined in the academic world as Afro-Japanese exchange. The twentieth century was the stage for some of the most intense expressions of Afro-Japanese solidarity and political exchange. Scholars have mapped the left-wing solidarities among Japanese and Black American and West Indian Marxists, the importance of Black literary aesthetics to Japanese postwar writers, and Japanese affective communities drawing on Rasta ideology.[2] This research has opened exploration into the cultural and political products created by Japanese people consuming and reflecting on Black cultural productions. In a similar vein, I show that Japanese and Ainu female writers from the 1980s and 1990s incorporated Black feminist thought into their political philosophies.

I will be focusing on two writers in this essay: Fujimoto Kazuko, an important translator of American literature, and Chikappu Mieko, an influential Ainu activist and clothwork artist. Fujimoto was essential to translating several novels written by Black American women and has written books on Black feminist practice. Chikappu published an essay on Alice Walker's *The Color Purple* in an essay collection by writers interpreting the works of Walker and detailing their personal relationship to her body of work. It is essential that we acknowledge the political writings that these women produced based on their own experiences of Japanese society, their understanding of Japanese history, *and* their interpretations of Black American feminist writers. This is at the heart of what I would like to term Afro-Japanese and Afro-Ainu feminist practice. The intellectual production of these two women has been deeply impacted by the intellectual production of Black feminists, as have the writings of other Japanese writers and translators.

Little has been written on the relationship between Japanese women and the works of Black women and Black American feminists. The relationship of which I speak is one in which Japanese women have read, translated, disseminated, and incorporated the philosophical and political practices of Black feminists into their own work. While there are many working definitions of Black feminism, the most influential remains that posited by the Combahee River Collective, who see Black feminism as the "struggle against racial, sexual, heterosexual and class oppression . . . and the development of integrated analysis and practice based upon the fact that the major systems of oppression are interlocking."[3] While neither Fujimoto nor Chikappu define the kind of Black feminism that they are interested in, they are specifically engaging with the works of influential Black feminist and womanist activists: Toni Cade Bambara, Toni Morrison, and Alice Walker. From engaging with these writers, Fujimoto and Chikappu highlight the importance of building community, transmitting generational knowledge, maintaining the ability to love in the fight against oppression, and fighting the oppressive systems of racism, heterosexism, and capitalism simultaneously. It is these specific attributes of Black feminists that Fujimoto and Chikappu believe were essential to transmit to a Japanese audience. Both Fujimoto and Chikappu saw that Japanese society was ignoring the racist elements in their society, and they are visceral in their critique of Japanese support for assimilationist policies.

While this essay will be exploring a small section of this body of work, these writers were by no means the only people seeking out Black political thought. In the postwar period, scholar Nukina Yoshitaka established the Black Studies Association (Kokujin Kenkyuu no kai) and the *Journal of Black Studies* in 1956 with the specific goal of interpreting and disseminating Black literary works to nurture a democratic intellectual movement and push against the American-imposed dictatorship.[4] Japan would eventually transition from being an occupied, impoverished state to one of the wealthiest countries in the world. Nevertheless, Japan's rapid postwar development, the mistreatment of Japan's ethnic minorities, Japan's role in supporting American military hegemony in Asia, and its economic exploitation of formerly colonized Asian countries created the conditions for uneasy reflection for many conscientious thinkers. Fujimoto, along with her professional peer, Atsuko Furomoto, were both members of Kokujin Kenkyuu no kai. They pushed to expand the reading of Black American literature to include Black American women.[5] Yoshida Ruiko, living in Japan, is a photojournalist famous for chronicling major events in Black American history for a Japanese audience. The period in which the Japanese female writers were most active in their engagement with Black feminism, the late 1970s and 1980s, was a period of intense development of Black internationalism and the decade that witnessed the start of Black American women writers achieving mainstream recognition.

Reading through Fujimoto and Chikappu's work shows that Japanese women's engagement with Black feminist literature was both varied and deeply enriching. Each writer interprets Black women in creative ways and uses Black feminist political practice to critique and change the shape of Japan's social movements. I would like to suggest that we call this interaction Afro-Japanese and Afro-Ainu feminist practice. It is possible that we can call this Japanese Black feminism, but as neither author is drawing their entire political practice from Black feminism, I do not wish to obscure the hybrid nature of their intellectual production. However, just as I do not want to obscure Fujimoto and Chikappu's own intellectual history, neither do I want to obscure their intellectual debt to Black American women; thus, there needs to be some acknowledgment of the importance of Black feminism to their body of work. Additionally, the use of "Afro-Japanese" and "Afro-Ainu" links the intellectual production of Japanese and Ainu women to the scholarly conversations on the intellectual production of Japanese men reading Black male political thought. Moreover, though I believe the practice should be named in this way, I do not want to suggest that I am labeling these women as feminist. Chikappu does not call herself a feminist for the same reason that many Black women did not call themselves feminist—because of the association of feminism with a white/Japanese liberal feminism that relied on racial and class subjugation.[6] However, as these women are drawing on the works of women who explicitly make clear their alignment with Black feminism or womanism, I am labeling the political practice itself. Finally, I am making a distinction between Afro-Japanese and Afro-Ainu. The Ainu is a collective name for the various communities that were indigenous to the northernmost territory of Japan, Hokkaido, and the Sakhalin Islands. As a result of the Japanese government's push for modernization and expansion during the Meiji era (1868–1912), Ainu communities were devastated and forcibly assimilated into the Japanese nation.[7] In reclaiming parts of their culture that were stolen from them, many Ainu activists, including Chikappu, do not acknowledge themselves as Japanese. Therefore, the combination of a Black feminist political practice with Japanese and Ainu social movements creates the hybrid of both Afro-Japanese and Afro-Ainu feminist practice.

It is within this history that we must interpret the Japanese and Ainu female writers who were moved by the political thought developed by Black American women. Fujimoto currently lives in the United States and also attended university there. Along with Atsuko Furomoto, she has translated several major literary works produced by Black American women. She was one of the lead translators of a seven-volume anthology collection published in 1981 and 1982. This collection includes the most famous writings of Toni Morrison, Alice Walker, Mary Helen Washington, Ntozake Shange, Zora Neale Hurston, and many others. This was the largest widespread dissemination of Black women authors in Japan. In addition to her efforts to build a team that would translate Black women's writings, Fujimoto trained her team and other women writers to engage in close reading and critical reflection of these texts.[8]

It is with the goal of nurturing collective learning in Japan that Fujimoto presents us with in-depth interviews of and conversations between Black American women and interpretations of the works of Toni Cade Bambara and Toni Morrison. In this book, *Even the Blues are Just Songs: Black Women's Manifesto*, Fujimoto opens the book with a meeting she had with Toni Cade Bambara. In this meeting, Fujimoto asks what Bambara meant by the term "salt eaters," referring to Bambara's 1980 novel, *The Salt Eaters*. Of Bambara's response, Fujimoto writes, "Salt is the metaphor tying our bitter and painful experiences together, tying our souls together. Moreover, as salt has the capacity to heal wounds, a salt-eater is also a person who can heal wounds."[9] In Bambara's novel, salt acts as a kind of magic, neutralizing the poison in the soul that festered from the disgrace and humiliation of slavery. Fujimoto interprets these words as reflecting a practice that would allow one to live a long life without losing one's dignity, moving beyond a practice of mere survival. These views are reflected by the women that Fujimoto interviews in Wisconsin. They state, "We want to be able to thrive," and, "We want to be able to live."[10] Fujimoto highlights repeatedly the degree to which the Black women she sits down with talk of dignity, of their optimism and hope for the future, despite all the indignities they had suffered throughout their lives. Fujimoto allows the stories and conversations between the women in the book to flow naturally and does not bring up a discussion about Japan's racism until the end of the book. The purpose of the book is to allow Black American women to tell their story and share their thoughts on the future of the Black community in the hope that engaging in the practice of careful listening will stir Japanese readers to reflect more carefully on America's race relations and, consequently, on Japan's.

One of the most stimulating conversations in the book occurs between Juliet Martin, a prison psychiatrist; Deborah Washington, co-owner of a television network; and Mary Hinkle, a broker. At the center of this conversation is the danger of the assimilationist propaganda that all the women agree has halted the progress of Black liberation. Martin recounts that during the 1960s, Malcolm X came to speak at Howard University. In his speech, he made clear that Black people will go on to gain doctorates and expect to be called Dr. X and Dr. Y but really will only ever be called "nigger." This speech, Martin recalls, made many in the audience angry, including Martin. It pushed against the entire notion of respectability politics, that the appropriate appearance and profession could protect Black people from the effects of racism. That same day after the speech, some kids yelled out "nigger bitch" to Martin when she was at an intersection, dressed in her best suit. "It was from that moment that I began to seriously consider Malcolm X's words. I had once thought the fight was over. I had deceived myself," she states.[11] For Washington, "these people didn't understand what the fight was about from the very beginning." She states, "to gain a good income, to have a good job, if people thought that was the goal all along, then they were wrong about the battle. Black people currently have no political power. They're still victims."[12] Within this conversation, we can see both the critique of respectability politics as a vehicle for Black liberation and a distinction being made between the achievement of socioeconomic success for *some* and Black liberation for *all*. Washington highlights that in professional settings when she is a client, the receptionist will never refer to her by last name, yet white clients will be referred to as Mrs., Mr., or Ms. "They resent the fact that I am a woman, and they hate the fact that I am black. Everyday is like this. Are we really finished with the struggle?" Washington states. Professional achievements yield a certain economic comfort, but the contempt of white people remains.

The achievement of economic success for some within the Black community has exacerbated the class divisions between Black people. Drawing on the influential Black American scholar and educator Carter G. Woodson, Martin states, "Education will separate you from your group. If we only study the classes we need to take for credit at university, we will only be drawing conclusions from that one ideological system. . . . we need to have a confrontation with ourselves." Hinkle adds, "if you can't maintain a relationship with the group you belong to, it's hopeless. You can assume that the color of your skin no longer exists as an issue for you, but all others see you as black."[13] They recognize that in a perverse manner, the more success a small group of Black people achieves, the more the ties between Black people fall apart. This is both injurious to the Black people who are left in poverty and to the newly rich Black people who deceive themselves into thinking their race no longer matters and who find themselves without the support of their community when faced with continued racial aggression. For Martin, it is not enough to make this only about white people and their racism: "we must be critical of ourselves . . . to avoid becoming complicit in the oppressive system."[14]

A recurring theme in the book is that Black liberation is not possible through achieving material success according to the logic of racio-capitalism, a key feature of Black feminist thought. Fujimoto writes that middle-class Black people enjoyed most of the socioeconomic gains made possible by the civil rights movement. She writes that "this situation has created what could be called an underclass. And we can see a pattern in the maintenance and reproduction of this underclass."[15] While the gap between middle-class and poor Black people has widened since the civil rights movement, there has always historically been a small elite of wealthy Black people—the Black bourgeoisie. For Martin, this Black bourgeoisie has always been a barrier to the progress of poor Black people. As a poor dark-skinned girl from Key West, Florida, Martin had gained entry to a boarding school on the East Coast and then briefly attended Fisk University before dropping out. In both places, Martin was treated with contempt by "white-ish" or "barely black" rich Black people.[16] This hateful treatment led Martin to the study of psychology. She wondered what it was about her skin (and ultimately theirs) that triggered this behavior, that attracted such contempt from her society. It is why she repeatedly comes back to the idea that only through rigorous self-critique will we be able to rid ourselves of the oppressive systems we live under. For Black people to merely try and copy the success of white people would maintain the white supremacist oppressive structure. Black feminists are not interested in achieving parity with white elites but in completely undoing the system that allowed for such a concentration of wealth and power.

Throughout the conversation is a very clear repudiation of the idea of assimilation. In her own words, Washington states that one of the defining characteristics of Black people is this ability to resist assimilation: "I call our unique characteristic our power, if discrimination, etc., disappeared, I don't think we would necessarily lose that power that kept us living. We must abandon the idea that we need to assimilate to survive, or we're screwed. This is in our history, there is so much wisdom on existence that we need to recover." Martin goes further and states, "In my sense, our survival necessarily includes the fact that we have not lost those qualities. Without them, we can't expect to survive. For everyday life, if we don't use our historical psychological legacy, we will not be able to live."[17] Both speak to the cultural legacy of Black communities that have developed to resist "being locked in a corner"—in other words, that have developed the power to resist assimilation and cultural extermination. The language, music, art, literature, and political organization are all part of a cultural legacy that has been nurtured from one generation to the next. The women that Fujimoto interviews in this book are inheriting not only the legacy of oppression but the creative expression and resistance of their forebears.

Fujimoto writes, "I listened, I wrote, on such cruel and painful topics. I once wrote that the process of listening can also change us."[18] Fujimoto believes that the process of listening and listening carefully is an ethical act. The refusal to listen, or to willfully misunderstand what an oppressed group is saying is itself an act of violence. She writes:

> Some conscientious and self-believing people say that black people can and should be fully assimilated when their economic status improves. Whether American or Japanese, I am hurt by such words, which are spoken in a friendly manner. When African-Americans say that their lives are in danger if they abandon their blackness, those who do not take them seriously are fundamentally violent. We have been using such violence as leverage against the people of the earth . . . in Japan and in the world.[19]

It is with a view to challenging this idea that Fujimoto produces this book for a Japanese audience. Fujimoto is no stranger to the idea of assimilation, the idea that the abuse minorities experience will go away if only they behave and mix fully with those who cause their suffering. Such language is rife in Japanese government propaganda that seeks to create a homogenous society. Assimilation puts the burden of oppression on the oppressed. As was made clear in the conversation between Martin, Washington, and Hinkle, all assimilation does is destroy the community from which one draws strength while allowing racism to endure. Such language also ignores the historical reality that assimilation is often forced and violent. Chikappu speaks to this experience very clearly. Where people are colonized, such as was the case with the Ainu and Okinawans, assimilation becomes banning the speaking of one's own language, banning fishing and hunting practices, destroying temples and artwork; entire cultures are destroyed to "encourage assimilation."

While there is a searing indictment of those who believe in the process of assimilation, Fujimoto also remarks on a very important characteristic of these Black American women. She was moved by the stories Black women had to tell, not simply because they trusted in her enough to expose their personal stories and vulnerabilities to her. Fujimoto saw in their language and in their demeanor a powerful transformative element. She writes, "When I heard the voices of black women in North America telling their stories, I felt their words stabbing and shooting at me. I felt their sense of crisis as well."[20] And yet, within this pain, there is also extraordinary joy and dignity. Despite the subject matter that Fujimoto is exposed to, she is astonished at the joy on display around her. She writes, "The women who have appeared in this volume know all about the mechanisms of such a world. And yet, they do not close their hearts. Their battles are endless and not optimistic, but they do not despair. They are women who laugh. And they laugh joyously."[21] The process of listening carefully to the pain and the joy, of being exposed to thought and spirit on display, stirs a transformation in the reader. Fujimoto hopes that a Japanese reader can be moved by the vulnerability and pain on display in this history and open their heart to resisting the violence Japanese society inflicts on its minority population.

The importance of vulnerability in Black women's language cannot be overstated. Chikappu had also been drawn in specifically by the vulnerability displayed by Alice Walker. *The Color Purple* was first translated into Japanese in 1984 and was part of the wave of Black American women's literature that was published during this decade. This followed the translation of Walker's novel *Meridian,* which was part of the Black American women's anthology Fujimoto and others published in 1981 and 1982.[22] Chikappu was an Ainu activist, famous for her role in pushing for the recognition and transmission of Ainu cultural heritage. She had done extensive work on teaching the practices of embroidery that were essential to transmitting the spiritual history and philosophy of different Ainu communities. She has written extensively on her experiences of Japanese imperialist violence and the effect this has had on Ainu families and especially on Ainu women. She has also written an essay on Walker, a nuanced and intimate reading of *The Color Purple*, in which Chikappu finds a kindred spirit with Walker. Chikappu understands and shares Walker's philosophies that all parts of the natural world have spirit and deserve respect, not merely the humans. It is a philosophy that places a love for life at the center of fighting oppression and believes that if oppression is truly to be undone, a desire to live a loving life is essential.

Chikappu, in her essay "The Color Purple is the Brilliance of Existence," writes deeply about personal experiences growing up Ainu: her community experience of violent discrimination, her reflections on her abusive father, her unhappy marriage, her spirituality, and how profoundly she related to several themes present in Walker's novel. Part of the reason why Chikappu was able to connect so deeply to Walker's novel is that Walker chooses to lay out the full scale of intimate partner violence experienced by Black women at the hands of Black men. Indeed, Walker's generation of Black women writers were the first to publicly write about the violence that occurred within Black families and communities. Walker's insistence in openly displaying the intracommunal violence present within Black communities attracted fierce critique from Black men who felt that Walker and other Black women writers were essentially playing into the hands of the white establishment by displaying Black community pain.[23] What these Black male critics failed to understand is that it is precisely due to the openness of these painful moments that Walker's writings have touched so many. Far from introducing more reasons for people to look down on Black communities, the vulnerability and strength of Walker's characters allowed others to connect to these experiences.

Chikappu finds multiple parallels between Ainu culture and Black American culture. One of these is the practice of Ainu embroidery, *ikarakara*, and Black American quilting. Chikappu states, "If the culture created by black people is quilts, the culture created by the Ainu is ikarakara. . . . [W]hat both quilts and ikarakara have in common is the thoughtfulness and overflowing love of their creators that has been poured in."[24] Love is at the center of quiltmaking, creating a blanket or item of clothing that has the dual purpose of enveloping a loved one and transmitting cultural history through the images, materials, and methods of sewing. ann-elise lewallen writes that "historically, Ainu women created motifs to protect loved ones and their own bodies."[25] lewallen shows that for contemporary Ainu revivalists, those determined to relearn and pass on traditional Ainu culture, relearning clothwork art and mimicking the traditional technique allows Ainu women to engage in memory creation and tap into a spiritual relationship with their ancestors. She writes, "engaging this spontaneous technical skill and tacit understanding with an unseen ancestral realm is empowering, therapeutic and redemptive."[26] Throughout her life, Chikappu has been trying to wrestle back aspects of Ainu beliefs and art that were stolen from her and her generation. From learning from her mother and looking at displays of Ainu clothing behind museum glass, she found ways to relearn *ikarakara*. Chikappu and other revivalists pushed against the currents of Japanese culture that would have seen knowledge of *ikarakara* destroyed. She writes, "People are similar to quilts, the passage of time passes as if the culture of the powerful is all that matters and those who stay quiet are eliminated. . . . However Walker says that if each of us is but a small dot, by connecting dots to lines, we can change the current."[27]

Chikappu exhibits a clear affinity with the spiritual ideas Walker displays in *The Color Purple*. She quotes Shug, the glamorous free-spirited woman who is constantly disrespected, as saying that "love is the call of love's spirit, when you cut down a tree, it is as if blood were flowing down your arm . . . the god on display here is one that is framed by a profound appreciation for existence, all of existence."[28] Central to Walker's philosophy (and indeed to many Black feminist activists) has been a vegan environmental practice that is deeply critical of the way humans have degraded nature to justify policies of resource extraction. In her essay "Everything is a Human Being," Walker writes, "But, in truth, Earth itself has become the nigger of the world. It is perceived, ironically, as other, alien, evil...While the Earth is poisoned, everything it supports is poisoned."[29] Chikappu shows that Walker's philosophy is about living and loving. Protecting and transmitting cultural knowledge from one generation to the next is an act of love and necessary for life; respecting the rest of the natural world around us is an act of love and necessary for life; and finally, for Chikappu, being vulnerable and sharing in pain is an act of love and necessary for life. She writes, "The act of sharing mental anguish, together with the act of continuing to live and cultivating love, nourishes people."[30]

In this, Chikappu shares a great deal with what drives Fujimoto to transmit Black women's knowledge. The act of being open with one's pain is a key component to building a community that can nurture love. Maintaining one's dignity and love is essential to surviving under oppressive systems and the key to undermining them. When Fujimoto talks of Bambara's *Salt Eaters*, she concludes that sharing and being exposed to a particular kind of pain is a creative act. It binds together those who have shared similar sufferings and shows that a life filled with love is not incompatible with a life filled with pain, and indeed, the strength of nurturing self-love, transmitting that self-love to those around you, is a powerful act. This is what Chikappu sees in the character Shug. Having experienced so much trauma in her life, Celie decries that "God is nothing but a man... He's small-minded, screwed up, lax in everything he does, and vulgar." To this, Chikappu quotes Shug's response: "This is what I believe, listen to me. God is in you. He is in everyone. When you are born into this world, you are born with God in you. But only those who look for it can find it."[31] Looking for God and nurturing love come to meld together here. For Shug, who spoke that "love is the call of love's spirit," the essence of a divine spirit and the essence of love are not separate. Shug's response to Celie is both an encapsulation of her belief system and an act of love toward Celie who is on the precipice of despair.

Both the idea that God and love are everywhere and that one has to actively seek it out resonate with Chikappu. She writes, "The Ainu *kamuy* and Shug's god are the same."[32] Chikappu found the Ainu *kamuy* (divine spirit) when she began the process to learn her family's traditional embroidery practices. She writes, "In the midst of such deep-rooted discrimination, we Ainu had to fight against ourselves, and in the midst of this struggle, we had the strength to regain our pride. Regaining Ainu culture will lead to regaining the pride of the Ainu people. I found the Ainu *kamuy* in Ainu *ikarakara* (embroidery)."[33] Regaining pride in one's heritage and fighting to rebuild a community that was destroyed allows one to become closer to a divine spirit and to love. It is the drive to do this, to fight for such a life, that moves Chikappu. *The Color Purple* encapsulates the brilliance of fighting for love and fighting to rebuild a community under constant assault. "I want to fight for this life," she writes.[34] At the end of the essay, there is a specific appeal to allies and comrades in Japan who must be moved to join forces with the Ainu: Japanese, Zainichi Koreans, Chinese, Taiwanese, South and North Koreans, Okinawans, and Burakumin. The Japanese are included in the new future she wishes to build, but only by fighting together will everyone find the "brilliance of life" that Walker showed was possible.

Fujimoto and Chikappu have each contributed to the dissemination of Black feminist work in Japan. Fujimoto's book was republished in November 2020 and sold so well that it was reprinted again in January 2021.[35] It was influential among writers of that generation and has since come back in the public mainstream as a result of the 2020 summer of racial justice following the murder of George Floyd. One young writer discusses the reprint as part of *Vogue Japan*'s book club.[36] Fujimoto's influence as a translator is probably most significant, having been indispensable to the translation of Black American women's work. Chikappu published her essay on Alice Walker in a special essay collection on Walker in 1991. As there is no information on how many copies this book sold, it is difficult to gauge the influence of this collection. However, Chikappu was a very important Ainu activist before passing away in 2010. She was involved in the establishment of *Rera no kai*, the Ainu Cultural Association, had fought and won court cases against the improper use of Ainu photos, and became well known for her clothwork art.

Both Fujimoto and Chikappu are explicit about what it is Black women have to offer Japanese political movements: the critique of assimilation, the critique of racial capitalism, how Black women communicate their suffering, how Black women resist by creating stronger community, by nurturing self-love and creating the space for others to join their philosophy. Fujimoto and Chikappu are examples of Japanese and Ainu women who show a nuanced and creative reading of Black women's work. They have produced political philosophies that meld their own historical understanding with the political thought of Black feminist writers. These texts critiqued racist and imperialist elements of Japanese society and aimed to convince readers of the transformative power within Black feminist writings and in turn encapsulate an Afro-Japanese and Afro-Ainu feminist practice.

## Notes

[1] Kaneko 2019, 129.

[2] Koshiro 2003, 190–94; Bridges 2020; Sterling 2015.

[3] Combahee River Collective 1977.

[4] Koshiro 2003.

[5] Onishi and Sakashita 2019.

[6] lewallen 2016.

[7] Bukh 2010.

[8] Onishi and Sakashita 2019, 107–108.

[9] Fujimoto 1986, 3.

[10] Ibid., 13.

[11] Ibid., 83–84.

[12] Ibid., 84.

[13] Ibid., 86.

[14] Ibid., 87.

[15] Ibid., 12.

[16] Ibid., 19.

[17] Ibid., 88.

[18] Ibid., 261.

[19] Ibid., 261.

[20] Ibid., 261.

[21] Ibid., 261.

[22] Onishi and Sakashita 2019.

[23] Davis 1987.

[24] Chikappu 1991, 49.

[25] lewallen 2016, 163.

[26] Ibid., 164.

[27] Chikappu 1991, 49.

[28] Ibid., 46.

[29] Walker 2011, 258–259.

[30] Chikappu 1991, 51.

[31] Ibid., 43.

[32] Ibid., 45.

[33] Ibid., 44–45.

[34] Ibid., 51.

[35] Takeshi 2021.

[36] Nakamura 2021.

## Bibliography

Bridges, William H. *Playing in the Shadows*. Ann Arbor: University of Michigan Press, 2020.

Bukh, Alezander. "Ainu Identity and Japan's Identity: The Struggle for Subjectivity." *The Copenhagen Journal of Asian Studies.* 28, no. 2 (2010): 35–53.

チカップ美恵子. 1991. 風のめぐみ：アイヌ民族の文化と人権. 東京：株式会社御茶の水書房.

Davis, Thulani. "Family Plots: Black Women Writers Reclaim Their Past." *The Village Voice*. 1987, Retrieved August 20, 2021. https://www.villagevoice.com/2020/01/11/black-women-writers-reclaim-their-past/.

lewallen, ann-elise. *The Fabric of Indigeneity: Ainu Identity, Gender, and Settler Colonialism*. Albuquerque: University of New Mexico Press, 2016.

Kaneko, Ayumu. "Studies of Black History in Post-War Japan." *Transpacific Correspondence: Dispatches from Japan's Black Studies*, ed. Yuichiro Onishii & Fumiko Sakashita. Basingstoke: Palgrave Macmillan, 2019.

藤本和子. 1986. ブルースだってただの唄：黒人女性のマニフェスト. 朝日新聞社.

河地和子. 1990. わたしたちのアリスウオーカー：地球上のすべての女たちのために. 株式会社御茶の水書房.

Koshiro, Yukiko. "Beyond an Alliance of Color: The African American Impact on Modern Japan." *positions: east asia cultures* critique. 11, no. 1 (2003): 190–198.

Nakamura, Yuko. 藤本和子著『ブルースだってだたの唄 黒人女性の仕事と生活』を、今、読むべき理由。(VOGUE BOOK CLUB | 中村佑子). *Vogue*. https://www.vogue.co.jp/change/article/vogue-book-club-blues-datte-tadano-uta. Retrieved 18 January 18, 2022.

Sterling, Marvin. "Race, Ethnicity and Affective Community in Japanese Rastafari." In *Traveling Texts and the Work of Afro-Japanese Cultural Production: Two Haiku and a Microphone*. Ed. William H Bridges & Nina Cornyetz. London: Lexington Books, 2015.

久野剛士. 2021. 斎藤真理子×八巻美恵 『ブルースだってただの唄』を今読む意味, *Cinra*. https://www.cinra.net/article/interview-202101-saitouyamaki_kngshcl. Retrieved January 18, 2022.

Walker, Alice. *In Search of Our Mother's Gardens*. Apple Books. Open Road Integrated Media, 2011.

Walker, Alice. *Living By the Word: Essays*. Apple Books. Open Road Integrated Media, 2011.

# 8

## BLACK JAPANESE STORYTELLING AS PRAXIS

### ANTI-RACIST DIGITAL ACTIVISM AND BLACK LIVES MATTER IN JAPAN

**Kimberly Hassel**

### "Racism Is Not a Trend"

Toward the end of my yearlong fieldwork in Tokyo, news hit Japan of the murder of George Floyd, a Black man, at the hands of white Minneapolis police officer Derek Chauvin, who knelt on Floyd's neck for nine minutes and twenty-nine seconds on May 25, 2020. As the Black Lives Matter (BLM) demonstrations unfolded in the United States and worldwide during the summer of 2020, Grace, a Black Japanese woman in her mid-twenties who had relocated to Tokyo from a rural prefecture in northeastern Japan, began to share videos and images of the demonstrations on her Instagram. Her phone calls to me became more frequent as she wished to express her pain and frustration. While this frustration was directed toward the violence enacted against Black people globally, it was also directed toward acquaintances who responded to her posts with the claim that racism does not exist in Japan. Grace had also noticed that there was a perception among Japanese users of social networking services (SNS), the localized term for social media, that BLM was just another "trend." "Racism is not a trend!" Grace angrily exclaimed to me over the phone.

In previous conversations about my fieldwork on SNS and smartphone culture in contemporary Japan, Grace and I had bonded over our identities as "mixed" Black women (I am Black Dominican and white American; she is Black American and Japanese). We often exchanged stories of the frustrating questions that we receive about our identity. Although Grace often spoke of her experiences humorously, this was a coping mechanism for some of her more disturbing experiences: "I can't take things seriously . . . if I did, I wouldn't survive." Grace spoke of these experiences with me during in-person hangouts or over the phone—these narratives did not make their way into her Instagram. That is, until the summer of 2020. In one Instagram post, Grace featured ten screenshots of paragraphs that she had typed on the Notes application of her smartphone. These paragraphs constituted reflections on discrimination in Japan, including several stories of anti-Black racism that she had encountered. Grace recounted that one teacher in her junior high school, believing that her curly hair was a perm and thus against the school's hair code, forcibly dunked her head beneath a running faucet to "wash it out." Grace's hair stayed curly—it was *her natural hair*, after all. The teacher left without a word, leaving Grace dripping wet in front of the sink.

Grace's storytelling was her own contribution to anti-racist activism in Japan and anti-racist movements on a global, networked scale. In the digital age, SNS have increasingly played a role in highlighting social and political issues. This is due to the capabilities of SNS, as they facilitate the dissemination of information on a wide scale and at a near-instantaneous rate. The use of SNS in movements raises multiple questions. When and how do SNS become tools for movements? In what ways can SNS serve as sites of critical resistance through the sharing of personal stories of injustice? How can these stories educate audiences and confront long-standing misconceptions? I approach these questions by focusing on SNS usage in the context of Japan and the BLM demonstrations of 2020, suggesting that we—as scholars and observers—may consider the acts of storytelling by Black Japanese SNS users as a form of intervention and resistance.[1] In this context, this storytelling aims to contest racialized stereotypes, address misunderstandings of BLM in Japan, and raise awareness of the racism experienced by Black people in Japan. Ultimately, storytelling constitutes an intervention against the perception that racism does not exist in Japan.

Scholars have discussed the caveats of centering interpersonal aspects of racism at the expense of its structural or institutional components—and vice versa.[2] In this chapter, I strive to reach a balance by discussing racism in the context of the perpetuation of racialized stereotypes, violent and discriminatory acts and words directed toward perceived racial and ethnic "others," and the act of othering—all of which must be contextualized in a history of racialized stereotypes in Japan and narrative discourses of Japan as "homogeneous."[3] I also include Sterling's discussion of structural racism as "racialized people's structurally facilitated inability to complexly represent themselves as full human beings."[4] By using storytelling to speak against racialized stereotypes, media misrepresentations of BLM, and the perception of Japan as devoid of racism, I suggest that Black Japanese users of SNS are seeking to *reclaim* agency in the representation of their identity and lived experience—and thus combat racism.

## Context Matters: Digital Activism in Post-3.11 Japan

When and how do SNS become tools for movements? The use of SNS as tools for activism can be attributed to the affordances of these platforms, or "how, for whom, and under what circumstances" these platforms "enable and constrain."[5] danah boyd characterizes persistence, visibility, spreadability, and searchability as the major affordances of SNS.[6] Hashtags (#) and livestreaming have played significant roles in digital activism. Hashtags denote a particular topic or message that can easily be attached to posts, shared, and searched. They can be characterized as an "indexing system."[7] Hashtags and their corresponding algorithms also "suggest" potential shared connections, though they do not necessarily force the user to engage.[8] Yet when users do engage, social and political movements may result. It is thus unsurprising that the term "hashtag activism" has been adopted into vernacular usage.[9] Livestreaming—often paired with hashtags—embodies unscheduled reporting at the hands of the user, and its nature as an "unfiltered" form of documentation produces a visceral air.[10] Such documentation may highlight an act of injustice occurring instantaneously near the user or an event in which the user is participating.

Since digital technologies are localized differently, despite their seemingly "universal" nature, examinations of digital activism must consider historical and societal context.[11] In examining digital activism and the digital circulation of personal narratives in Japan, we must begin with the Triple Disaster of March 11, 2011, also known as 3.11. The disaster involved the catastrophic trifecta of a magnitude 9.0 earthquake, a tsunami, and the meltdown of the Fukushima Daiichi Nuclear Plant. 3.11 was also fully covered on SNS; shortly after the disaster, cell phone transmitters became inundated with calls, leading to massive call failures. SNS thus served as key tools in confirming the safety of loved ones, exchanging accounts of the disaster, and crowdsourcing information in the wake of media distrust. SNS were also used to critique the government's response to the disaster and mobilize antinuclear demonstrations.[12] Slater, Nishimura, and Kindstrand suggest that this political engagement can be attributed to the ability of SNS to recruit individuals around "explicitly oppositional and political causes" and establish "connections among already organized groups in common causes."[13] This also held true for the BLM demonstrations of 2020, which constitute a significant moment within the genealogy of digital activism in post-3.11 Japan.

The message of the BLM movement—namely, the necessity to protect Black lives against police brutality, violence, and racism—was pertinent long before the creation of the hashtag #BlackLivesMatter. This hashtag came into existence after the 2012 murder of Trayvon Martin, an unarmed Black teenager, by George Zimmerman. In response to Zimmerman's later acquittal, Alicia Garza, Patrisse Cullors, and Opal Tometi created #BlackLivesMatter.[14] #BlackLivesMatter has since become a rallying hashtag in activism against anti-Black racism and violence. The continuity of this digital movement was highlighted in the resurgence of BLM demonstrations following the 2020 murder of George Floyd. A video recorded by witness Darnella Frazier was circulated on SNS, showing Chauvin kneeling on Floyd's neck—Floyd's cries and pleas could be heard vividly, yet Chauvin continued to kneel. Floyd's murder and the murder of countless other Black Americans triggered nationwide and global demonstrations. News of the murder and demonstrations eventually reached Japan.

As I watched broadcasts of the demonstrations on Japanese media, I noticed that the images and the narrations by newscasters focused on the destruction of property rather than systemic racism and the murder of Black people. I would later learn that this was not unlike the coverage taking place *within* the United States. Nevertheless, such coverage impacted impressions of the demonstrations in Japan. On June 7, 2020, the *Nippon Hōsō Kyokai* (NHK), a leading broadcaster, aired a segment on the BLM demonstrations as part of *Kore de Wakatta! Sekai no Ima* (*Now I Understand! The World Today*), an international affairs program directed toward a younger audience. I was exposed to the segment via the circulation of its controversial animated clip on Twitter. In the clip, a muscular Black man with cornrows strangles a coin purse as he angrily speaks of economic inequity disadvantaging Black Americans, especially against the backdrop of COVID-19.[15] The clip, which heavily relied on caricatures and stereotypes of Blackness, was a shock to my system. The *Sekai no Ima* broadcast and the ensuing criticism serve as one case study of localized representations of the BLM demonstrations. There were moments in which BLM was highlighted on SNS, such as the marches that took place in Tokyo and Osaka on June 14 and June 7, respectively.[16] While these marches brought attention to anti-Black racism, the marches also faced backlash, including assertions that BLM was "an American issue"—that racism does not exist in Japan.[17] Here, it is necessary to explore several moments and themes in Japan's encounters with Blackness.

## Japan's Encounters with Blackness

Scholars have noted the arrival of enslaved Black people with Portuguese traders in the mid-1500s as perhaps Japan's first encounter with Blackness.[18] While the enslaved were initially viewed with marvel, Leupp explains that by the late eighteenth century, dark skin carried negative connotations. Exposure to

Western depictions of Black people as subhuman—evident in the minstrel show enacted for Japanese officials by white sailors in blackface aboard Commodore Matthew Perry's ship in 1854—especially impacted Japanese views on race.[19] Later encounters with Blackness encompassed various exchanges and representations. There is the engagement of Black American intellectual-activists such as W. E. B. Du Bois with Japan; the consumption of Black culture, ranging from hip-hop to Rastafarianism; and the fetishization of the Black body and racist portrayals of Blackness, evident in literature such as *Chibikuro Sambo (Little Black Sambo)*.[20]

With regards to mixed-race identity in Japan relevant to this study on the anti-racist digital activism of Black Japanese users of SNS, scholars take the interracial relationships between European traders and Japanese women as a starting point.[21] Historical discourse on Black Japanese identity focuses on the context of World War II and the U.S. occupation of Japan. In this discourse, Black Japanese children born from Black American GIs and Japanese women are often painted in a tragic light as "mixed-blood" orphans.[22] Contemporary discussions of Black Japanese identity have taken on more nuanced forms. Carter, for example, has discussed how mixed Black Okinawans are "interpellated into militarized spaces in ways Black Japanese mainland people are not."[23] A common theme in examinations of mixed-race identity in Japan is marginalization through othering. This othering takes place in the context of ideologies such as *nihonjinron*: the theory of "Japaneseness" that centers on the "cultural, racial, and ethnic homogeneity of Japan."[24] Shaitan and McEntee-Atalianis explain that such a discourse impacts identity construction—mixed-race Japanese individuals who live in Japan are sometimes treated as "foreigners" and must navigate "self" and "other" ascriptions.[25]

Recent amplified coverage of Black Japanese public figures has brought issues of identity and othering to the public eye. Ariana Miyamoto, who is Black American and Japanese, received the title of Miss Universe Japan 2015. Miyamoto faced backlash for her victory, including assertions that Miss Universe Japan should "have a real Japanese face."[26] Nevertheless, Miyamoto expressed a resolve to represent mixed-race and Black Japanese identity and "challenge the definition of being Japanese."[27] Black Japanese athletes have also captured attention—notably, tennis champion Naomi Osaka, who is of Haitian and Japanese heritage. Razack and Joseph have discussed how Osaka's status as representing Japan sometimes results in the erasure of her Haitian heritage; at the same time, her Japanese heritage is frequently questioned, and she is the target of racist comments regarding her Blackness.[28]

Concurrent with these experiences is the attempted erasure of Osaka's activism. She has utilized Twitter as a platform to share her own thoughts regarding anti-Black racism and to amplify BLM in the wake of the 2020 global demonstrations. In particular, her messages have centered on accountability, as she critiques inaction and silence. "Just because it isn't happening to you doesn't mean it isn't happening at all," Osaka posted on May 29, 2020.[29] Osaka's digital activism was met with criticism from Twitter users—within and beyond Japan— who asserted that sports should not be entangled with "politics." However, these assertions did not deter Osaka. During the US Open in September 2020, which took place in the midst of the COVID pandemic, the tennis star wore seven black masks bearing the names of Black Americans killed by the police and/or white racists: Breonna Taylor, Elijah McClain, Ahmaud Arbery, Trayvon Martin, George Floyd, Philando Castile, and Tamir Rice.[30]

We see that Black Japanese public figures have used their visibility in the media to challenge discourse on so-called "Japaneseness" and spread awareness about anti-Black racism. But what about those who do not bear celebrity status?

## Beyond Trending: Storytelling as Anti-racist Pedagogy

Can SNS serve as a site of critical resistance through the sharing of personal stories of injustice? If so, in what ways? Black Japanese storytelling is a testimony of dissent against historical racial narratives that are not only incorrect but also erase particular lived experiences. For example, the narrative of Japan as "homogeneous," and thus devoid of racism, erases their experiences of anti-Black racism occurring throughout their lives. These acts of storytelling are also taking place in a post-3.11 moment characterized by media distrust, growing reliance on crowdsourced information, and the digital circulation of narratives. Against the backdrop of the COVID-19 pandemic, the digital has become *the* medium for activism. We may consider how the individual, including their stories, becomes the message—a spin on Marshall McLuhan's assertion of the medium as message.[31] Here, we turn to storytelling among Black Japanese users of SNS who are keenly aware that anti-Black racism is an issue relevant to Japan.

### Grace

Grace was born to a Black American mother and Japanese father in a rural prefecture in northeastern Japan. For Grace, Instagram proved to be a helpful means of meeting fellow *hāfu*, or mixed-race individuals.[32] Grace often adds identity markers as hashtags in her posts, such as #blasian. She recalled multiple times when she met other *hāfu* by happenstance in Tokyo and they recognized her from her public posts. The BLM demonstrations in the summer of 2020 motivated Grace to use her Instagram as a platform to spread awareness about anti-Black racism and the BLM movement itself. Within her Instagram Stories, which often took the form of video narrations recorded in Japanese during her lunch break, Grace emphasized shared humanity and the importance of "spreading love, not hate." In her first series of videos, she brings in her positionality:

I'm half Asian, half Black. I'm a Japanese-American *hāfu*. So I have a lot of thoughts about this. And when you ask why, it's because the issue in America is that Black people are getting targeted and killed. I want to think "I don't live in America, I live in Japan so I'm safe!" But I can't. It hurts so much to see Black people getting beat, killed . . . looked at with harsh looks. It absolutely hurts.

"What's happening now is not 'somebody else's problem,'" Grace continues. She urges her viewers to imagine what they would do if they experienced such violence, or if their loved ones were killed. She concludes with a call for her viewers to carefully consider their words and actions and to speak and act with reciprocity in mind.

While Grace received positive responses after her first series of videos, she also received responses from followers that demonstrated a lack of understanding and empathy. In one of her near-daily narrations on Instagram, Grace spoke of the confusion she felt upon receiving a reply from a user that stated, "I don't think that there is discrimination in Japan." Grace postulated that the user reached this conclusion because they have not experienced discrimination, have not discriminated against others, and have not witnessed discrimination. In another video, Grace spoke of her frustration upon hearing a colleague state, "Whenever I open SNS, it's discrimination this, discrimination that. . . . I want this trend to be over soon." Grace recalled her internal thought process: "This is not a trend!" She wondered aloud how an individual could possibly see videos of police brutality and not feel *anything* in response.

Through her Instagram Stories, Grace resolved to amplify the movement through continuous posting while also encouraging her followers to do the same. In one video, Grace commented that her followers' acts of sharing her videos had resulted in strangers contacting her with words of gratitude for her insight and vulnerability. Grace then encouraged her followers to act: "If you have your own thoughts, I want you to put them into words and put them out there . . . if you don't say anything or do anything, I think that's the same as turning a blind eye to the issue." This statement highlights accountability in the age of SNS: a call to engagement following exposure to a message or issue.

## Joel

Joel is a college student, born and raised in Tokyo. He made an interesting reference to his Japanese-Guyanese identity when first introducing himself to me during a video interview: "I'm from Japan, even though I don't look like I'm from Japan." Joel had experienced bullying as a child, along with incessant questions regarding his background. He explained that in kindergarten, he was called "gorilla" or

"Obama." While he joked that being called Obama made him feel presidential, he also explained the complexity of his childhood experiences:

> But as a kid I didn't really feel good, of course. In Japan, if you're *hāfu*, you don't have to be Black or white, the fact that you're *hāfu* is just being different from Japanese, so you're gonna get bullied. If you look different, you're gonna get bullied. As I grew up I felt kind of discriminated against just because I'm Black. But I got used to it.

For Joel, the positive feature of SNS was the prevalence of information. He explained that SNS such as Instagram and TikTok had been influential in spreading information about BLM among Japanese youths. Joel indicated that he wished to amplify BLM on SNS in a way that reiterated that this was not just a fleeting "moment":

> On SNS, one of my friends made this website for BLM and asked us to spread it. But I haven't done it yet, just because I don't want this to be just a "moment" thing. You know? So, I'm planning to post that when people start to forget it. So maybe a week later or two weeks later.

This assertion connected to a later point that Joel made about societal dynamics: the tendency to "forget about things and move onto the next fiery topic." Joel's decision to amplify his acquaintance's BLM website *after* it was trending hints at an intervention against performative, ephemeral engagement in digital activism.

Joel remarked that he was shocked that racism was so blatantly present in the United States, in contrast to racism in Japan, which he viewed as more discreet yet insidious. The stories told by Black Japanese individuals highlight othering encounters, both blatant and discreet, occurring throughout their lives in Japan. Such encounters can be so pervasive that they are accepted as an unfortunate yet unavoidable component of lived experience—or as Joel described them, something that one gets "used to." These encounters, combined with the myth that Japan is "homogeneous," and thus devoid of racism, are reminiscent of what Nixon characterizes as "slow violence." Nixon explains that while violence is frequently perceived as "immediate" and "explosive," slow violence "occurs gradually and out of sight."[33] The narratives of Joel and Grace constitute a form of resistance against racism in Japan, slow and otherwise. The act of ignoring the issue or treating the issue as a "trend" is a form of violence that, in the eyes of Joel and Grace, cannot continue.

## @cocoalizzy

Instagram user @cocoalizzy, called Lizzy by her followers, has played a significant role in disseminating information on BLM in Japanese and spreading awareness of racism in Japan. On June 2, 2020, Lizzy posted a video on IGTV, Instagram's video platform, that has now been viewed over two million times.[34] In the video, Lizzy cries as she explains that Black people in the United States are killed just because of their skin color. She also discusses her experiences as a Black Japanese woman:

> I'm Japanese in terms of heart (*kokoro*) and citizenship, but since my skin color is Black I've been a target of discrimination. There are many people who think that I'm a villain just because of that, and there are people who have been killed because of that . . . people who are the same age as me, people who are younger than me . . . people have been killed while just going out shopping, or while just jogging.

Lizzy describes the discrimination she experienced in Japan, recalling how customers at one of her part-time jobs expressed that they did not wish to buy products from a Black person. Ultimately, Lizzy wishes for her Japanese viewers to realize that the issue is a *global* marginalization of Black individuals. "It does not matter if you are Black, white, or Japanese, what do *you* think of this situation?" she asks, emphasizing that anti-Black racism is not the concern of only one demographic. Lizzy urges her audience to think more deeply about the meaning of the demonstrations. For example, rather than hyperfixating on the destruction of property when viewing media coverage, she urges viewers to consider *why* this is taking place. Lizzy also prompts viewers to imagine if *their* friends were discriminated against—or worse, murdered. What is interesting is Lizzy's direct appeal toward Japanese individuals who consume Black culture. We may consider this to be a form of accountability toward those who enjoy Black culture but do not acknowledge the burdens of being Black.[35]

Lizzy's video is significant not only because of its raw emotion but also because of its acknowledgment of the power of SNS in sharing information. Lizzy encourages her audience to learn from her video and circulate it. She also suggests individual actions that her viewers can take, including searching for keywords such as "*kokujin sabetsu* (anti-Black racism)" and "America, George Floyd"; reading related content; and uploading this content onto their Instagram. By highlighting Black Japanese storytelling on Instagram, I wish to emphasize that Instagram should also receive attention as a site of activism. Twitter is often the object of studies on digital activism due to its centrality in movements such as the Arab Spring uprisings of 2011.[36] Instagram's popularity among youths in Japan, combined with the appeal of its visuality, mark the platform as an effective means of sharing stories and spreading awareness of injustice. Activists can record videos or create informative visuals that are accessible for a broader audience. The ability to directly share Instagram Stories to acquaintances or to one's own feed facilitates the circulation of activist messages. Grace had shared Lizzy's video onto her own Instagram Stories with the caption, "She's *hāfu* just like me, so proud of her!" Although Grace does not personally know her, Lizzy's visibility as a Black Japanese woman, combined with her vulnerable storytelling, created an empathetic bond. These acts also coalesced with storytelling by Black Japanese figures such as Naomi Osaka—fostering opportunities for community-building and the development of a Black Japanese digital network.

## Japan as Site of Inquiry: Counterpublics and Black Digital Networks

How can personal stories of injustice educate audiences and confront long-standing misconceptions in society? The past decade has seen an increase in works centering the intersections of Blackness and digital media. This literature has approached topics such as the racial biases of algorithms, #BlackLivesMatter, and "Black Twitter."[37] The current literature, however, focuses on Blackness from the perspective of the United States, along with hardware and software developed within this context. There is a need to expand this focus. As Sobande highlights, Black (digital) experiences cannot be reduced to a monolith—although the digital seems "borderless," one must not neglect the impact of "social constructions of the nation-state, citizenship, ethnicity, racial identity and borders."[38]

The stories shared by Black Japanese users of SNS demonstrate Japan's potential as a site of inquiry in transnational Black digital networks and counterpublics, or "the alternative networks of debate created by marginalized members of the public."[39] Users such as Lizzy and Grace speak against those who consume Black culture in Japan yet remain silent on the issue of anti-Blackness. It is also worth noting the invocation of empathy in their videos: a call for Japanese viewers to imagine *themselves* or their loved ones in the position of Black people who are endangered every day. Furthermore, it is worth noting users' manipulation of temporality, as evidenced by Joel's resolution to circulate his acquaintance's website at a later date.

The complicated reception of BLM in Japan and the action taken by Black Japanese SNS users offer multiple points for analysis. Of particular interest are the claims against which Black Japanese users are taking action: the perception of BLM as a "trend" and the perception that anti-Black racism is not relevant to Japan. It is possible that the perception of BLM as a "trend" results from the conflation of the hashtag with "trendy" participatory culture. Surface-level engagement with digital activism may also set the ground for confusion. Grace's discussion of her colleague who viewed BLM as a "trend" took place within the context of #BlackoutTuesday, a media event that took place on June 2, 2020, in which SNS users posted a black box to draw attention to BLM.[40] This event harmed activism; when searching for essential information by typing "#BLM" in search functions, activists instead encountered rows of black boxes.[41]

It is also possible that concentrated coverage of demonstrations in the United States creates a sense of distance from the movement in Japan, paired with the idea that racism is a problem in the US and not in Japan, as evident within the *Sekai no Ima* clip. However, Lizzy's call for users to search "*kokujin sabetsu*" online suggests that perhaps it is no longer excusable to *not* know of the movement. Similarly, Jackson, Bailey, and Foucault Welles assert that "not knowing where to look for alternative narratives is no longer an excuse for those in the mainstream."[42] Thus, while (mis)representations may have sowed the seeds of confusion, users can invest time in understanding anti-Blackness locally and globally. At the same time, there are nuances here regarding accessibility to information and media literacy.

Another dynamic that potentially impacts the reception of BLM among Japanese users of SNS is the imagination of Japan as "homogeneous." However, Japan is *not* homogeneous, as we see from the presence of, for example, *zainichi* (ethnic Korean) communities, which include Korean and Japanese *hāfu*. Black Japanese users are resisting dominant ideologies and racialized stereotypes that still have a hold in contemporary Japan. The establishment of a Black digital network in Japan via SNS can potentially weaken or eradicate this hold. We cannot know or prove if their storytelling truly changed each viewer's racial consciousness, and this is the challenge of digital activism. However, what we *do* know is that these narratives are out there, being watched and circulated—in Lizzy's case, over two million times.

Black Japanese individuals are striving to reclaim their agency in their own representation, and this is significant. Indeed, in their examination of Naomi Osaka's use of social media in resisting "racial binary or fixed Japanese identity classifications," Razack and Joseph suggest that social media can provide athletes "with chances to re-write the racialized story of their success."[43] I suggest that Black digital networks in Japan are worth continued examination well beyond the temporal moment of 2020 because of their potential in fostering activism and community-building. These digital networks become especially crucial when "in-person" opportunities for connection become difficult or impossible—for example, during a global pandemic.[44]

## Conclusion: "There Is No Racism in Japan"

Toward the end of my fieldwork, an acquaintance invites me to eat at a restaurant in my neighborhood. On the day of the dinner, I ultimately decide to leave my hair in an afro rather than take an extra twenty minutes to comb it down. Upon opening the door to the restaurant, my acquaintance looks at me with widened eyes: "*Kin-chan!* Your hair!"[45] As I eat, I notice two children staring and smiling at me. I wave hello, and both children then yell: "So scary (*kowai*)!" Taken aback, I look around and notice that the surrounding individuals, including my acquaintance, are laughing. Before the children leave, they look back at me once more. I wave again, and they once again yell "*kowai!*" before leaving with their mother. I tell my acquaintance that the incident left me upset. "They probably have never seen a foreigner before," he shrugs. I have my doubts, given our location in Tokyo.

I have always been aware that my various intersecting identities—Dominican American, Black, "mixed," woman—impact my experiences in the field. This awareness sometimes leads to a numb acceptance of interactions that are responses to my identities. Yet, the incident at the restaurant leaves me with a sinking feeling in my stomach. Distressed, I message Grace. I have reservations about relying on interlocutors for emotional support, as this can result in the performance of emotional labor. However, Grace and I have developed a close connection, and I do not know to whom else I should turn. Grace responds quickly and thoughtfully in a mixture of English and Japanese:

> Honestly, I know that feeling, I have experienced that so many times or hella worse.
> Sometimes, kids can be too honest and innocent . . .
> Good parents will correct them on the spot but if not, oh well, it's the parents' fault.
> They have to educate and teach their kids what's 👍👍/👎👎.
> 80% of the time, if things like that happen I will just let it go.
> Although, case by case I will talk to them and teach them in a fun way maybe haha.
> I know in Japan, people will stare at us a lot. People say things that they shouldn't.
> If I were you, I would think of it like this:
> "This kid is the luckiest kid to see MY afro for the first time! I became his hair role model so I hope this kid will never forget me" haha
> But at the same time, I'm sorry that happened and it must hurt your feelings.
> But don't forget, no matter what people say, you're beautiful!
> And it's normal to look different, so be unique. We aren't the same. We are all different people. Looking similar isn't that fun.
> Always be yourself, there is only one *Kin-chan* in existence.
> No one can change you from being you!

In closing with this vignette, I include my own storytelling to open a conversation on positionality and fieldwork. I am now aware of the nuances of that moment in the restaurant and I feel less of a visceral response. However, I wish that my training as an ethnographer—a method well-represented in Asian Studies— included a discussion of how to process these moments. These moments, while difficult, can also be opportunities for dialogue. Discussions of racism, including the racism experienced by Black scholars, are still approached with trepidation by scholars in Asian Studies. However, these conversations need to happen. Scholars must reflect on their positionality, their own potential complicity in systemic inequity, and their commitment to activism. Perhaps this should be incorporated into both Asian Studies and ethnographic training—how to confront racism, how to support interlocutors and mentees in times of distress, and how to intervene in the face of injustice.

## Notes

[1] I wish to emphasize that the opinions and narratives within this chapter are not representative of all Black Japanese individuals. The interviews within this chapter were conducted as part of an ongoing project on digital sociality and smartphone culture in contemporary Japan. The project features thirty-five interviewees, many of whom were young women university students or postgrads in their early twenties. The study sample also features Japanese students who had returned to Japan after living abroad (*kikokushijo*) and mixed-race individuals. Grace and Joel had agreed to participate in the project to discuss their SNS and smartphone usage; since our interviews and conversations coincided with the BLM demonstrations, their responses centered on digital activism. Both consented to discuss their experiences and participate in another ongoing project that I am conducting on mixed-race identity in Japan. The comments made by Grace and Joel coalesced with the narratives of Black Japanese celebrities (such as Ariana Miyamoto), users with public SNS profiles, and influencers (such as @cocoalizzy). The similarities in these narratives demonstrate a need for further scholarship on the experiences of Black Japanese people in Japan—a population that is growing, although we do not know the exact number since the Japanese government does not maintain statistics related to race.

[2] Rosa and Díaz 2019; Sterling 2010.

[3] Befu 2001; Oguma 2002[1995]; Russell 2020; Shin 2010.

[4] Sterling 2010, 27.

[5] Davis 2020, 11.

[6] boyd 2014, 10–11.

[7] Bonilla and Rosa 2015, 5.

[8] Cotter 2019.

[9] Jackson, Bailey, Foucault Welles 2020, xxxii.

[10] Tufekci 2017, xxv.

[11] Ito 2005; Miller 2012; Miller et. al 2021.

[12] Petrovic 2019; Petrovic 2020; Slater, Nishimura, and Kindstrand 2012; Steinberg 2020.

[13] Slater, Nishimura, and Kindstrand 2012, 21-22.

[14] Florini 2019, 22.

[15] Russell 2020; Takeda 2020.

[16] While a discussion of the marches is beyond the scope of this chapter, the literature would benefit from an examination of the use of SNS by organizers and participants.

[17] Rich and Hida 2020.

[18] Leupp 1995; Russell 2020.

[19] Leupp 1995, 7.

[20] Onishi 2013; Cornyetz 1994; Condry 2006; Sterling 2010; Bridges 2016; Russell 1991; Russell 1998.

[21] Earns 2017; Leupp 2017.

[22] Hamilton 2017; Koshiro 1999; Roebuck 2016; Sawada 2001.

[23] Carter 2014, 649.

[24] Befu 2001, 68–69.

[25] Shaitan and McEntee-Atalianis 2017.

[26] Fackler 2015.

[27] Ibid.

[28] Razack and Joseph 2021.

[29] The original tweet may be found here: https://twitter.com/naomiosaka/status/1266514627934015489.

[30] Calow 2021; Mansoor 2020.

[31] McLuhan 1994[1964], 7.

[32] The term "*hāfu*" has been contested, due to its centering of a supposed "half" nature of identity. Some, including Grace, have accepted the term and use it only because it is so widely used in Japan. Throughout this chapter, I use *hāfu* because of its ubiquity and use by Black Japanese interlocutors, although I acknowledge the issues surrounding the term.

[33] Nixon 2011, 2.

[34] @cocoalizzy's video caught the attention of news outlets such as NHK World (2020) and scholars such as Alexis Dudden (2021).

[35] Tate 2003.

[36] Tufekci 2017.

[37] Benjamin 2019; Brock 2020; Florini 2019; Hamilton 2020; McIlwain 2019; Noble 2018; Jackson, Bailey, and Foucault Welles 2020.

[38] Sobande 2020, 6.

[39] Florini 2019; Jackson, Bailey, Foucault Welles 2020, xxxiii.

[40] #BlackoutTuesday diverged from its original initiative, #TheShowMustBePaused, which was started by Jamila Thomas and Brianna Agyemang to protest anti-Black

racism in the music industry and "disrupt the work week" to motivate reflection. #TheShowMustBePaused's mission statement can be found here: https://www. theshowmustbepaused.com/about.

[41] Coscarelli 2020; Willingham 2020.

[42] Jackson, Bailey, and Foucault Welles 2020, 198.

[43] Razack and Joseph 2021, 302.

[44] Hassel 2021.

[45] My nickname, derived from my name (*Kinbari*). The "*-chan*" within my nickname is an endearing honorific that is typically used when addressing close friends, children, and/or girls.

## Bibliography

Befu, Harumi. *Hegemony of Homogeneity: An Anthropological Analysis of "Nihonjinron."* Melbourne: Trans Pacific Press, 2001.

Benjamin, Ruha. *Race after Technology: Abolitionist Tools for the New Jim Code.* Cambridge: Polity, 2019.

Bonilla, Yarimar, and Jonathan Rosa. "#Ferguson: Digital Protest, Hashtag Ethnography, and the Racial Politics of Social Media in the United States." *American Ethnologist* 42, no. 1 (2015): 4–17.

boyd, danah. *It's Complicated: The Social Lives of Networked Teens.* New Haven: Yale University Press, 2014.

Bridges, William H. "The Sun Never Sets on *Little Black Sambo*: Circuits of Affection and the Cultural Hermeneutics of *Chibikuro Sambo*—A Transpacific Approach." In *The Affect of Difference: Representations of Race in East Asian Empire*, edited by Christopher P. Hanscom and Dennis Washburn. Honolulu: University of Hawai'i Press, 2016, 304–327.

Brock, André L. *Distributed Blackness: African American Cybercultures.* New York: New York University Press, 2020.

Calow, Emma. "'Well, What Was the Message *You* Got?': The Discursive Power of Naomi Osaka and Her Peaceful Protest at the 2020 U.S. Open." *European Journal for Sport and Society* (2021): 1–21.

Carter, Mitzi Uehara. "Mixed Race Okinawans and Their Obscure In-Betweeness." *Journal of Intercultural Studies* 35, no. 6 (2014): 646–661.

@Cocoalizzy. "*Nihonjin no minna ni shitte hoshii kokujin sabetsu ni tsuite* #BLACKLIVESMATTER." Instagram TV, 2020. https://www.instagram. com/tv/CA7TyTeF8Jb/.

Condry, Ian. *Hip-Hop Japan: Rap and the Paths of Cultural Globalization*. Durham: Duke University Press, 2006.

Cornyetz, Nina. "Fetishized Blackness: Hip Hop and Racial Desire in Contemporary Japan." *Social Text*, no. 41 (1994): 113–139.

Coscarelli, Joe. "#BlackoutTuesday: A Music Industry Protest Becomes a Social Media Moment." *The New York Times*. June 2, 2020. https://www.nytimes.com/2020/06/02/arts/music/what-blackout-tuesday.html.

Cotter, Kelley. "Playing the Visibility Game: How Digital Influencers and Algorithms Negotiate Influence on Instagram." *New Media & Society* 21, no. 4 (2019): 895–913.

Davis, Jenny L. *How Artifacts Afford: The Power and Politics of Everyday Things*. Cambridge: MIT Press, 2020.

Dudden, Alexis. "Masks, Science, and Being Foreign: Japan during the Initial Phase of COVID-19." In *The Pandemic: Perspectives on Asia*, edited by Vinayak Chaturvedi. Ann Arbor: Asia Shorts, Association for Asian Studies, 2021, 49–62.

Earns, Lane. "Mixed Messages: Interracial Couples and Biracial Children From the Nagasaki Foreign Settlement Period to World War II." In *Hapa Japan: History (Volume 1)*, edited by Duncan Ryūken Williams. Los Angeles: Ito Center Editions, an imprint of Kaya Press, 2017, 85–102.

Fackler, Martin. "Biracial Beauty Queen Challenges Japan's Self-Image," *The New York Times*, May 29, 2015. http://www.nytimes.com/2015/05/30/world/asia/biracial-beauty-queen-strives-for-change-in-mono-ethnic-japan.html.

Florini, Sarah. *Beyond Hashtags: Racial Politics and Black Digital Networks*. New York: New York University Press, 2019.

Hamilton, Amber M. "A Genealogy of Critical Race and Digital Studies: Past, Present, and Future." *Sociology of Race and Ethnicity* 6, no. 3 (2020): 292–301.

Hamilton, Walter. "'Enemies in Miniature': The Mixed-Race Children from the Allied Occupation of Japan." In *Hapa Japan: History (Volume 1)*, edited by Duncan Ryūken Williams. Los Angeles: Ito Center Editions, an imprint of Kaya Press, 2017, 293–327.

Hassel, Kimberly. "Digital Sociality in COVID-19 Japan." *Anthropology News* website, December 7, 2021. https://www.anthropology-news.org/articles/digital-sociality-in-covid-19-japan/.

Ito, Mizuko. "Introduction." In *Personal, Portable, Pedestrian: Mobile Phones in Japanese Life*, edited by Mizuko Ito, Daisuke Okabe, and Misa Matsuda. Cambridge: MIT Press, 2005, 1–16 .

Jackson, Sarah J., Moya Bailey, and Brooke Foucault Welles. *#HashtagActivism: Networks of Race and Gender Justice*. Cambridge, Massachusetts: MIT Press, 2020.

Leupp, Gary. "'Placed on a Par with All Other Japanese': Hapa Japanese in Japan and the World, 1543–1859." In *Hapa Japan: History (Volume 1)*, edited by Duncan Ryūken Williams. Los Angeles: Ito Center Editions, an imprint of Kaya Press, 2017, 17–44.

———. "Images of Black People in Late Mediaeval and Early Modern Japan, 1543–1900." *Japan Forum* 7, no. 1 (1995): 1–13.

Koshiro, Yukiko. *Trans-Pacific Racisms and the U.S. Occupation of Japan*. New York: Columbia University Press, 1999.

Mansoor, Sanya. "Naomi Osaka Says She Wore 7 Masks About Black Lives During This Year's U.S. Open to 'Make People Start Talking.'" *Time*, September 13, 2020. https://time.com/5888583/naomi-osaka-masks-black-lives-matter-us-open.

McIlwain, Charlton D. *Black Software: The Internet and Racial Justice, From the Afronet to Black Lives Matter*. New York: Oxford University Press, 2019.

McLuhan, Marshall. *Understanding Media: The Extensions of Man*. First MIT Press edition. Cambridge: MIT Press, 1994[1964].

Miller, Daniel. "Social Networking Sites." In *Digital Anthropology*, edited by Heather A. Horst and Daniel Miller. London, New York: Berg, 2012, 146–161.

Miller, Daniel, Laila Abed Rabho, Patrick Awondo, Maya De Vries, Marília Duque, Pauline Garvey, Laura Haapio-Kirk, Charlotte Hawkins, Alfonso Otaegui, Shireen Walton, and Xinyuan Wang. *The Global Smartphone: Beyond a Youth Technology*. London: UCL Press, 2021.

NHK World. "Teen who Fled Racism in Japan, Returns with a Message that Resonates." Web, June 22, 2020. https://www3.nhk.or.jp/nhkworld/en/news/ataglance/988.

Nixon, Rob. *Slow Violence and the Environmentalism of the Poor*. Cambridge, Massachusetts: Harvard University Press, 2011.

Noble, Safiya Umoja. *Algorithms of Oppression: How Search Engines Reinforce Racism*. New York: NYU Press, 2018.

Oguma, Eiji. *A Genealogy of "Japanese" Self Images.* Translated by David Askew. Melbourne: Trans Pacific Press, 2002[1995].

Onishi, Yuichiro. *Transpacific Antiracism: Afro-Asian Solidarity In Twentieth-Century Black America, Japan, and Okinawa.* New York: NYU Press, 2013.

Petrovic, Sonja. "Tracing Individual Perceptions of Media Credibility in Post-3.11 Japan." *The Asia-Pacific Journal: Japan Focus* 18, no. 10 (2020): 1–26. https://apjjf.org/2020/10/Petrovic.html.

———. "A Sense of Communal Belonging in Digital Space: The Case of the 3.11 Disaster." *New Voices in Japanese Studies* 11 (July 2019): 74–98.

Razack, Sabrina, and Janelle Joseph. "Misogynoir in Women's Sport Media: Race, Nation, and Diaspora in the Representation of Naomi Osaka." *Media, Culture & Society* 43, no. 2 (2021): 291–308.

Rich, Motoko, and Hikari Hida. "In Japan, the Message of Anti-Racism Protests Fails to Hit Home." *The New York Times*, July 1, 2020. https://www.nytimes.com/2020/07/01/world/asia/japan-racism-black-lives-matter.html.

Roebuck, Kristin. "Orphans by Design: 'Mixed-blood' Children, Child Welfare, and Racial Nationalism in Postwar Japan." *Japanese Studies*, 36, no. 2 (2016): 191–212.

Rosa, Jonathan and Vanessa Díaz. "Raciontologies: Rethinking Anthropological Accounts of Institutional Racism and Enactments of White Supremacy in the United States." *American Anthropologist* 122, no. 1 (2020): 120–132.

Russell, John G. "'Mindo' and the Matter of Black Lives in Japan." *The Asia-Pacific Journal: Japan Focus* 18, no. 17 (2020): 1–11. https://apjjf.org/2020/17/Russell.html.

———. "Consuming passions: Spectacle, Self-Transformation, and the Commodification of Blackness in Japan." *positions: asia critique* 6, no. 1 (1998): 113–177.

———. *Nihonjin no kokujinkan: Mondai wa "Chibikuro Sanbo" dake de wa nai.* First edition. Tōkyō: Shinhyōron, 1991.

Sawada, Miki. *Kuroi hada to shiroi kokoro: Sandāsu Hōmu e no michi.* Tōkyō: Nihon Tosho Sentā, 2001[1963].

Shaitan, Alexandra and Lisa J. McEntee-Atalianis. "*Haafu* Identity in Japan: Half, Mixed or Double?" In *Mixed Race in Asia: Past, Present and Future*, edited by Zarine L. Rocha and Farida Fozdar. New York: Routledge, Taylor & Francis Group, 2017, 82–97.

Shin, Hwaji. "Colonial Legacy of Ethno-racial Inequality in Japan." *Theory and Society* 39 (2010): 327–342.

Slater, David H., Nishimura Keiko, and Love Kindstrand. "Social Media, Information, and Political Activism in Japan's 3.11 Crisis." *The Asia-Pacific Journal: Japan Focus* 10, no. 24 (2012): 1–33. https://apjjf.org/2012/10/24/David-H.-Slater/3762/article.html.

Sobande, Francesca. *The Digital Lives of Black Women In Britain.* Cham, Switzerland: Palgrave Macmillan, 2020.

Steinberg, Marc. "LINE as Super App: Platformization in East Asia." *Social Media + Society* 6, no. 2 (2020): 1–10.

Sterling, Marvin D. *Babylon East: Performing, Dancehall, Roots Reggae, and Rastafari in Japan.* Durham, NC: Duke University Press, 2010.

Takeda, Okiyoshi. "NHK and 'Black Lives Matter': Structural Racism in Japan." *The Asia-Pacific Journal: Japan Focus* 18, no. 18 (2020): 1–12. https://apjjf.org/2020/18/Takeda.html.

Tate, Greg. *Everything but the Burden: What White People Are Taking From Black Culture.* New York: Broadway Books, 2003.

Willingham, A.J. "Why Posting a Black Image with the 'Black Lives Matter' Hashtag Could Be Doing More Harm than Good." CNN. June 2, 2020. https://www.cnn.com/2020/06/02/us/blackout-tuesday-black livcs-maller-instagram-trnd/index.html.

# 9

# FROM BLACK BROTHER TO BLACK LIVES MATTER

## PERCEPTION OF BLACKNESS IN VIET NAM

### Phuong H. Nguyen and Trang Q. Nguyen

On a Friday morning in May 2020, a news report filled the screens of major news channels around the United States: *George Floyd, forty-six-year-old African American male, killed by police in Minneapolis, Minnesota*. The news reports continued over the weekend, playing a bystander's video in a loop that we would come to know as a critical piece of evidence in the murder trial of the police officers involved. For many, footage of the suspects was unsettling: an Asian officer was part of the police squad that confronted Mr. Floyd.

A year on, as we started writing this essay in the summer of 2021, we know now that this event marked a critical point in racial history, not just in the United States but also around the world. The murder of George Floyd, and the overwhelming, renewed attention to the Black Lives Matter (BLM) movement that followed, meant an opportunity to reflect on anti-Black racism within Asian and Asian diasporic communities. During protests against anti-Asian racism in America in 2020 and 2021, many shouted, "Asian Lives Matter. Black Lives Matter," signifying that they go hand in hand. Many of us within these communities had our first serious dialogues with parents and grandparents about race and our relationships with our Black friends. We passed out pages and pages of educational resources on the history of the Black Lives Matter movement and its cultural significance. All over the popular social media website Instagram, we saw countless infographics—a method of sharing information via text overlaying pictures—on how to be a better ally and address anti-Blackness within your own communities. Each tiny square being shared was a glimmer of hope for a more racially informed social circle. The events of May and June 2020 had, hopefully and ideally, forever changed our understanding of our nuanced historical relationship with our friends of African descent.

Back home in Viet Nam, we observed a division in the media space. On one side, Vietnamese youths voiced support for the BLM movement on their social platforms, explaining the intricacies of racial relations and existing racial tensions that brought about the protests. Some rallied to host fundraising events for the global movement. A suite of activist platforms and groups were created in the form of social media public accounts to share educational resources and translate race-related terms that were virtually nonexistent in the Vietnamese daily vocabulary. On the other side, news coverage of videos showing the violent encounters between the police and protesters in American cities was received with anger and disgust. Many Vietnamese netizens flocked to those social media accounts to question the authority and validity of the BLM movement, while dismissing the need for Vietnamese to care about such matters.

This essay unpacks some of the tensions seen during the period of heightened BLM activities and the strongly opinionated—yet fleeting—responses from the Vietnamese public to this movement. Against the backdrop of the cultural, political, and historical meanings through which Blackness is understood in Viet Nam, we dissect the responses to an awareness-raising campaign on social media and the representation of BLM in the media space, while including perspectives from Vietnamese activist groups and other social commentators. We argue that while racism is usually considered nonrelevant in Vietnamese society, subtle forms of discrimination against darker skinned groups still exist as a result of a combination of factors: a long history of practiced and normalized colorism shared with other Asian cultures, colonial legacies, and the lack of exposure to racial dialogues in a largely homogenous population. By highlighting the short yet heated debate about BLM in 2020 in the Vietnamese media space, the essay will show that there is potential for the young Vietnamese generation to start addressing our own racial biases and connecting global movements like BLM to issues closer to home.

## A Note on Methodology

This essay is primarily based on interviews with community activists and organizers involved in the Black Lives Matter movement in Viet Nam. During the course of writing this paper, we engaged with the three most eminent, youth-run organizations in Hanoi and Ho Chi Minh City: Viet Activism, Viets for Change, and Black Lives Matter Hanoi.[1] We employed semistructured interviews to understand their experiences when executing their information campaigns and to gauge the overall attitude of the Vietnamese population that they observed at the time. Before starting to work on this chapter, we had been following these groups for a period of time out of an informal interest in Vietnamese activism. We then decided to formally reach out to schedule online interviews with them as neither of us (nor some of the interviewees) were physically in Viet Nam. In the end, we interviewed three of them and also talked to a few others who were vocal during this period.[2] From these three organizations, we focused on dissecting the public comments posted to the Facebook page named "Black Lives Matter Hanoi."

We considered the ethical dimensions of using the names of these organizations. Even though they have public pages on social media, presenting their names could trigger hostile new media traffic to their sites, especially considering the public outrage examined in the latter half of this chapter. However, with the groups' consent, we decided to retain the organizations' names and to use pseudonyms for our interlocutors/interviewees, having explained the risk of disclosure of their identities. This ensures that we can honor these groups' important work as Vietnamese youth activists who are raising awareness on racial issues in Viet Nam. We humbly intend for this small contribution to motivate a longer conversation and a call for more extensive research into race in Viet Nam and in Asia more broadly.

## Whiteness and Blackness in Viet Nam

### From Colorism to Racism

Growing up in Viet Nam, we were taught that white equals beauty. Every skin care product advertised on television tells us that the best skin care is one that helps your skin to be "trắng hồng rạng rỡ," radiant blushy white, or "trắng chuẩn Hàn Quốc," white by Korean standards, so you would never worry about having dark skin again.[3] "White beauty"—as written on these skin-brightening cream jars—means your face now has a head-turning effect, unlike those of the women whose skin is just a few shades darker!

Colorism, defined by Alice Walker as the "prejudicial or preferential treatment of same-race people based solely on their color," is no new phenomenon among Asian, Asian diasporic, and other ethnic and racial groups.[4] Even as whitening products reportedly might include dangerous if not potentially lethal chemicals, they are widely available in every Vietnamese cosmetic market segment, promising to lighten Southeast Asian skin tones to align with the global standards of beauty.[5]

Figure 9.1: Whitening product advertisements are prevalent in the Vietnamese cosmetics market (Photos by author). Ponds, an American brand, has one of the widest ranges of whitening products, which are almost exclusively produced in and marketed for Asian markets. Similar situation is observed with European brands such as L'Oréal. Other influences come from Korean and/or Japanese brands such as Bioré. Most (if not all) of these products and advertisements for them usually use the word "white" or "whitening" in their branding.

This refers to, if not a White Western face shown widely in television commercials, then at least a bright, pigment-free, Korean-like complexion, which is deemed as desirable by many Vietnamese people, especially young women, under the influence of the *hallyu* (Korean Wave).[6] Han, a representative from Viet Activism, sees this as the Vietnamese's "white obsession," the idea that being attached to a white person will move you up in the Vietnamese social hierarchy.[7]

Understanding colorism in Viet Nam and in Asia more generally helps reveal the (hidden) racism in our society. Darker skin tones in Viet Nam are associated with a lower social status: if one works in the field all day under the sun, there is little chance one could have the fair complexion that can be flaunted by the class of intellectuals and royalists sheltered indoors, an attitude which journalist Raymond Zhou calls "an offshoot of class discrimination."[8] In their extensive oral history interviews with Asian communities in the US, Joanne L. Rondilla and Paul Spickard offered anecdotal evidence from Japanese, Cambodian, Filipino, Vietnamese, and Thai groups, confirming a common theme of light skin preference.[9] Researchers explain that the preference for lighter shades of skin does not automatically equate to wanting to be racially White but rather signals the desire to be part of the wealthy classes of these Asian societies.[10]

Colorism has existed across Asia, especially East Asia, long before Western domination.[11] Some early literary works and cultural artifacts can serve as a sign of this fair skin preference. Bai Juyi, a renowned poet during the Tang dynasty, penned a famous poem, *Chang hen ge*, in which he described a beautiful woman chosen as one of the king's wives as "warm water from the lake caressing the white skin."[12] The significance of skin color as a determinant of class is believed to have traveled from ancient China to the rest of East Asia—for example, in Japan as early as the Nara period in the late eighth century.[13] Until quite recently, mid-nineteenth-century Japanese men and women still put on white lead powder to create "ivory-skin that is 'like a boiled egg'—soft, white and smooth on the surface."[14] The Korean Cultural Heritage Administration also sees the obsession with "white" skin in Korea as dating back thousands of years, evidenced in murals depicting pale skin from the Goguryeo kingdom (AD 37–668) era, or in folklore presenting beautiful people—men and women alike—as having "white" skin.[15] Vietnamese folk literature also reserved a special place for the fair skin of the woman, with Hồ Xuân Hương, the Queen of Nôm poetry, writing in the eighteenth century: "Thân em vừa trắng lại vừa tròn," ("My body is white and plump") in *Bánh trôi nước*, one of the most famous poems written in the Vietnamese Nôm scripture.[16] The Vietnamese, descendants of dragons and fairies, with their red blood and yellow skin—as the legends of Vietnamese origins go—take pride in their roots yet also retain an attitude toward fair skin similar to other East Asian neighbors.

The century of French colonization brought new meanings to the black/white (or dark/fair) dichotomy in Viet Nam.[17] The fair skin of Westerners is now the standard of beauty and with it, other physical features associated with racial whiteness, including a high nose arch, large double-lidded eyes, and tall stature. Margaret Hunter sees the establishment and maintenance of white supremacy by colonial rulers as being "predicated on the notion that dark skin represents savagery, irrationality, ugliness, and inferiority" as opposed to whiteness, which is associated with "civility, rationality, beauty, and superiority."[18] In Viet Nam, both of these forces—social class discrimination and the colonial legacy—come together to influence the way Vietnamese see people who are different. As the French colonizers saw the "Annamese" as inferior, the Vietnamese now would see darker skin—whether associated with African-descended people, other Asian groups, or even Viet Nam's own ethnic minorities—as dirty, barbaric, and less desired.[19]

## Blackness in Vietnamese History

In Viet Nam, most Vietnamese will tell you: there is no racism; that we don't see race because we are all the same; that race is only relevant in multiracial societies like the United States. There is a general consensus in the Vietnamese academic community that ethnicity—not race—is the key to understanding the Vietnamese people.[20] The decennial nationwide census of 2019 confirmed this generally accepted idea of homogeneity, where 85.7% of the population identified as belonging to the Kinh ethnic majority, with a large share of the remaining fifty-three ethnicities concentrated in just a few provinces.[21] Even with many ethnicities, Vietnamese still look similar overall, and the everyday Vietnamese person is rarely exposed to people who look evidently racially different from them.

That is not to say that, historically, Vietnamese society is totally ignorant about race or about Black people, especially considering its colonial struggles. At the Fifth Congress of the Communist International (Comintern) in 1924, President Ho Chi Minh—then Nguyen Ai Quoc—delivered a report, *On Lynching and the Ku Klux Klan*, announcing solidarity with the struggle of African Americans—the very race he called "the most oppressed and the most exploited of the human family"—against white supremacy in the US.[22] His 1925 book, first published in Paris as *Le Procès de la colonisation française* (*French Colonialism on Trial*), draws strong similarities between the struggle against colonial rule of Black peoples in African nations and that of the "Annamese."[23] In this revealing text exposing the crimes of the French, Ho Chi Minh's call was loud and clear: to survive and to thrive, the Vietnamese need to sympathize and unite with other oppressed groups around the world (for example, other colonized peoples like those of African descent) against the system of white supremacy and colonialism. Both of these texts authored by the country's first president had a great influence on Vietnamese political thinking that continues to this day.

The First Indochina War between French troops and the Việt Minh-led revolutionary forces in the 1940s and 1950s brought the first wave of Black soldiers onto Vietnamese soil in modern history.[24] The Senegalese officers who were recruited from Africa to fight on behalf of the imperial power in Indochina were subject to violent attacks due to both the French's fear mongering rumors about the *tây* đen (for example, that these Black westerners "ate their enemies' dead bodies") and the Vietnamese's anti-French, anti-colonial rhetoric.[25] Meanwhile, Việt Minh military leaders engaged in psychological warfare tactics to "convinc[e] African soldiers that they were fighting on the wrong side . . . to join the anticolonial movement and forsake their colonial oppressors."[26] Part of this war's legacies still exists in everyday life in Africa today—for example, as told through generations of family (hi)stories of how *nem* (springroll), a traditional Vietnamese delicacy, found its way to becoming a favorite street food in Dakar thanks to the migration of these Senegalese officers' Vietnamese wives to West Africa.[27]

The Second Indochina War, known more commonly as the Vietnam War and, in Viet Nam, as the War against American Imperialists, once again brought

Figure 9.2. A photo of the encounter between the famous Vietnamese monk
Thich Nhat Hanh and Dr. Martin Luther King Jr. Dr. King was a prominent
figure in Vietnamese history associated with the anti-war movement in the 1960s
(Photo copyright: Plum Village Community of Engaged Buddhism via Thich
Nhat Hanh Foundation).

another wave of soldiers of African descent to Viet Nam. While the Vietnamese
battled with the idea of fighting yet another "invader"—as often mentioned in
Vietnamese official history books—Americans in their own accounts grapple with
the fact that "Vietnam was the first major conflict in which the armed services were
fully racially integrated, and the first conflict after the civil rights revolution of the
1950s and early '60s."[28] Once again, Black soldiers were in the position wherein
they felt like they were fighting the wrong war, the white man's war, against the
backdrop of the civil rights movement back home.[29] During the racial reckoning of
2020, material including Dr. Martin Luther King Jr.'s 1967 "Beyond Vietnam" anti-
war speech and Muhammad Ali's quote, "No Vietnamese ever called me n****r,"
were passed around by Vietnamese and Vietnamese American youths together
with our own translation of the *Letters for Black Lives*.[30] They serve as reminders
of the historical significance that Black American and Vietnamese communities
shared in the decades of violence and war. To the Vietnamese, Black soldiers were
a part of the enemy in the war era, yet they were simultaneously an ally in the fight
against imperialism.

The legacies of over a century of continuous wars against Western powers left Viet Nam with a generation of mixed-race children, including the children of Black US soldiers and Vietnamese women, who faced discrimination not just during wartime but also to this day. In presenting a "Black Testimony" on their displacements, Bernard Scott Lucious considered this group of Afro-Amerasians to have "experienced the most discrimination because their black skin was perceived as relatively darker than the skin color of other Vietnamese people (especially White Euro-Amerasians) . . . because their black skin made them physically conspicuous" and made them stand out from the rest of their generally homogenous Vietnamese communities.[31] From being the "children of the enemy" to being seen as "dirty" due to their dark skin, journalistic accounts have recorded the struggles of this generation of "children of the dust" stuck between two worlds and belonging to neither.[32] It is easy to attribute the discrimination either to "the color-line" or colorism. In the Vietnamese context, anti-Black racism is an amalgamation of a myriad of factors: the association of lighter skin with higher social class ideals rooted in ancient history, and the imposition of Western and white standards of beauty through decades of colonization and occupation, compounded by both local and white people's prejudiced narratives against Black people, who are seen as brutal and inhumane in war.

### Blackness in Viet Nam Today

Fast-forwarding to 2020, Viet Nam has moved beyond its primary association as a country synonymous with the wars of the twentieth century. Globalization and the opening of foreign businesses in Viet Nam allowed the migration of thousands of expatriates. From 2004 to 2021, the number of foreigners working in the country increased from 12,000 to over 100,000, concentrating mostly in Hanoi and especially Ho Chi Minh City.[33] According to the General Office of Population and Family Planning, two-thirds of these foreigners come from East Asia (China, Taiwan, Korea, and Japan, due to the dynamics of trade and investment) and therefore can largely pass as locals.[34] Nonetheless, the movement of new migrants from overseas has definitely contributed to the Vietnamese's understanding of the world outside of its borders. This is, however, still very much influenced by stereotypes delivered through the entertainment business and media that the country has access to. When asked about where they think the source of our people's understanding about Black people comes from, all of our interviewees would cite the influx of Western media that has accompanied this process of globalization. This is evident in the consumption of popular culture, most eminently Hollywood movies that are often produced by white artists, which usually depict people of African descent as either dangerous criminals or weak characters who are ameliorated by white saviors.[35]

Unlike our neighbor China, whose legacies of violent anti-Black policies throughout history remain evident to this day, Viet Nam's racism and racial issues are more subtle.[36] Minh, an informant who worked with a Western country's embassy in Hanoi, revealed to us the hierarchy in English-teaching communities in which most (non-Asian) foreigners are engaged in Viet Nam. Guided by a natural law of supply and demand, as most parents prefer for their children to be educated by a *Tây trắng* ("Western white"), English centers would—whether secretly or openly—advertise and pay white teachers a higher salary compared to those of other races, if they hire them at all, regardless of whether the employee's native language is actually English. This is corroborated by anecdotes told elsewhere. For example, Angee Floyd, an African American former English teacher who is now an entrepreneur and comedian living in Ho Chi Minh City, says that in this country, "white is king."[37]

For the past two decades, Vietnamese consumers enjoy and support Black entertainers and profit off of Black humor, likenesses, and culture. One prime example is the anonymous but popular Facebook page "Anh Da Đen" ("Black Brother"), which posts daily, translating memes and videos featuring Black people to its audience.[38] The page boasts a following of almost 2.9 million people as of December 2021—almost 3 percent of the Vietnamese population—and was "liked" more than 800,000 times, making it prime real estate for on-demand paid commercial advertising and promotions.[39] On a cultural zeitgeist level, a genre of music recently attracted mainstream Vietnamese attention: rap. Two reality show contests recently dedicated to finding the best rapper in Viet Nam—*Rap Viet* and *King of Rap*—are among the most successful entertainment shows in Vietnamese television history, attracting millions in viewership each week and with *Rap Viet* voted the "TV Show of the Year" in 2020.[40] The judges on the shows are popular rappers, with coaches who have been rapping since the early 2000s. The only female coach in *Rap Viet*, Suboi, has been dubbed "Queen of Hip-hop" in Viet Nam by the international media. The rise of rap and the popularity of these TV shows have sparked controversy surrounding cultural appropriation among Vietnamese netizens, but those have gone unaddressed, as commenters voiced that there are more important domestic issues to worry about in Viet Nam than cultural appropriation. Despite the link to Black culture, these popular entertainment programs did not mention anything about the history of their inspiration, as well as the BLM movement, in any of their posts or shows.

There are also Black people who attach their image to their art and use their Blackness to differentiate themselves and offer a new perspective in Viet Nam. One example is entertainer Nnadozie Uzor Nadis, who adopted the Vietnamese name "Nam." Nadis broadcasts his daily life in Ho Chi Minh City to his 71,900 subscribers on a YouTube channel called AfroVietTV. He is widely known by his fans as *Nam Đen* or "Black Nam." His channel's purpose is to bring together the beauty of African and Asian cultures, with his most popular videos being the series "Welcome to Vietnam," which attracted millions of views. Nadis is among a group of foreign entertainers from Africa who are experiencing a rise of fame in Viet Nam. The entertainment space that was occupied mostly by white people before is opening up, albeit slowly, to Black artists like him.

## Black Lives Matter in Viet Nam
### *Through the Media Looking Glass*

In the political and news sphere, the Vietnamese media coverage of the global protests in the wake of George Floyd's death and the BLM movement, like elsewhere in the world, was extensive. Of course, it did not take up the front pages as much as it did in the United States, but it was prominent enough on online newspapers' homepages to grab the Vietnamese audience's attention.

The online newspaper *Dân Trí*, one of Viet Nam's most respectable online news sources, covered the protests from May 28, 2020, and published a total of seventeen articles in June 2020. The newspaper focused on neutral, fact-based reporting, sometimes translating already published articles from international sources such as Reuters, the AP, the BBC, or Sputnik. All the articles covering the protests and the incidents with American police were tagged with "người da màu"—Vietnamese for "people of color"—as Vietnamese do not consider themselves to be "of color."[41] The articles during this period attracted two camps of thought, at least by the people who cared enough to type comments on online news articles: support for Black people and condemning the police for their use of force, and in contrast, condemning Black people for committing crimes and condemning the protests for being an opportunity for looting.

*Vietnamnet*, the official newspaper of Viet Nam's Ministry of Information and Communications, published thirty-three articles tagged "biểu tình ở Mỹ" ("protests in America") in June of 2020. The articles are mostly neutral original content, as the ministry has reporters on the ground in the US. The tag "phân biệt chủng tộc," or "racism," on the other hand, mostly focused on the racial violence Asian people faced during the height of the COVID-19 pandemic, with three articles detailing racism against Asians and only one article about Black Wall Street. *Vietnamnet* also allows comments on its articles, but the articles did not attract any from its readers.

The official website of the Communist Party in Viet Nam published an article at the height of the protests in America on June 15, 2020. The article was titled "'Black Lives Matter' and the dream of eradicating racism in America," in which the author discusses the history of racism in America and ponders if racism could really be eradicated despite America having had its first Black president.[42] The overarching sentiment from official Vietnamese media outlets seemed to be that of a neutral tone with fact-based reporting, letting readers draw conclusions for themselves and voice their opinions if they felt the urge to.

## A Tale of Two Cities

Political sources and news outlets aside, the court of public opinion took to social media to voice their thoughts on the BLM movement. On June 11, 2020, a Facebook page was created by a group of young Hanoians, called *Black Lives Matter Hanoi*, with the specific mission to voice support for the BLM movement and "raise awareness and educate Vietnamese youths on the issues of systemic racism and police brutality," as written in their page description. However, what stood out about this campaign was not the uplifting fact that Vietnamese youths are now talking about race but the tsunami of negative responses to a Black Lives Matter, awareness-raising effort. Besides the blatantly racist and derogatory commentary, some argued that anti-Black racism has nothing to do with Vietnamese and that it is meaningless to push a BLM agenda in Viet Nam. One commenter summed it up:

> The page is hypocritical. Injustice [against] people in the country [Viet Nam] [is] abundant. Police violence in the police station. Discrimination among classes, regions, and ethnicities is piling up. . . . But be busy-bodies. Indeed, the entire population supports hypocrites.

In Ho Chi Minh City, or Saigon as many of its dwellers and adorers still call it, on June 21, 2020, an event titled "Saigon is Listening: Black Lives Matter" was hosted by Viet Activism in collaboration with other groups, attracting a large following from the expat and Vietnamese communities. The event received surprisingly positive responses with a huge turnout, despite happening on a rainy Sunday summer evening.[43] It created a safe space for reflection and encouraged the groups involved in expanding their activist work and connecting them with one another to elevate their voices.[44]

Despite the two wildly different responses from the audience in these two cities (we do not consider these voices to be representative of entire cities), we noted the two opposite reactions to a BLM campaign in Viet Nam.[45] Due to the volume of responses to the Black Lives Matter Hanoi Facebook page, we choose to focus on this platform while also situating our understanding of the activism landscape in Viet Nam during this period with input from other groups and individuals. The next section integrates these data sources with the social content from Black Lives Matter Hanoi as our primary point of departure.

## A Social Echo Chamber

Black Lives Matter Hanoi was created in June 2020, at the height of the Black Lives Matter protests around the world. Their aim was to help create conversations and raise awareness among Vietnamese netizens about systematic racism and police brutality. Two of Black Lives Matter Hanoi's most popular posts were its first profile-picture change to a logo, and its first post indicating the organization's purpose and mission. The logo incorporates the Black power fist with an illustration of the Temple of Literature in solidarity. The Temple of Literature was Viet Nam's first ever university, and it is a temple dedicated to Confucius. The choice to include this Vietnamese symbol of a place with deep history, and arguably one of Hanoi's most recognizable landmarks, seems to signify the activists' intentions that they as Hanoians support BLM. Unfortunately, this inclusion drew backlash from some of the page's passersby, and some of them called the logo offensive because it depicted the power fist coming out on top of the temple as though it had punched through the roof. Some went so far as to ask the activists to remove the word "Hanoi" from the page name as they did not think this page represented all the people of Hanoi.

We extracted the comments from these two posts and parsed through them to glean the common themes or keywords that these comments shared, using "web scraping" techniques by manually downloading, copying and pasting the content, and then removing personally identifiable details.[46] Harvesting the publicly available comments in these two most popular posts, we employed a process that Franz et al. designated as "passive analysis" to unpack the thematic grouping of the comments (it is "passive" because the commenters are not involved in our analyzing process) by color coding the comments in Vietnamese, cross-checking among the authors, and then translating important texts into English.[47]

Three key themes emerged from the 898 comments we collected: (1) the observation that there are no Black people in Viet Nam as we are a homogenous society, and therefore, there is no need for BLM; (2) the whataboutism that there are bigger issues in Viet Nam and we should focus on internal affairs; and (3) the ignorance that Black people "had it coming" as they are no good. The scarce comments supporting the page were drowned out by a sea of negativity, with dogpiled comments questioning why Vietnamese people in Viet Nam care about a movement that is halfway across the globe, and why the page is fundraising for such a cause.

The sentiment that Viet Nam is homogenous and the whataboutism go hand in hand, as evident by their frequency of appearances in the comment section. The commenters pondered if Hanoi and Viet Nam had a big enough population of Black people for this topic to be of interest, asking, "Oh? Does Viet Nam have Black people? And if we do, who cares about them?" and, "What a joke, when did Hanoi discriminate against Black people?" The commenters failed to acknowledge the existence of Black Vietnamese, anti-Black racism, as well as discrimination that Black people faced in Viet Nam with employment. These comments were made despite the recent surge in interest in shows like *King of Rap* or *Rap Viet* as mentioned above.

After asking these questions, the next crop of commenters suggested that activists should care about what is currently happening at home first, pleading "Why aren't you doing something nice for your own homeland, your fellow countrymen, who are dying? . . . Humbly change the page name to VIETNAMESE LIVES MATTER?" Some resorted to questioning the page's motive, asking who they were fundraising for or who they were fighting for when people in Viet Nam were still facing many problems. One retorted:

> [Dear] dozens of page admins. Innocent people lost their land, lottery ticket sellers lost their jobs during the pandemic[48] and did not receive any support. China occupies the sea and islands. Why don't you guys demonstrate these things but protest for a Black criminal overseas? Are the people of Vietnam happy and prosperous?

The image of Black people or the idea that darker skin is bad had been perpetuated in Viet Nam through the country's history with colorism and a desire to align with whiteness, as analyzed in the earlier section. One commenter repeatedly posted what they deemed "evidence" of Black people engaging in illegal activities, insinuating that the page was applauding bad behaviors and that Black people had it coming to them when they chose to commit crimes. They belittled the page and its supportive commenters, saying, "[these are] your African American idols," suggesting that the supporters were actually idolizing criminal activities. As our interlocutor Minh noted, the Vietnamese, who generally valorize a respect for authority, would likely have had a "mental struggle" upon seeing images of protestors—rioters and looters as the media portrays them—and trying to empathize with them, a message that Black Lives Matter Hanoi was pushing. These commenters, although only a mere group of around three hundred, voiced their attitude toward Blackness in Viet Nam loudly and clearly. They do not care about Black people in Viet Nam, much less all the way across the world in the US.

The racist and bullying commentaries got so bad that the page's administrator had to put up a post saying a comment would be deleted and the author privately messaged if it contained violence, reactionist sentiment against the government, or hate speech. Despite their warning and subsequent deletions, hate speech was still rampant, with comments calling Black people *lũ da đen phá hoại* ("Black people [are] wreckers of havoc"). The comments we found in Vietnamese were coated with a layer of disdain, a hatred so deep like the kind you would find in the depths of forums like 4chan or r/TheDonald (a Donald Trump-supporting, alt-right subreddit). They found like-minded, albeit racist and ignorant, individuals, and formed their own echo chamber on post after post of a page dedicated to show Vietnamese support for BLM. They resorted to calling Black people *lũ*, a quantifier in Vietnamese to signify the resentment reserved for enemies and trivialities. After a month of defending themselves against almost three hundred hostile and persistent commenters, the dozen administrators of the Facebook page for Black Lives Matter Hanoi became inactive in July 2020.

## Conclusion

So, are Vietnamese people in Viet Nam racist against Black people? The answer is more complicated than a simple yes or no. Anti-Blackness in Viet Nam comes from both colorism and its colonial legacy to form a subtle, subconscious form of bias rather than a painful history of institutionalized discrimination based purely on race. Due to the common national sentiment that we don't have "race" in Viet Nam, Vietnamese people are largely "racially" homogeneous; and while the presence of other ethnic and racial groups is growing, that is not happening fast enough for the country to adjust its attitude. Interwoven with colorism, as well as imperialism and its colonial legacy, "racial" issues in Viet Nam appear in the form of subtle discrimination against darker-skinned groups, including the country's ethnic minority groups.

Race education in Viet Nam is limited to historical rather than contemporary events. Racism is thought of as an issue of the past, eradicated after Black people were freed from slavery and no longer an embedded institutionalized problem. Therefore, except for those with foreign exposure through traveling and staying abroad where these issues are evident, it remains a blind spot for many. As one of our informants remarked, "If we don't go out of the place where we're the majority, how do we know we're also marginalized and discriminated against?" This majority status is sometimes reflected in the desire to align with whiteness, which further deepens prejudice against Black people. To alleviate the issue and change the outlook of Vietnamese in Viet Nam, we need more diverse representation of people of all races through cultural exchange, conscious media reporting, and nationalized education. It also helps Vietnamese to understand discrimination against ourselves when we go abroad, be it for business or pleasure.

Racial movements like BLM have sparked heated discussion but are often short-lived because they are viewed as not directly relevant to the life of the average person in Viet Nam. Our essay briefly shows how successful activist groups started out discussing BLM but branched out and sought to educate Vietnamese audiences on a suite of directly relevant issues. This includes connecting anti-Black racism with discrimination against ethnic minorities in Viet Nam, an effort that might intersect with issues of gender and sexuality. To be sustainable in their growth, these groups chose to hit closer to home, addressing problems in Viet Nam's backyard. This shows some hope that the next generation of young Vietnamese are taking the lead in addressing the unspoken biases that exist in the country, opening the space for the Vietnamese people to have an honest conversation about complex and nuanced issues in a globalized world.

NOTE: In an effort to reclaim the spelling of our country's name, Viet Nam, in the English language, this has been how we write in this chapter instead of the more commonly seen "Vietnam". Vietnamese is a mono-syllabic language, where each sound has its own meaning. According to the late photojournalist Philip Jones Griffiths, the shortening of *Viet Nam* into *Vietnam* in the 1940s and 1950s (and subsequently other Vietnamese geographic names) was due to a cost-saving reason when transmission via telex was charged by the number of words. To borrow the words of the American historian Ted Engelmann in a letter to the OAH, writing Viet Nam "help[s] readers, mainly Americans, realize that Viet Nam is a country, not a war." Aside from the fact that our government has been advocating for the official name of the country to be written so, we encourage a gradual change in accepting "Viet Nam" as the correct way to write the country name in English, to remind everyone of our roots, the beauty of our language and the identity that we write to ourselves.

## Notes

[1] We only engaged with Black Lives Matter Hanoi via written Facebook messages on their page as the group had been inactive for over a year by the time we reached out and the administrators did not want to be interviewed as Black Lives Matter Hanoi.

[2] Interestingly, the people we interviewed and those involved in these initiatives are mostly, if not always, those who have been abroad and/or are part of Generation Z (those born in or after 1996). Their backgrounds are similar: most are current or former students at international schools or "high schools for the gifted," which are designated specialized public high schools for students gifted in the study of natural sciences, social sciences, and foreign languages. Many students in these magnet high schools would then go on to study abroad. The educational backgrounds of these activists are important, as they highlight the potential exposure to people of different races and ethnicities they would have encountered in their school curriculum and their social circles. This contrasts with their circle of friends doing their studies in Viet Nam who usually tend to see issues motivating the BLM movement as international matters that are not relevant to their lives.

[3] A good selection of these television commercials can be found here: https://youtube.com/playlist?list=PLza6wDkW7daGn_vlso7TueCfgEKdV0sKO.

[4] See Walker, *In Search*, 290; Chou, *Asian American Sexual Politics*; Norwood, *Color Matters*; Wahyuwidaya, *Colorism*. Cultural influences from East Asia, predominantly through the *hallyu* (Korean Wave), arguably have the most impact on Vietnamese's beauty standards. Kim ("Understanding 'Koreanness'") wrote from within the Korean society,

where Vietnamese is the second-largest migrant group of foreign residents, assigning the Vietnamese into the "Collective Dark"/"Collective Blacks" category.

[5] Khan, "Skin-lightening creams."

[6] The Korean influence in Viet Nam started in the early 2000s with the introduction of Korean television dramas and pop music (K-drama and K-pop). See Jang, Nguyen and Kwon, "Women's empowerment." In addition, Japanese influence is also significant in the skincare product market.

[7] All informants' names in this chapter are pseudonyms in order to protect their anonymity; however, we decided to keep the real names of the platforms so that their work can be elevated and reviewed (with the teams' informed consent).

[8] Zhou, "Seeing."

[9] Rondilla and Spickard, *Is Light Better?*

[10] Jones, "Significance"; Lee, "Lessons"; Rondilla and Spickard, *Is Light Better?*

[11] Dixon and Telles, "Skin Color"; Li, Hyun and Belk, "Skin Lightening."

[12] This is a rough English translation from the original text: 春寒賜浴華清池 / 溫泉水滑洗凝脂. We read from the Sino-Vietnamese/Vietnamese translation by Tản Đà ("Xuân hàn tứ dục Hoa Thanh trì / Ôn tuyền thuỷ hoạt tẩy ngưng chi" or "Tiết xuân được tắm ở hồ Hoa / Nước ấm vuốt da trắng mịn màng" [English word-by-word translation: 'In springtime bathing in Flower lake / Warm water caressing white smooth skin']).

[13] Wagatsuma, "Social Perception," note 3.

[14] Glenn, "Consuming Lightness," 179.

[15] Yoon, "Tracing." It is also interesting to note that during the ancient time in Joseon (as well as in other parts of East Asia), westerners were not called or seen as white.

[16] The name of the poem is literally the name of the sweet dish "glutinous rice ball," which is eaten across Viet Nam and East Asia. It acts as a euphemism for the woman's fate and dignity through the ups and downs of life. It is believed that in this period, the ideal standard for women included a plump body (presenting fertility) and white, pale skin (presenting beauty).

[17] Black/white (the race) and dark/fair (the skin colors) are described with the same word pair, đen/*trắng*, in Vietnamese.

[18] Hunter, "Persistent," 238.

[19] Annam is the pejorative term French colonialists used to call the land that is now Viet Nam (though sometimes specifically central Viet Nam during some periods). Discrimination against people with darker skin in Viet Nam now is obviously less blatant and more subtle compared to French treatment of its colonial subjects. Some examples of this tendency include stereotypes of Black people as dangerous, or a preference for lighter-skinned East Asians over other darker-skinned Asian groups in South and Southeast Asia as standards of beauty, or the treatment of the ethnic minority groups as needing to "catch up" with Kinh people as evidenced in government programs (a popular mantra is "Đưa miền núi tiến kịp miền xuôi," or bringing the mountainous areas—inhabited

by many ethnic minorities—on par with the plains, which are mostly populated by the Kinh majority). Nonetheless, in our opinions, these unaddressed biases and this subtle discrimination could lead to deep social issues and unfettered racism—the tiniest manifestation of which is through the response to BLM discussed later in this essay.

[20] Vương and Vũ, "Nhân học."

[21] Dang, "Does Horizontal Inequality"; Huy Thắng, "Công bố." The majority of Vietnamese ethnic minority population live in the northwest regions, northeast mountains, and central highlands, with other (very densely populated) regions largely inhabited by the Kinh majority. Pischedda et al. ("Phylogeographic") explains from a different perspective the genome-based ethnic origin makeup of the present-day Vietnamese population, arguing that while there are genetic variations among different ethnic groups in Viet Nam, they all belong to the geographic location of and around the Indochinese Peninsula and southern region of China. It is also worth noting that Viet Nam's reports to the OHCRC Committee on the Elimination of Racial Discrimination (CERD) have focused on ethnic minorities as the subject of discrimination in question, while acknowledging the discrimination that Vietnamese citizens face overseas (Duy Ly, "Công tác").

[22] A full record of the English translation of this essay as well as other related texts can be retrieved from a recently published selection introduced by Nguyen Dai Trang (see Nguyen, "The Black Race").

[23] Ho Chi Minh described the Vietnamese using this pejorative term in a sarcastic sense. An excerpt of the Vietnamese translation of this text (titled "Bản án chế độ thực dân Pháp," or "The Sentence of the French Colonial Regime") has been widely taught in the modern Vietnamese secondary school curriculum until now. It serves as a reminder for the young generation of the country's colonial past while positioning the Vietnamese struggle in a bigger world picture, especially in its relationship with African nations that were then French colonies.

[24] We understand that how we define who "Black people" are historically can be slippery. For example, it may include groups inhabiting marine Southeast Asia or the Pacific Islands in ancient and current times. In this section, we focus on more recent history with the movement of African and African-descended mercenaries into Viet Nam through wars.

[25] Ginio, "African Troops," 99.

[26] Ibid., 100.

[27] Peyton, "How Spring Rolls."

[28] Goodwill, "Black and White."

[29] Chow and Bates, "Da 5 Bloods"; Terry, "Bloods."

[30] We are aware of accounts that say this quote has been misattributed to Mr. Ali and that it probably wasn't him who said it, but we find that its significance still stands in the Vietnamese/Vietnamese American rhetoric during the awareness campaigns in 2020.

[31] Lucious, "In the Black Pacific," 133.

[32] Emerson, "Part Vietnamese"; Winn, "Vietnam War Babies."

[33] Người Lao Động, "Hơn 100,000"; Viet Nam News, "Number." As these statistics are from official MOLISA reports, they did not take into account the population of migrants into Viet Nam that stay on quarterly tourist visas (or commonly known as "visa runs" in the community). Recently, the Vietnamese government has started imposing more stringent restrictions on foreigners working in Viet Nam to avoid loopholes in labor laws (see Decree 152/2020/ND-CP).

[34] Tổng cục, "Lao động."

[35] Superhero movies are usually very popular in Vietnamese cinemas, and most of the time, they feature white protagonists, especially against Black antagonists (the *Kingsman* franchise is an example). DC's *Suicide Squad* was also popular, next to the suite of movies that make up the Marvel cinematic universe. While the film industry itself has improved on diversity in recent years, it is worth mentioning the impact of some of these stereotypes, especially in a society not racially diverse itself, like Viet Nam.

[36] Ouassini, Amini and Ouassini, "#ChinaMustExplain"; Sautman, "Anti-Black Racism."

[37] The Black Experience Japan, "You Have Freedom," 13: 52.

[38] While the page name is still "Black Brother," recent publications in the last few years have stopped featuring Black people exclusively, and the page has become a more common "meme" page for entertainment, though contents featuring people of African descent are still the most abundant and prominent.

[39] This is one of the most common transactions for social media content creators and advertisers in Viet Nam, with branded content on Facebook created on demand for payments (with Facebook being the most common social media platform in Viet Nam at 65 million users in 2021, according to Statista. The "Black Brother" administrator team mentions it accepts requests via direct messages to the page.

[40] Bell Shino, "Vì sao."

[41] In Vietnamese colloquial as well as formal language, the word "người da màu" ("people of color") is usually used as a euphemism to refer to people of African descent and less likely for Asian groups, even darker-skinned South Asians. This might be seen as a more polite way of saying "người da đen" ("black-skinned people"), but it also means Vietnamese people are unlikely to count ourselves as people of color.

[42] Hoài Hà, "Black Lives Matter."

[43] From the event's Facebook record, over five hundred people showed interest in participating (i.e., by clicking "Going" or "Interested"). From the event photos published by Saigon is Listening afterward, the event looked like it was attended by around one to two hundred people. It's critical to note that Saigon is Listening was created by a group of foreigners of African descent, mostly African American, living in Ho Chi Minh City, but according to their event description, the event engaged with Vietnamese youth activist groups to facilitate conversations between the communities. The organizers also reported having to change to a bigger venue due to an overwhelming audience. We only engaged with Viet Activism and not Saigon is Listening when writing this essay. See event page: https://www.facebook.com/events/1189259914753185/.

[44] For example, Viet Activism and Viets for Change (formerly Viets for BLM) recently hosted a joint event on understanding ethnic minorities biases by Vietnamese.

[45] These groups all started around the same time of heightened BLM activities globally and were all initially focused on BLM/anti-racism content, but Viet Activism and Viets for Change eventually expanded their coverage to stay relevant for longer. Our interlocutors also attributed the positive responses to their campaigns to the dominant platform they were using (Instagram instead of Facebook, where the number of Vietnamese well surpassed the former).

[46] Mancosu and Vegetti, "What You Can Scrape." While we acknowledge the slippery nature of using pseudonyms to call the commenters (see Gerrard, "What's in a (Pseudo) name?"), and in our cases using no names at all, we see that this is a public platform that any (Vietnamese-speaking) person on or outside of Facebook can access, and therefore, the scraping process did not violate the limited ethical and legal general guidelines in academic literature. During the scraping process, we could not access some of the comments that were deleted and turned off by the Facebook page administrators, and this caused some disruptions to the comment threads, which we see as a limitation to our research.

[47] Franz et al., "Using Facebook."

[48] Viet Nam employs a wholesale system for lottery tickets, which big lottery ticket companies sell to wholesalers in big cities, who sell the tickets to local stores, who then sell the tickets to individual sellers. Those individual sellers then go around the cities to sell the ticket to anyone who would buy it before it expires (see Anton Abroad, "Vietnam's Lottery Wholesale"). During the COVID-19 pandemic, Viet Nam entered strict lockdowns, which caused these street sellers to lose their jobs.

## Bibliography

Anton Abroad. "Vietnam's Lottery Wholesale—An Exploiting System on Cost of Those Who Live on the Edge of Existence." *Anton Abroad*, n.d., accessed December 28, 2021. https://antonabroad.com/vietnams-lottery-wholesale-an-exploiting-system-on-cost-of-those-who-live-on-the-edge-of-existence/.

Bell Shino. "Vì sao Rap Việt xứng đáng trở thành TV Show của năm?" ("Why *Rap Viet* deserves to be the TV Show of the Year"), *Channel 14*, January 24, 2021, https://kenh14.vn/vi-sao-rap-viet-xung-dang-tro-thanh-tv-show-cua-nam-20210123122602458.chn.

The Black Experience Japan. "You Have Freedom Out Here, Like Real Freedom . . . (Black in Vietnam) | MFiles" Interview by the Black Experience Japan. Youtube. January 9, 2020, video, https://www.youtube.com/watch?v=VlsKDIn6ecs.

Chou, Rosalind S. *Asian American Sexual Politics: The Construction of Race, Gender, and Sexuality*. Lanham. Rowman & Littlefield, 2013.

Chow, Andrew R. and Josiah Bates. "As Da 5 Bloods Hits Netflix, Black Vietnam Veterans Recall the Real Injustices They Faced During and After the War." *TIME Magazine*, June 12, 2020, https://time.com/5852476/da-5-bloods-black-vietnam-veterans/.

Dang, Thi Thu Hoai. "Does Horizontal Inequality Matter in Vietnam?" *Social Indicators Research* 145, no. 3 (2019): 943–956.

Dixon, Angela R., and Edward E. Telles. "Skin Color and Colorism: Global Research, Concepts, and Measurement," *Annual Review of Sociology* 43, no. 1 (July 2017): 405–424. https://doi.org/10.1146/annurev-soc-060116-053315.

Duy Ly. "Việt Nam nỗ lực thực hiện công ước quốc tế "Chống phân biệt chủng tộc" ("Vietnam's Efforts in Executing CERD)", *Báo Dân tộc* (Ethnic Periodical), April 19, 2021, https://baodantoc.vn/viet-nam-no-luc-thuc-hien-cong-uoc-quoc-te-chong-phan-biet-chung-toc-1618388596332.htm.

Emerson, Gloria. "Part Vietnamese, Part Black—And Orphans." *New York Times*, February 7, 1972, 26. Archived version, https://www.nytimes.com/1972/02/07/archives/part-vietnamese-part-blackand-orphans.html.

Franz, Daschel, Heather Elizabeth Marsh, Jason I. Chen, and Alan R. Teo. "Using Facebook for Qualitative Research: A Brief Primer." *Journal of Medical Internet Research* 21, no. 8 (2019): e13544. https://doi.org/10.2196/13544.

Gerrard, Ysabel. "What's in a (Pseudo) Name? Ethical Conundrums for the Principles of Anonymisation in Social Media Research." *Qualitative Research* 21, no. 5 (2021): 686–702. https://doi.org/10.1177/1468794120922070.

Ginio, Ruth. "African Troops in the Wars of Decolonization: Indochina, 1946–1954." In *The French Army and Its African Soldiers: The Years of Decolonization*, 77–104. Lincoln: University of Nebraska Press, 2017. https://doi.org/10.2307/j.ctt1hfr1hf.10.

Glenn, Evelyn Nakano. "10 Consuming Lightness: Segmented Markets and Global Capital in the Skin-Whitening Trade." In *Shades of Difference: Why Skin Color Matters* edited by Evelyn Nakano Glenn, 166–187. Redwood City: Stanford University Press, 2009. https://doi.org/10.1515/9780804770996-012.

Goodwill, Gerald F. "Black and White in Vietnam." *The New York Times*. July 18, 2017, https://www.nytimes.com/2017/07/18/opinion/racism-vietnam-war.html.

Hoài Hà. "'Black Lives Matter' và giấc mơ xóa bỏ tình trạng phân biệt chủng tộc tại Mỹ" ("Black Lives Matter" and the dream of eradicating racism in America). Official website of the Communist Party of Vietnam, updated

June 15, 2020, accessed May 30, 2021, https://dangcongsan.vn/the-gioi/tin-tuc/black-lives-matter-va-giac-mo-xoa-bo-tinh-trang-phan-biet-chung-toc-tai-my-557060.html.

Hunter, Margaret. "The Persistent Problem of Colorism: Skin Tone, Status, and Inequality." *Sociology Compass* 1, issue 1 (September 2007): 237–254. https://doi.org/10.1111/j.1751-9020.2007.00006.x.

Huy Thắng. "Công bố kết quả Tổng điều tra dân số 2019" (Reports on the result of the National Census 2019). July 11, 2019, http://tongdieutradanso.vn/cong-bo-ket-qua-tong-dieu-tra-dan-so-2019.html.

Jang, Haeyoung, Ngoc Tram Oanh Nguyen, and Seung-Ho Kwon. "Women's Empowerment and Transnational Consumption of Hallyu in Vietnam," *Asian Journal of Women's Studies*, 27, no. 2 (2021): 184–207. https://doi.org/10.1080/12259276.2021.1924482.

Jones, Trina. "The Significance of Skin Color in Asian and Asian-American Communities: Initial Reflections", *UC Irvine L. Rev* 3, issue 4 (December 2013): 1105–1123. https://scholarship.law.uci.edu/ucilr/vol3/iss4/11.

Khan, Coco. "Skin-Lightening Creams Are Dangerous—Yet Business is Booming. Can the Trade Be Stopped?" *The Guardian.* April 23, 2018. https://www.theguardian.com/world/2018/apr/23/skin-lightening-creams-are-dangerous-yet-business-is-booming-can-the-trade-be-stopped.

Kim, Hyein Amber. "Understanding "Koreanness": Racial Stratification and Colorism in Korea and Implications for Korean Multicultural Education." *International Journal of Multicultural Education* 22, no. 1 (2020): 76–97. http://dx.doi.org/10.18251/ijme.v22i1.1834.

Lee, Sharon Heijin. "Lessons from 'Around the world with Oprah': Neoliberalism, Race, and the (Geo)politics of Beauty," *Women & Performance: A Journal of Feminist Theory* 18, no. 1 (March 2008): 25–41, https://doi.org/10.1080/07407700801902809.

Li, Eric P. H., Hyun Jeong Min, and Russell W. Belk. "Skin Lightening and Beauty in Four Asian Cultures," *NA—Advances in Consumer Research* 35 (2008), eds. Angela Y. Lee and Dilip Soman, Duluth: Association for Consumer Research, 444–449.

Lucious, Bernard Scott. "In the Black Pacific: Testimonies of Vietnamese Afro-Amerasian Displacements." In *Displacements and Diasporas: Asians in the Americas*, edited by Wanni Wibulswasdi Anderson and Robert G. Lee. New Brunswick: Rutgers University Press, 2005, 122–155.

Mancosu, Moreno, and Federico Vegetti. "What You Can Scrape and What is Right to Scrape: A Proposal for a Tool to Collect Public Facebook Data." *Social Media+ Society* 6, no. 3 (2020). https://doi.org/10.1177/2056305120940703.

Người Lao Động. "Hơn 100.000 lao động nước ngoài làm việc tại Việt Nam" ("More than 100,000 Foreigners Working in Vietnam"). *Người Lao Động (The Labour)*, April 21, 2021, https://nld.com.vn/cong-doan/hon-100000-lao-dong-nuoc-ngoai-lam-viec-tai-viet-nam-20210420195219116.htm.

Nguyễn Ái Quốc. *Bản án chế độ thực dân Pháp*—Vietnamese translation of *Le Procès de la colonisation française*. Truth Publishing House reprints 1975 (original script written in French in 1925).

Nguyen, Dai Trang. T*he Black Race by Ho Chi Minh and Selected Works on Systemic Racism*. Toronto: New Vietnam Publishing, 2021.

Norwood, Kimberly Jade, ed., *Color Matters: Skin Tone Bias and the Myth of a Postracial America*. London: Routledge/Taylor & Francis Group, 2014.

Ouassini, Anwar, Mostafa Amini, and Nabil Ouassini. "#ChinaMustexplain: Global Tweets, COVID-19, and Anti-Black Racism in China." *The Review of Black Political Economy* (2021), https://doi.org/10.1177/0034644621992687.

Peyton, Nellie. "How Spring Rolls Got to Senegal." *Slate*, November 7, 2016, https://slate.com/news-and-politics/2016/11/the-strange-story-of-how-spring-rolls-became-senegals-go-to-snack.html.

Pischedda, Sara, Ruth Barral-Arca, Alberto Gómez-Carballa, J. Pardo-Seco, M. L. Catelli, Vanesa Álvarez-Iglesias, J. M. Cárdenas et al. "Phylogeographic and Genome-Wide Investigations of Vietnam Ethnic Groups Reveal Signatures of Complex Historical Demographic Movements." *Nature: Scientific Reports* 7, no. 1 (2017): 1–15. https://doi.org/10.1038/s41598-017-12813-6.

Rondilla, Joanne L., and Paul Spickard. *Is Lighter Better?: Skin-Tone Discrimination among Asian Americans*. Lanham: Rowman & Littlefield Publishers, 2017.

Sautman, Barry. "Anti-Black Racism in Post-Mao China." *The China Quarterly* 138 (June 1994): 413–437. http://www.jstor.org/stable/654951.

Statista. "Facebook Users in Vietnam," updated July 20, 2021, accessed December 10 2021, https://www.statista.com/forecasts/1136459/facebook-users-in-vietnam.

Terry, Wallace. *Bloods: Black Veterans of the Vietnam War: An Oral History*. New York: Random House Publishing Group, 1984.

Thich Nhat Hanh Foundation. "When Giants Meet," January 11, 2017, accessed August 10, 2021, https://thichnhathanhfoundation.org/blog/2017/8/9/when-giants-meet.

Tổng cục Dân số—Kế hoạch hoá gia đình (General Office for Population and Family Planning). "Lao Động Nước Ngoài Ở Việt Nam—Nhìn Từ Các Góc Độ Pháp Lý Và Quyền Con Người" (Foreign Labor in Vietnam—From a Legal and Human Rights Perspective). 2 July, 2018, http://gopfp.gov.vn/chi-tiet-an-pham/-/chi-tiet/lao-%C4%91ong-nuoc-ngoai-o-viet-nam-%0Anhin-tu-cac-goc-%C4%91o-phap-ly-va-quyen-con-nguoi-8402-3309.html.

Tran, Linh K. "Người Việt mình có phân biệt chủng tộc?" ("Are We, Vietnamese, Racist?"). *Vietcetera*, June 3, 2020, https://vietcetera.com/vn/nguoi-viet-minh-co-phan-biet-chung-toc.

Vietnam News. "Number of foreign workers in Vietnam on the rise." *Vietnam News*, June 21, 2017, https://vietnamnews.vn/society/378649/number-of-foreign-workers-in-viet-nam-on-the-rise.html#0x3A4G9EZgHPrejY.97.

Vương, Xuân Tình and Vũ Đình Mười. "Nhân học tộc người" ("Ethnicity Anthropology"), *Viet Nam Academy of Social Sciences*, February 3, 2021, https://vass.gov.vn/nghien-cuu-khoa-hoc-xa-hoi-va-nhan-van/Nhan-hoc-toc-nguoi-119.

Wagatsuma, Hiroshi. "The Social Perception of Skin Color in Japan." *Daedalus*, 96, no. 2 (Spring 1967): 407–443.

Wahyuwidayat, Radha. Colourism in South and South-East Asia. *Green Left Weekly*, issue 1093 (2016): 6, https://search.informit.org/doi/10.3316/informit.057108501131980.

Walker, Alice. *In Search of Our Mothers' Gardens*. San Diego: Harcourt, 1983.

Winn, Patrick. "Vietnam War Babies: Grown Up and Low on Luck." *GlobalPost*, September 2, 2011, https://theworld.org/stories/2011-09-02/vietnam-war-babies-grown-and-low-luck.

Yoon, Min-sik. "Tracing the Root of Koreans' 'White Skin Obsession,'" *The Korea Herald*, December 24, 2021, http://www.koreaherald.com/view.php?ud=20211223000883.

Zhou, Raymond. "Seeing Red over Black Angel," *China Daily Opinion*. September 18, 2009. https://www.chinadaily.com.cn/opinion/2009-09/18/content_8711576.htm.

# 10

## "WE HAVE A LOT OF NAMES LIKE GEORGE FLOYD"

### PAPUAN LIVES MATTER IN COMPARATIVE PERSPECTIVE

### Chris Lundry

Inspired by the Black Lives Matter (BLM) movement in the United States, the Papuan Lives Matter (PLM) movement emerged in the summer of 2020, around one year after racist incidents against West Papuans sparked protest and violence in East Java that spread to West Papua and other parts of Indonesia. This paper contextualizes the colonial and postcolonial history of West Papua through the lens of race in order to understand the emergence of PLM. Initially described by European explorers and then colonizers as "Black," West Papuans—and Melanesians more broadly—came to embrace this designation in solidarity with African Americans, the African diaspora, and with Africa itself.[1] PLM is an extension of this solidarity, arising within the specific context of racism and discrimination in Indonesia.

West Papuans share many of the same grievances expressed by African Americans through BLM: a history of slavery that continues to influence their treatment; institutional and personal racism; disenfranchisement; structural conditions that keep them poorer than their fellow citizens; and violence at the hands of police, military, and security institutions that is often committed with impunity.[2] The situation of West Papuans is complicated by their problematic incorporation into Indonesia in 1969, including the disenfranchisement of more than 99 percent of the population and the presence of separatist sentiment among a large portion of the population that desires independence from Indonesia. While the study of racism in the West has a long history, studies of racism in Asia are much rarer. Furthermore, as Indonesian anthropologist Veronika Kusumaryati notes, "the place of Black Melanesians in Asian Studies is still ambiguous, as they are not considered to be proper 'Asians.'"[3] It is my hope that this brief article adds to these bodies of work. It should also be noted that many West Papuans embrace their Blackness as a given in their work; more of their voices would be a welcome addition to Asian studies.[4]

## Background

West Papua, under Indonesian control since 1962, is the western half of the island named Papua or New Guinea, the latter a name given to the island by Spanish explorers in the sixteenth century who decided that the inhabitants resembled those of Africa's Guinea.[5] The Dutch called it "Nieuw Guinea," the Indonesians "West Irian" and then "Irian Jaya" ("Glorious Irian") before renaming it Papua in 1999. In 2003, Indonesia divided the region into two provinces, Papua and West Papua. I will refer to the region focused on in this essay as West Papua for simplicity.[6]

Prior to European contact in the sixteenth century, parts of West Papua were a source for slaves to the nearby sultanates of Tidore and Ternate, but most residents had little contact with outsiders. As other Europeans encroached, the Dutch asserted themselves, and West Papua eventually became part of the Dutch East Indies, ruled indirectly through the Sultan of Tidore. Dutch sovereignty, however, was tenuous.[7] Although slavery was banned in the Indies in 1863, it remained in practice into the twentieth century in West Papua and peripheral regions of the Dutch East Indies.[8] The border with the eastern half of the island, now Papua New Guinea, was formalized in 1884.[9]

The colonial administrative presence was light, and it was mostly missionaries who traveled to the interior. Beginning in the 1930s, the Dutch envisioned West Papua as a place for Eurasians or "Indos," children of mixed Dutch and Indonesian parentage. Their position in the colonial hierarchy was threatened by the increase in Dutch immigration and the education of native Indonesians, and as the products of miscegenation, they were "problematic." Dutch fascists also envisioned West Papua as a new homeland.[10] Attempts at transmigration and establishing farms mostly ended in failure, and the Japanese invasion during World War II ended the experiment.

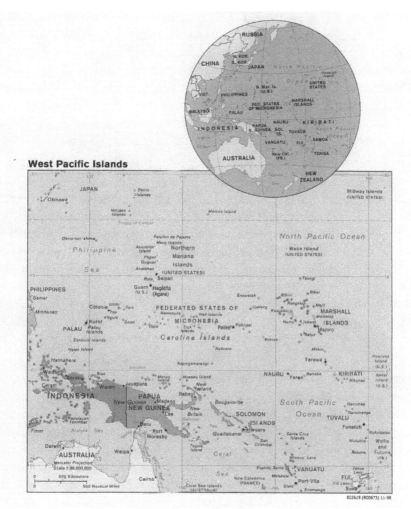

Figure 10.1. "West Pacific Islands." Washington, D.C.:
Central Intelligence Agency 1998, Print.

The Japanese occupation was brief, and the Allies fought and retook the
territory with the help of Papuans, who captured or killed Japanese enthusiastically
because of their harsh treatment and the rewards that were offered. Papuans saw
African American soldiers working alongside whites, the first time they saw people
with dark skin and hair like theirs in such positions, and it helped expose the lie of
white supremacy—a justification for European colonialism—that the Dutch had
promoted.[11] Of course, the segregated American armed services of the period were
far from egalitarian (and remain so),[12] but it inspired Papuans.

In the series of talks between the Dutch and Indonesians during the revolution,
a Papuan was present in an official capacity only at the Malino Conference in 1946.

Frans Kaisiepo, a Dutch-educated elite, originally favored the Dutch but soon converted to the Indonesian position and was rewarded by being named governor of the province in 1964. In subsequent conferences until independence in 1949, Papuans were sidelined, and their fate was left for others to determine. The Dutch and the Indonesians argued that because of the low overall levels of education and development, Papuans were unable to contribute meaningfully. Papuans have argued that Indonesia in 1949 shared these attributes following centuries of Dutch colonialism and that there existed a similar stratum of educated elites.

The fate of West Papua was to be settled in 1951; it was not. Indonesia's President Soekarno labeled West Papua "a colonial sword poised over the neck of Indonesia," and the issue contributed to the nationalization of Dutch assets.[13] Dutch political scientist Arend Lijphart described the "trauma of decolonization" that the Dutch felt over West Papua, losing the last vestige of empire, but they began programs to educate West Papuans and prepare them for self-government. The Dutch created political councils and trained police, bureaucrats, and a civil service and hoped that 90 to 95 percent of all civil service positions would be held by Papuans by 1970.[14] Yet, as Indonesia and Holland were in increasingly belligerent conflict, the United States came to favor the Indonesian position (to court Soekarno), and Papuans remained left out of discussions about their fate.

In 1962, as the civil rights movement was gaining ground in the United States following the "Freedom Rides" one year earlier, West Papua's fate was handed to Indonesia, albeit nominally under a United Nations transition and with the promise of a plebiscite. But the UN was sidelined, and "Indonesianization" began rapidly. Papuan civil servants were dismissed and replaced, Papuan police were confined to barracks, political expression that was not explicitly pro-Indonesia was forbidden, and Papuan nationalists were imprisoned, tortured, and murdered. Soekarno withdrew from the UN over confrontation with Malaysia, and he abrogated the decision to hold a referendum, arguing that there was no need because Papuans wanted to be Indonesian—a non-Papuan speaking for West Papuans.

After Suharto's rise in 1965 (and Indonesia's turn to the West), he assented to an "Act of Free Choice" to be held in 1969. The referendum was a stage-managed sham by all accounts. The UN representatives were made fools, and Cold War appeasement won out again.[15] Just 1,022 Papuans out of an estimated population of 800,000 were selected by Indonesia to vote, and those who spoke out were intimidated, imprisoned, or killed with impunity.[16] The sham results were unanimous for integration with Indonesia. Thus the "Act of Free Choice"—certainly an "act," though definitely not "free" nor an exercise of "choice"—denied self-determination and possibly independence to West Papuans, but the international community had its "referendum," and the region's fate was sealed.

In 1965, one year before the Black Panthers took up arms in self-defense in the United States—and created self-help social programs in the face of apathy or hostility from the American state—armed separatism emerged in West Papua, although some Papuans had been pro-Indonesia all along and others were swayed to join the pro-Indonesia side for opportunistic reasons. Many pro-Indonesia Papuans, including the territory's first governor, reversed course, however, when they saw how Papuans were being treated and the policies that sent Indonesians to settle West Papua. Nationalist symbols, such as the *Bintang Kejora* (Morning Star) flag, were banned, and cultural expression was curtailed. Papuans have held that cultural differences also support their claims for self-determination. For example, Papuans are predominantly Christian while Indonesians are Muslim. As Octovianus Mote and Danilyn Ritherford argue, Indonesians were enamored with West Papua's wealth—the world's largest open-pit gold mine and second-largest copper mine are in West Papua—but not its people.[17]

Indonesia's logic, which held that in 1969, Papuans had to choose representatives to vote for them because they were uneducated, was ignored in the presidential election just two years later. Some 379,531 West Papuans voted in the 1971 national elections for Indonesia. Yet rather than reflecting the enfranchisement of the Voting Rights Act just six years prior in the United States, this election was also a farce; every representative elected was from Suharto's political vehicle, Golkar.[18] Subsequent elections were similarly rigged, essentially disenfranchising Papuans. Yet the idea that West Papuans are unable to participate fully in voting persists among some, just as some in the United States are promoting laws specifically designed to disenfranchise African Americans and other minorities, something that BLM is fighting. When observers in the Carter Center delegation, who had been sent to monitor the 2004 Indonesian presidential election, wanted to include a section in the report that noted, similar to Aceh, the overwhelming military presence and intimidation in the region, former US ambassador to Indonesia John Monjo blurted out, "For god's sake, they're naked!" His statement raised more than a few eyebrows.

West Papuans viewed the reforms associated with Indonesian democratization that began in 1998—as well as the referendum that led to Timor-Leste's independence—with optimism. The ban on the *Bintang Kejora* was lifted, and the press was freer—for a while. The Papuan Presidium Council was formed, and leaders went to Jakarta, where even those presumed to be pro-Indonesia requested a referendum on independence. Theys Eluay, a traditional chief and a former Golkar politician and Suharto loyalist, emerged as a uniting figure for West Papuans. His assassination at the hands of Indonesian security personnel in November 2001 was viewed by many as a death knell for the resurgent demand for a referendum. Subsequent reforms have been mostly symbolic.

## Papuan "Blackness" and Global Connectedness

Papuans have long identified as Black, and Black movements have long sought to identify with Papuans and Melanesians more generally, including with claims of a shared African ancestry and diaspora.[19] Seeing African American soldiers in World War II stoked this sentiment. In the period between 1949 and 1962, Papuans used this identity to lobby for support for their independence.

Papuans' "race" had been debated for centuries prior to this, including by preeminent thinkers such as Alfred Russel Wallace, whose Wallace Line drew a distinction between flora and fauna but whose racial line was a few islands eastward, differentiating Sumba, Flores, Timor, and Papua from the rest of the Indonesian archipelago. In the colonial era, anthropologists argued over racial distinctions, and often, classification came down to the impressions of individual surveyors that included assumptions about mental and moral capacities.[20] Classifying Papuans as inferior was a convenient *ex post facto* justification for their slavery, including "blackbirding," or taking Papuans captive to work in Australia and elsewhere.[21]

Despite being left out of the negotiations about their future, between 1949 and 1962, Papuan nationalists lobbied for recognition, especially in Africa. Nicolaas Jouwe published *Voice of the Negroids in the Pacific to the Negroids throughout the World* in April 1962, after US Attorney General Robert Kennedy visited Jakarta and support for the Dutch position was crumbling. The pamphlet asserts Papuans' separate identity from Indonesia as well as their right to self-determination, and it notes the presence of elected councils throughout the territory. It appeals for support from other "Negroid" countries and includes an open letter to Ethiopian leader Haile Selassie, with copies sent to several other African countries. It also includes a copy of a telegraph sent to US President John F. Kennedy, condemning his brother's remarks calling Papuans backward during his trip to Jakarta.

The Papuan position put some postcolonial nations in a bind. Some, in the spirit of the 1955 Bandung Conference, found it hard to criticize the Indonesian position. Because some Papuan nationalists identified with the Dutch, and the Dutch were still in control of the territory, some viewed Papuans as colonial puppets. Although identifying with African and Black movements was an attempt to build solidarity, it also allowed racists to view Papuans as they viewed Black people in general: unable to govern themselves, or even as "sons of Ham."[22] Despite common Indonesian portrayals of Papuans as primitive, Representative to the UN Sudjarwo mocked the Dutch, stating, "It may, in fact, be asked: what kind of racial links have the Dutch with the West Irians (sic)? Certainly, I look much more like a West Irian or Papuan than do my Dutch friends!"[23] Portraying himself as Papuan, Major J. Diamara of the Indonesian Defense Council submitted to the United Nations a document addressed to "all the peoples of Africa" that "West Irian is an integral part of Indonesia"—another case of an Indonesian speaking for Papuans.[24]

Although some African countries voiced support for West Papua, nobody who determined their fate paid Papuans much attention. The African American press reported on events, including a visit by Jouwe, but the mainstream American press portrayed the Papuans as primitive headhunters and cannibals.[25] Despite the "Act of Free Choice," West Papuan nationalists raised the *Bintang Kejora* and declared independence on July 1, 1971, lobbying for support in Africa and among African Americans, including from the National Association for the Advancement of Colored People (NAACP).[26] West Papuans continue this lobbying, including with the Congressional Black Caucus (CBC) and the Congressional Asian Pacific American Caucus, whose former chair, Eni Faleomavaega, a nonvoting member from American Samoa, was a staunch supporter of West Papuan self-determination before his death in 2017. In 2004, the CBC and Faleomavaega submitted letters to Secretary of State Condoleezza Rice, asking her to review the "Act of Free Choice" and quoting Nelson Mandela.[27] In 2010, Faleomavaega and others urged the Obama administration to prioritize West Papua, and that same year, West Papuans and other activists and academics spoke to the Subcommittee on Asia, the Pacific, and the Global Environment about abuses in West Papua.[28]

## Contemporary Racism toward Papuans

Although one Dutch official portrayed Papuans as "sweet, timid,"[29] by far the predominant portrayals of Papuans include "stupid," "dirty," "lazy," "vicious," "hostile," and "savage," their land "godforsaken."[30] They "lived like wild beasts, had no religion, nor kings and superiors, lived from their land, ate pigs, etc."[31] Ligia Giay shows how "native informants," predominantly Moluccan, established the initial stereotypes that became fixed and intertextual.[32] Colonial portrayals of other natives frequently used these stereotypes, in part to justify the colonial project and the duty to "uplift" their subjects.

Yet these stereotypes persist. I have heard educated Indonesians say they cannot be racist because Indonesia is a postcolonial society, yet they have referred to Papuans using these stereotypes, justified by the low economic indicators in West Papua.[33] Papuans are referred to as "pigs," "dogs," "monkeys," and other dehumanizing slurs, as noted in the African American press.[34] Papuans' Blackness is enough for Indonesian landlords to reject them as potential renters.[35]

Portrayals of Papuans in popular culture reflect these stereotypes. Images of the "typical" inhabitants of the thirty-four provinces of Indonesia include West Papuans in *koteka*, or penis gourds. Although worn by some members of predominantly highland groups, they are not reflective of the traditional garb of the entire region. However, the image works to reinforce these stereotypes in the classrooms of Indonesia outside of West Papua.[36] Predominantly Muslim Indonesians view the *koteka* as immodest and a sign of backwardness, offensive along with Papuans' consumption of pork, both of which become fodder for jokes. These repeated images turn all Papuans into *koteka*-wearing "savages." In 1971, Indonesia launched "Operation Koteka" to get highland Papuans to wear pants and dresses; it failed.[37] The portrayals of Papuans as lazy or stupid can be internalized by West Papuans, leading to low self-esteem.[38]

The historical section noted the absence of Papuan voices in determining their future; this voicelessness continues. Following the outbreak of violence in August 2019, most of the mass media in Indonesia reporting on it—and its causes—included interviews with non-Papuan officials, the military, and the police. In the context of PLM, one analysis of Indonesian media conducted by faculty of Universitas Udayana showed that although images of West Papuans continue to propagate stereotypes, some media claim that there is no racism toward West Papua because the region is sent special autonomy funding, an assertion that makes no sense.[39] One has to look at foreign sources to hear Papuan voices on the unrest and PLM.

Political representation has proved problematic as well. Soekarno appointed an Ambonese, Zainal Abidin Syah, as governor-in-exile in 1956, who was succeeded by a Javanese, Pamoedji (1961–1963). Elias Bonay, the first governor of West Irian, was Papuan, but he was removed after eighteen months for criticizing Indonesian transmigration. But in 1973, Suharto began appointing Sundanese and Javanese military officers as governors. The provinces have Papuan governors now, but outsiders remain in positions of influence, especially the military.

In the latest offering to mollify Papuans, Jakarta named Singgerei Rumagesan a national hero in 2020. Although he lived in Papua for a time, Rumagesan was Seramese and Moluccan. As a local king selected by the Dutch, he tried to forcefully convert Christians to Islam, was later imprisoned and exiled by the Dutch, and raised a militia to fight for West Papua's integration with Indonesia. National heroes are meant to epitomize an element of Indonesian history, such as nationalist struggle. In conversations with politically active Papuans, none knew who Rumagesan was nor that he was declared a national hero from Papua.[40]

West Papuans—including religious figures—continue to be arrested, tortured, and murdered with impunity by Indonesian military and police personnel. A recent event was eerily similar to the murder of George Floyd. Following a disagreement in a food stall between West Papuan Steven Yadohamang and the proprietor, two uniformed air force officers accosted Yadohamang, wrestling him to the ground while one put his boot on his head to restrain him. Like Floyd, the abuse was filmed and disseminated. Though not fatal, the media made the connection to Floyd, and the government apologized and dismissed the officers.[41] Given the environment of impunity for abuses in West Papua in general, one wonders if the case would be known were there not cell phone video.

Yet even if filmed, other cases, including death at the hands of the police, do not guarantee justice. In May of 2020, a West Papuan laborer named Marius Betera was beaten by a police officer, an act also captured on video. Yet the coroner's report was suspiciously inconclusive, and the police went on a social media offensive to deny responsibility, labeling the accusation a "hoax."[42] It is much easier to find cases such as this than Yadohamang's, given the environment of impunity, or even cases where the police brag that their violence is legitimate.[43] "In Papua, we have a lot of names like George Floyd," stated Elvira Rumkabu, a lecturer at Jayapura's Cendrawasih University.[44] On police abuse, Benny Wenda, the president of the United Liberation Movement for West Papua, remarked, "There is no difference between what happens to African Americans in the US and what happens to West Papuans."[45] Although the situation with West Papuans in Indonesia reflects local political and social contexts, the African American experience continues to be a touchstone.

## Papuan Lives Matter

Papuan Lives Matter emerged as a hashtag after the death of George Floyd and nearly a year after the incidents of racist violence directed at West Papuans in Indonesia, starting at a university in East Java in August 2019. Reacting to a perceived slight, Javanese students—soon joined by security forces as well as militia groups—attacked West Papuans in their dormitories. The violence quickly spread to West Papua and other areas in Indonesia. Images of the protests saturated Indonesian media for weeks and led to violence, arrests, and killings. The hashtag spread, and so did the use of PLM signs at demonstrations. Some West Papuans wrote "monkey" on themselves to draw attention to the racism, and the use of the *Bintang Kejora* was also widespread. PLM is drawing attention to the structural racism directed at West Papuans in Indonesia, complicated by the situation in West Papua itself.

Although there are people who speak on behalf of PLM, it is similar to BLM in that it is amorphous. The availability of cell phones enables images of abuse as well as demonstrations to spread rapidly. Assa Aso, an activist and member of the National Committee for West Papua, stated, "We have studied digital movements. We realize that it's not enough to encourage people to join the protest but also to let people outside know what we are doing, and then they feel involved. When the news spreads to the international community, we feel satisfied."[46] In a tacit acknowledgement of the power of new media, the Indonesian government shuts down the internet in West Papua during periods of unrest, employs disinformation campaigns, and uses "troll farms" to attack West Papuans' messages. Activists skirt the shutdowns through connections at hotels with their own satellite internet service.[47]

Indonesia has been undergoing democratization since 1998 and has made tremendous progress with regard to freedom of expression, including protest. In West Papua, this freedom is suppressed, making Papuans question their place in Indonesia—are they full citizens? Why, then, is the government denying them the rights it extends to other Indonesians? Why the double standard? Immigration from more densely populated regions of Indonesia to West Papua is also stoking resentment—and fears that West Papuans will soon be a minority in their own land.

Papuan activists and journalists have also capitalized on the interest stoked by PLM to spread their message, and stories have appeared in online and mainstream media in the United States, Great Britain, Australia, and around the world. BLM activists in the United States have displayed *Bintang Kejora* flags in solidarity with West Papua and have told Papuan activists with PLM placards that they should just use Black Lives Matter—an acknowledgement of shared Blackness and experience despite the unique context of the West Papuan struggle.[48]

In West Papua itself, little has changed despite the campaign. PLM is known and respected, but as one confidential source told me, "People who want to make change are doing so by joining NGOs and organizations that provide relief for Papuans," including combating what he described as a racially motivated lack of distribution of COVID aid to ethnic Papuans, similar to BLM claims in the United States.[49] Among many Indonesians, there is an unwillingness to admit that racism exists.[50] Yet others are more sanguine. Rumkabu noted that although there is resistance from conservative and older Indonesians, younger Indonesians are more willing to discuss race and express solidarity with Papuans. PLM, she stated, has opened a much-needed dialogue about race in Indonesia.[51]

## Conclusion

This essay has explored the similarities of experience and circumstance of West Papuans to African Americans in the United States, including slavery, disenfranchisement, economic exploitation, political marginalization, lack of representation, and institutional and structural racism. It also shows the influence that African Americans have had in West Papua. West Papuans continue to draw inspiration from civil rights and African American movements in the United States, connected by shared Blackness and "a sense of common oppression and painful collective memories,"[52] and they continue to lobby for support.

Originally denigrated for the color of their skin, West Papuans (and Melanesians more broadly) have embraced the term "Melanesia" and are actively working to "re-present" themselves in the context of a proud Blackness. The long history of internalized racism due to racist representation means that the "challenges for re-presenting Melanesia are therefore not just socioeconomic but epistemological."[53] West Papuans' identification with Blackness is one way to challenge old representations, and it "demonstrates that the global Black movement has been responded to locally and is shaped by the productions of Black epistemologies."[54]

The current situation in West Papua has been shaped by colonial history, Cold War realism, and contemporary Indonesian, regional, and international politics. Traditionally, the political discontent in West Papua has been blamed on factors such as the economy or low levels of development. The shocking racist violence of 2019 and the emergence of PLM, however, may reframe the issue. Rumkabu notes that PLM "has highlighted the most fundamental problem of the Papuan conflict, which is racism."[55] Whether PLM will be successful in the long term at getting Indonesians to acknowledge the racism that exists there toward Papuans and spur significant and positive change remains to be seen, but it appears to be sparking conversation—the first step. Perhaps it will also provoke those of us who study Asia to more deeply interrogate how race and racism fit into our work and acknowledge the marginalized minorities who are frequently overlooked.

## Notes

[1] Melanesia is a region in the Pacific that includes Papuans, and the term originates from the Greek for "black." The term differentiates Melanesians from Polynesians and Micronesians. It is the only region in Oceania designated for the perceived color of its inhabitants' skin, and the name was given to reflect European opinions of racial hierarchy, which considered Polynesians and Micronesians more developed. Tarcisius Kabutaulaka, "Re-Presenting Melanesia: Ignoble Savages and Melanesian Alter-Natives," *The Contemporary Pacific* 27, no. 1 (2015): 110, 116.

[2] Amnesty International, "'Don't Bother, Just Let Him Die': Killing with Impunity in West Papua," (2018), https://www.amnesty.org.au/wp-content/uploads/2018/07/Dont-Bother-Just-let-Him-Die.pdf. I am in no way trying to compare the suffering of two persecuted peoples in order to weigh which is worse, and I am well aware that, should the comparison include other marginalized peoples in other regions, we would also find similarities. Although each person's suffering is unique, patterns of cruelty nonetheless exist, reflecting power, position, status, and perceptions of race.

[3] Veronika Kusukaryati, "#Papuanlivesmatter: Black Consciousness and Political Movements in West Papua," *Critical Asian Studies* 53, no. 4 (2021): 456.

[4] Under Suharto's New Order, discussions of race and ethnicity were banned in the name of harmony, but this ban effectively silenced West Papuans and others who wished to draw attention to racism.

[5] Melanesians were also called "niggers." Gerald Horne, *The White Pacific: U.S. Imperialism and Black Slavery in the South Seas* (Honolulu: University of Hawai'i Press, 2007): 12; 134. This is, of course, not the first time Europeans looked at newly encountered, soon-to-

be-conquered people, and decided that they resembled some other group: just ask the "Indians" of North America.

[6] West Papuan anthropology PhD student Ligia Giay notes that, "The usage of the term Papuans as an umbrella term for all native inhabitants of the present day Radjaampat Islands and the western-half (sic) of New Guinea is problematic on account of the diversities of ethnicities and culture in the area." Ligia Giay, "Native Informants and the Construction of Stereotypes of Papuans in the 17th–18th Century" (MA Thesis, University of Leiden, 2014), 2 (fn 2).

[7] Danilyn Rutherford, "Laughing at Leviathan: John Furnivall, Dutch New Guinea, and the Ridiculousness of Colonial Rule," in *Southeast Asia over Three Generations (Essays Presented to Benedict R. O'G. Anderson)*, eds. James T. Siegel and Audrey R. Kahin (Ithaca: Cornell University, Southeast Asia Program, 2003), 50–78.

[8] Quito Swan, "Blinded by Bandung? Illumining West Papua, Senegal, and the Black Pacific," *Radical History Review*, 131 (2018): 62. Gerald Horne describes how hundreds of thousands of Pacific Islanders and Melanesians were "blackbirded" or captured as slave labor and shipped to Australia, Fiji, and elsewhere, where they faced devastating death tolls. Papuans were preferred because of their ability to learn English. As an Australian cleric noted, "It is a remarkable thing . . . that just in the decade that the terrible American Civil War . . . the traffic in Papuan savages arose." Horne, *The White Pacific*, 2, 33.

[9] After World War I, Australia governed the entire region until its independence in 1975.

[10] C. L. M. Penders, *The West New Guinea Debacle: Dutch Decolonization and Indonesia, 1945–1962* (Adelaide: Crawford House, 2002), 56–57; Arend Lijphart, *The Trauma of Decolonization: The Dutch and West New Guinea* (New Haven: Yale University Press, 1966), 79–81.

[11] Penders, *West New Guinea*, 89–90. Yosua R. Mansoben, personal interview, August 5, 2006, Abepura, West Papua.

[12] James Burk and Evelyn Espinoza, "Race Relations within the US Military," *Annual Review of Sociology*, 38 (2012): 401–22.

[13] Soekarno, "Major Address by President Sukarno to the Fifteenth United Nations General Assembly, New York, 30 September 1960. NST 1327/60, Pidato Presiden, Arsip 223" (Jakarta: Indonesian National Archives, 1960).

[14] Penders, *West New Guinea*, 390–92.

[15] John Saltford, *The United Nations and the Indonesian Takeover of West Papua, 1962–1969: The Anatomy of Betrayal* (New York: Routledge Curzon, 2003), 98–120.

[16] This is counting the entire population of West Papua at the time, reflecting an estimate, and not those who would have been deemed eligible to vote. In Indonesian national elections in 1971, 379,531 Papuans voted.

[17] Octovianus Mote and Danilyn Rutherford, "From Irian Jaya to Papua: The Limits of Primordialism in Indonesia's Troubled East" *Indonesia*, 72 (2001): 122.

[18] Biro Humas Komisi Pemilihan Umum. *Pemilu Indonesia Dalam Angka dan Fakta Tahun 1955–1999*. Jakarta: Biro Human Komisi Pemilihan Umum, 2000.

[19] According to W. E. B. Du Bois, one could trace "the African black from the great lakes of Africa to Melanesia." Swan, "Blinded," 62. Despite sharing the island and whatever personal sympathies its residents may have, Papua New Guinea has supported Indonesia politically with regard to West Papuan claims for self-determination. Kusumaryati, "#Papuanlivesmatter," 462.

[20] Fenneke Sysling, "The Human Wallace Line: Racial Science and Political Afterlife," *Medical History* 63, no. 3 (2019): 314–329.

[21] Ibid., 318. Gerald Horne has written an expansive account of Melanesian slavery in the Pacific entitled *The White Pacific*.

[22] David Webster, "Race, Identity and Diplomacy in the Papua Decolonization Struggle, 1949–1962," in *Race, Ethnicity and the Cold War: A Global Perspective*, ed. Philip Muehlenbeck (Nashville: Vanderbilt University Press, 2012); Horne, *The White Pacific*, 22.

[23] Sysling, "The Human Wallace Line," 328.

[24] Swan, "Blinded," 62. Statements of support for Indonesia delivered to the UN purportedly written by Papuans were predominantly written by immigrants to the region. Socrates Sofyan Yoman, "Injustice and Historical Falsehood: Integration of the Territory of Papua into Indonesia in 1969," in *Comprehending West Papua*, eds. Peter King, Jim Elmslie, and Camellia Webb-Gannon (Sydney: Center for Peace and Conflict Studies, the University of Sydney, 2011): 116.

[25] Swan, "Blinded," 65–67. This section of Swan's article paints a stark juxtaposition between portrayals of West Papuans in the Black and mainstream presses.

[26] The NAACP wrote to the UN in 1969 to protest the "Act of Free Choice." Kusumaryati, "#Papuanlivesmatter," 456.

[27] The East Timor and Indonesia Action Network, "Congressional Black Caucus (CBC) Joins with Faleomavaega in Urging U.S. Secretary of State and UN Secretary General to Support West Papua's Right to Self-Determination" (2005), https://etan.org/news/2005/03blkcau.htm.

[28] The East Timor and Indonesia Action Network, "50 Members of U.S. Congress Call Upon Obama Administration to Make West Papua One of Its Highest Priorities" (2010), https://etan.org/news/2010/08faleo.htm; "Crimes Against Humanity: When Will Indonesia's Military be Held Accountable for Deliberate and Systematic Abuses in West Papua?" Hearing before the Subcommittee on Asia, the Pacific and the Global Environment of the Committee on Foreign Affairs, House of Representatives, September 22, 2010, https://www.govinfo.gov/content/pkg/CHRG-111hhrg58430/html/CHRG-111hhrg58430.htm.

[29] Rutherford, "Laughing," 63.

[30] An NPR story on Carl Hoffman's book *Savage Harvest* (New York: William Morrow, 2014), a sensationalist and speculative look at the death of Michael Rockefeller that itself perpetuates these stereotypes, emphasized the region's headhunting as though it remained widespread. "A Tragic Disappearance (Mostly) Solved in 'Savage Harvest,'" NPR Weekend Edition, (2014), https://www.npr.org/2014/03/15/289828793/a-tragic-disappearance-

mostly-solved-in-savage-harvest. See also Maile Arvin, "The Polynesian Problem and its Genomic Solutions," *Native American and Indigenous Studies* 2, no. 2 (Fall 2015): 27–56.

[31] Leupe, in Giay, "Native Informants," 30.

[32] Giay, "Native Informants," 2.

[33] These reflect, however, exploitation at the hands of Indonesians, including migrants, as well as foreign corporations such as Freeport McMoRan. The economy is controlled by outsiders, and Papuans are marginalized. Ikrar Nusa Bhakti, "A New Kind of Self-Determination in Papua: The Choice Between Independence and Autonomy," in *Violent Internal Conflicts in Asia Pacific: Histories, Political Economies and Policies*, ed. Dewi Fortuna Anwar, et al. (Jakarta: Yayasan Obor Indonesia, 2005), 227–228.

[34] David Love, "'Monkeys, Dogs, and Pigs': After Years of Racial Abuse, Genocide, West Papuans Continue to Fight for Freedom from Indonesia," *Atlanta Black Star*, September 2, 2019, https://atlantablackstar.com/2019/09/02/monkeys-dogs-and-pigs-after-years-of-racial-abuse-genocide-west-papuans-continue-fight-for-freedom-from-indonesia/.

[35] Ashley Westerman, Ryan Benk, David Greene, "In 2020, Protests Spread Across the Globe with a Similar Message: Black Lives Matter," National Public Radio, December 30, 2020, https://www.npr.org/2020/12/30/950053607/in-2020-protests-spread-across-the-globe-with-a-similar-message-black-lives-matt.

[36] For representations of Melanesians more broadly, see Kabutaulaka, "Re-Presenting," 118–119.

[37] Note the similarity with settler colonialism's attempt to change culture and even "breed out" indigeneity. Arvin, "The Polynesian Problem," 36.

[38] Elvira Romkabu, personal interview, December 20, 2021.

[39] Ni Luh Putu Murni Oktaviani, I Gusti Agung Alit Suryawati, Ni Made Ras Amanda Gelgel, "Konstruksi Realitas Isu Papuan Lives Matter di Media Online," *Jurnal Ilmu Komunikasi* 1, no. 2 (2021), https://ojs.unud.ac.id/index.php/komunikasi/article/view/73760.

[40] W. F., personal communication, August 12, 2021; J. H., personal communication, July 11, 2021. I am using initials to protect the identity of these sources as they live in West Papua and could face retaliation for statements deemed critical of Indonesia. Octovianus Mote, personal communication, August 8, 2021.

[41] Ezra Sihite, "Anggota TNI AU Injak Kepala Warga Papua, Tragedi George Floyd Diungkit," July 28, 2021. Viva.co.id, https://www.viva.co.id/berita/nasional/1390830-anggota-tni-au-injak-kepala-warga-papua-tragedi-george-floyd-diungkit.

[42] The Gecko Project and Mongabay, "'Potentially Lethal' Police Assault on indigenous Papuan Man was Caught on Camera," *Mongabay*, October 27, 2020, https://news.mongabay.com/2020/10/potentially-lethal-police-assault-on-indigenous-papuan-man-was-caught-on-camera/.

[43] Marni Cordell, "Australia Trained Indonesia Police Officer Accused of West Papua Violence," *The Guardian*, August 2, 2021, https://www.theguardian.com/world/2021/aug/03/australia-trained-indonesian-police-officer-accused-of-west-papua-violence.

[44] Krithika Varagur, "Black Lives Matter in Indonesia, too," *Foreign Policy*, June 16, 2020, https://foreignpolicy.com/2020/06/16/black-lives-matter-papua-indonesia/.

[45] "ULMWP Calls for Suspension of Indonesia from UN Rights Council over Assault on Deaf Papuan," *Asia Pacific Report*, July 31, 2021, https://asiapacificreport.nz/2021/07/31/ulmwp-calls-for-suspension-of-indonesia-from-un-rights-group-over-deaf-man-assault/.

[46] Febriana Firdaus, "The Silent Song," Rest of World.com, https://restofworld.org/2021/the-silent-song/.

[47] Ibid.

[48] Lisabeth Ryder, founder, West Papua Action Network USA, personal communication, August 13, 2021.

[49] W. F., personal communication, August 12, 2021. Jenny Munro has noted that "technocratic racism" and a "settler colonial context" have worked to exclude Papuans from HIV prevention work in the region. Jenny Munro, "Global HIV Interventions and Technocratic Racism in a West Papuan NGO," *Medical Anthropology* 39, no. 80 (2020): 716.

[50] Kusumaryati, "#Papuanlivesmatter," 456.

[51] Elvia Rumkabu, personal communication, December 20, 2021.

[52] Rumkabu in Kusumaryati, "#Papuanlivesmatter," 465–466.

[53] Kabutaulaka, "Re-Presenting," 110.

[54] Kusumaryati, "#Papuanlivesmatter," 456.

[55] Ibid., 470.

## Bibliography

Amnesty International. "'Don't Bother, Just Let Him Die:' Killing with Impunity in West Papua." (2018). Accessed from https://www.amnesty.org.au/wp-content/uploads/2018/07/Dont-Bother-Just-let-Him-Die.pdf.

Anwar, Dewi Fortuna, Bouvier, Helene, Smith, Glenn, and Tol, Roger, eds. *Violent Internal Conflicts in Asia Pacific: Histories, Political Economies and Policies.* Yayasan Obor Indonesia, 2005.

Arvin, Maile. "The Polynesian Problem and its Genomic Solutions." *Native American and Indigenous Studies* 2, no. 2 (Fall 2015): 27–56.

Biro Humas Komisi Pemilihan Umum. *Pemilu Indonesia Dalam Angka dan Fakta Tahun 1955–1999.* Jakarta: Biro Human Komisi Pemilihan Umum, 2000.

Burk, James, and Espinoza, Evelyn. "Race Relations Within the US Military." *Annual Review of Sociology* 38 (2012): 401–22.

Cordell, Marni. "Australia Trained Indonesia Police Officer Accused of West Papua Violence," *The Guardian*, August 2, 2021, Accessed from https://www.theguardian.com/world/2021/aug/03/australia-trained-indonesian-police-officer-accused-of-west-papua-violence.

"Crimes Against Humanity: When Will Indonesia's Military Be Held Accountable for Deliberate and Systematic Abuses in West Papua?" Hearing before the Subcommittee on Asia, the Pacific and the Global Environment of the Committee on Foreign Affairs, House of Representatives, September 22, 2010. Accessed from: https://www.govinfo.gov/content/pkg/CHRG-111hhrg58430/html/CHRG-111hhrg58430.htm.

The East Timor and Indonesia Action Network. "50 Members of U.S. Congress Call Upon Obama Administration to Make West Papua One of Its Highest Priorities." Accessed from https://etan.org/news/2010/08faleo.htm.

The East Timor and Indonesia Action Network. "Congressional Black Caucus (CBC) Joins with Faleomavaega in Urging U.S. Secretary of State and UN Secretary General to Support West Papua's Right to Self-Determination." Accessed from https://etan.org/news/2005/03blkcau.htm.

Firdaus, Febriana. "The Silent Song," Rest of World.com. Accessed from https://restofworld.org/2021/the-silent-song/.

The Gecko Project and Mongabay. "'Potentially Lethal' Police Assault on Indigenous Papuan Man was Caught on Camera," *Mongabay*, October 27, 2020. Accessed from https://news.mongabay.com/2020/10/potentially-lethal-police-assault-on-indigenous-papuan-man-was-caught-on-camera/.

Giay, Ligia. "Native Informants and the Construction of Stereotypes of Papuans in the 17th–18th Century." MA Thesis, University of Leiden, 2014.

Hoffman, Carl. *Savage Harvest*. New York: William Morrow, 2014.

Horne, Gerald. *The White Pacific: U.S. Imperialism and Black Slavery in the South Seas*. Honolulu: University of Hawai'i Press, 2007.

Kabutaulaka, Tarcisius. "Re-Presenting Melanesia: Ignoble Savages and Melanesian Alter-Natives." *The Contemporary Pacific* 27, no. 1 (2015): 110–146.

King, Peter, Elmslie, Jim, and Webb-Gannon, Camellia, eds. *Comprehending West Papua*. Sydney: Center for Peace and Conflict Studies, the University of Sydney, 2011.

Kusukaryati, Veronika. "#Papuanlivesmatter: Black consciousness and political movements in West Papua." *Critical Asian Studies* 53, no. 4 (2021): 453–475.

Lijphart, Arend. *The Trauma of Decolonization: The Dutch and West New Guinea*. New Haven: Yale University Press, 1966.

Mote, Octovianus Mote and Rutherford, Danilyn. "From Irian Jaya to Papua: The Limits of Primordialism in Indonesia's Troubled East." *Indonesia*, 72 (2001): 115–140.

Muehlenbeck, Philip, ed. *Race, Ethnicity, and the Cold War: A Global Perspective*. Nashville: Vanderbilt University Press, 2012.

Munro, Jenny. "Global HIV Interventions and Technocratic Racism in a West Papuan NGO." *Medical Anthropology* 39, no. 8 (2020): 704–719.

Ni Luh Putu Murni Oktaviani, I Gusti Agung Alit Suryawati, Ni Made Ras Amanda Gelgel. "Konstruksi Realitas Isu Papuan Lives Matter di Media Online." *Jurnal Ilmu Komunikasi* 1, no. 2 (2021). Accessed from https.//ojs. unud.ac.id/index.php/komunikasi/article/view/73760.

Penders, C. L. M. *The West New Guinea Debacle: Dutch Decolonization and Indonesia, 1945–1962*. Adelaide: Crawford House, 2002.

Ryder, Lisabeth. Founder, West Papua Action Network USA. Personal communication, August 13, 2021.

Saltford, John. *The United Nations and the Indonesian Takeover of West Papua, 1962–1969: The Anatomy of Betrayal*. New York: Routledge Curzon, 2003.

Siegel, James T., and Kahin, Audrey R., eds. *Southeast Asia over Three Generations (Essays Presented to Benedict R. O'G. Anderson)*. Ithaca: Cornell University, Southeast Asia Program, 2003.

Sihite, Ezra. "Anggota TNI AU Injak Kepala Warga Papua, Tragedi George Floyd Diungkit." July 28, 2021. Viva.co.id. Accessed from https://www.viva.co.id/ berita/nasional/1390830-anggota-tni-au-injak-kepala-warga-papua-tragedi-george-floyd-diungkit.

Soekarno. "Major Address by President Sukarno to the Fifteenth United Nations General Assembly, New York, 30 September 1960. NST 1327/60, Pidato Presiden, Arsip 223." Jakarta: Indonesian National Archives, 1960.

Swan, Quito. "Blinded by Bandung? Illumining West Papua, Senegal, and the Black Pacific." *Radical History Review* 131 (2018): 58–81.

Sysling, Fenneke. "The Human Wallace Line: Racial Science and Political Afterlife." *Medical History* 63, no. 3 (2019): 314–329.

"A Tragic Disappearance (Mostly) Solved in 'Savage Harvest.'" NPR Weekend Edition. Accessed from https://www.npr.org/2014/03/15/289828793/a-tragic-disappearance-mostly-solved-in-savage-harvest.

"ULMWP Calls for Suspension of Indonesia from UN Rights Council over Assault on Deaf Papuan." *Asia Pacific Report*, July 31, 2021. Accessed from https://asiapacificreport.nz/2021/07/31/ulmwp-calls-for-suspension-of-indonesia-from-un-rights-group-over-deaf-man-assault/.

Varagur, Krithika. "Black Lives Matter in Indonesia, too." *Foreign Policy*, June 16, 2020. Accessed from https://foreignpolicy.com/2020/06/16/black-lives-matter-papua-indonesia/.

Westerman, Ashely, Benk, Ryan, and Greene, David. "In 2020, Protests Spread Across the Globe with a Similar Message: Black Lives Matter," National Public Radio, December 30, 2020. Accessed from https://www.npr.org/2020/12/30/950053607/in-2020-protests-spread-across-the-globe-with-a-similar-message-black-lives-matt.

# About the Editors

**WILL BRIDGES** is Associate Professor of Japanese, Arthur Satz Professor of the Humanities, and a Core Faculty member with the Frederick Douglass Institute for African and African-American Studies at the University of Rochester. His first monograph, *Playing in the Shadows: Fictions of Race and Blackness in Postwar Japanese Literature* was published by the University of Michigan Press in 2020.

**NITASHA TAMAR SHARMA** is a professor of Black Studies and Asian American Studies at Northwestern University, where she directs the Asian American Studies Program. She is the author of *Hip Hop Desis: South Asian Americans, Blackness, and a Global Race Consciousness* (Duke UP 2010) and *Hawai'i Is My Haven: Race and Indigeneity in the Black Pacific* (Duke UP 2021).

**MARVIN D. STERLING** is Associate Professor of Anthropology at Indiana University, Bloomington. He is author of *Babylon East: Performing Dancehall, Roots Reggae, and Rastafari in Japan* (Duke UP 2010).

# About the Contributors

**HODA BANDEH-AHMADI** is an anthropologist. She earned her Ph.D. from the University of Michigan in 2018. She was then Director of Social Research at the Center for Surgical Training and Research (C-STAR) in the University of Michigan Department of Surgery. She is currently an independent scholar. Her research focuses on the ethnography of academic and scientific institutions. In addition to her projects on anthropologists in India and the US, she has studied a range of topics, such as: the solar energy industry, US presidential campaigns, and the development of predictive analytics in surgical education.

**CAROLYN THOMPSON BROWN** is Chair of the Board of Trustees of the Fetzer Institute, a medium-size foundation located in Kalamazoo, Michigan. In that capacity, she leads the board in providing spiritual, strategic, and fiduciary oversight of the Institute. Previously, she served in various positions at the Library of Congress. These included directing cultural programming, including public relations, visitor services, publications, and exhibits; and leading the Collections and Services Directorate, which provided oversight of collections development, collections management, reference, and public outreach for the general, special, and Area Studies Collections. She retired from the library as director of the Office of Scholarly Programs and the John W. Kluge Center. In that capacity, she managed the $1 million Kluge Prize and directed residential fellowship programs for U.S. and international scholars. In addition, she organized conferences, seminars, teachers' institutes, and other scholarly events. The Poetry and Literature Program, which hosts the Poet Laureate of the United States, was also under her direction. Prior to joining the Library of Congress, Carolyn was Associate Dean for the Humanities at Howard University. Her professional writings examine the interrelationship of literature, culture, and psychology, with special focus on modern Chinese literature. She is the author of *Reading Lu Xun through Carl Jung* (2018), a book on spiritual healing in the short stories of twentieth-century China's most famous writer. Carolyn holds a BA in Asian Studies and an MA in Chinese literature both from Cornell University, and a Ph.D. in literature from American University.

**GUANGTIAN HA** is Assistant Professor of Religion at Haverford College. His latest book, *The Sound of Salvation: Voice, Gender, and the Sufi Mediascape in China*, is published by Columbia University Press. He is also the co-editor of *Ethnographies of Islam in China* (Hawai'i 2021) and *The Contest of the Fruits* (MIT 2021). His new project uses Arabic, Persian, and Chinese sources to examine the essential role of B/black laborers—sailors and slaves—in enabling the maritime voyages of Muslim merchants in medieval times. He is a failed comedian who ended up in academia and found resonances between laughter and mystical truth. In March 2022 he collaborated with Musa Sulaiman in organizing a unique stand-up comedy special in downtown Philadelphia (https://www.seetickets.us/event/Muslim-Kings-of-Comedy-SOLD-OUT/467252) featuring some of the major African American Muslim comedians in the US. His interest in African American Muslim comedy dovetails with his research on medieval B/black sailors and laborers: they are distant in time (medieval vs. contemporary) and geography (trans-Atlantic vs. trans-Pacific), yet so close as though linked through a wormhole.

**KIMBERLY HASSEL** is Assistant Professor in the Department of East Asian Studies at the University of Arizona. She is an anthropologist and digital ethnographer specializing in the intersections of digital culture, youth culture, and identity in contemporary Japan. Hassel also specializes in diaspora studies, critical mixed-race studies, and Afro-Japanese encounters. Her current book project, tentatively titled *Mediating Me: Digital Sociality and Smartphone Culture in Contemporary Japan*, examines the relationships between Social Networking Services (SNS), smartphones, and shifting notions of sociality and selfhood in Japan, especially among young people. Her examination of the impact of COVID-19 on digital sociality in Japan and ethnographic methods on a broader scale has appeared in *Anthropology News*. Hassel received a Ph.D. in East Asian Studies from Princeton University. Her dissertation fieldwork was funded by a Japan Foundation Japanese Studies Doctoral Fellowship. She is an alumna of the Mellon Mays Undergraduate Fellowship and the Institute for Recruitment of Teachers.

**ISABEL HUACUJA ALONSO** is Assistant Professor at Columbia University's Department of Middle Eastern, South Asian, and African Studies (MESAAS). She is the author of *Radio for the Millions: Hindi-Urdu Broadcasting Across Borders,* (Columbia University Press, 2013), and has published articles and translations about modern South Asian history and sound studies in several journals, including *Public Culture, Bioscope,* and *South Asia*. She completed her Ph.D. from the University of Texas at Austin in 2015, and prior to joining Columbia, taught at California State University, San Bernardino.

**CHRIS LUNDRY** is a profesor-investigador in the Centro de Estudios de Asia y África at El Colegio de México, Mexico City. His work focuses on Indonesia and Timor-Leste, but also on the Southeast Asian region in general. His publications cover revolution and separatism, conflict and reconciliation, religion and politics, terrorism, and elections. He co-authored *Narrative Landmines: Rumor, Islamist Extremism, and the Struggle for Strategic Influence,* (Rutgers, 2013, with Daniel Leonard Bernardi, Pauline Hope Cheong, and Scott W. Ruston), an award-winning book on rumors and terrorism, and he has published in *Asian Studies, American Behavioral Scientist, Small Wars Journal, Estudios de Asia y África, Studies in Conflict and Terrorism, Asian Politics and Policy, Contemporary Islam,* and *Situations: Cultural Studies in the Asian Context,* among others. He was a United Nations-accredited observer in the 1999 referendum in Timor-Leste and a Carter Center delegate in the 2004 presidential election in Indonesia. His forthcoming book, *Confrontando al Leviatán: Soberanías en disputa en Indonesia Oriental* (El Colegio de Mexico Press, 2022) explores factors that spur and maintain separatism in eastern Indonesia as well as elements that allow it to decline and for the state to cohere.

**M. BILAL NASIR** is currently the Chau Mellon Postdoctoral Fellow in the Intercollegiate Department of Asian American Studies at Pomona College. His research examines Muslim American social movements in Greater Los Angeles, CA, aimed at abolishing the War on Terror. Bilal's writings have been published or are forthcoming in *Anthropological Quarterly, Nova Religio,* and *Political Theology*.

**PHUONG HA NGUYEN** (she/her) is a doctoral researcher at the Department of Social Anthropology and Cultural Studies (Institut für Sozialanthropologie und Empirische Kulturwissenschaft) at the University of Zurich, Zurich, Switzerland. Her research focuses on the urban ethnography of innovation, children and youths, and the interaction between social actors in social transformation processes in the context of modern Viet Nam. Phuong holds a Master of Development Studies degree with First Class Honours from the University of Melbourne (Australia) and a Bachelor's degree in Economics and Finance from RMIT University Vietnam. Her current doctoral project investigates the Vietnamese digital sharing economy in the narrative of the Fourth Industrial Revolution.

**TRANG QUYNH NGUYEN** (she/her) is an independent researcher and cybersecurity engineer born and raised in Hanoi, Viet Nam and currently based in New York City. Her research interests include race, human perceptions, the media, and the human element in cybersecurity. Her previously published research discussed framing theory and media manipulation. Trang has an MS in Information Systems from Pace University, NY, and a BA in Social Psychology and Communications from Mercyhurst University, PA.

**SOHAM PATEL** is a Visiting Assistant Professor of Comparative Ethnic Studies at Pitzer College. He received his Ph.D. from the Department of American studies at the University of Minnesota. His research interests include anti-Muslim racism, border imperialism, Black-Brown solidarities, and radical internationalism. Soham's current book project, *Muslim Worldmaking: Race and Culture in the Shadow of War,* examines how South Asian/American Muslim filmmakers and visual artists have envisioned and practiced radical care and solidarity in the global struggle against anti-Muslim racism.

**KRISTIN ROEBUCK** is Assistant Professor and Howard Milstein Faculty Fellow in the Department of History at Cornell University. After completing her Ph.D. in East Asian History at Columbia University in 2015, Roebuck worked as Mellon Diversity Postdoctoral Scholar at Cornell University. In 2019, she won a Fulbright U.S. Scholar Grant for research on racial nationalism in Japan. In 2021, she led a team of colleagues to win a Mellon Migrations Grant, applied toward founding an interdisciplinary Laboratory on Human Trafficking, Its Origins, and Remedies. A historian of modern Japan, Roebuck's research interests encompass the history of the body, slavery and kinship, medicine and law, race and gender, and international relations. Her book manuscript, *Japan Reborn: Race and Eugenics from World War to Cold War*, is forthcoming with Columbia University Press. Roebuck has also published in such venues as *The Harvard Journal of Asiatic Studies, Japanese Studies*, and *Asia Pacific Perspectives*; her public-facing work has appeared in *NBC News, The Hill, Time Magazine*, and National Public Radio's *Global Journalist*.

**FELICITY STONE-RICHARDS** is a scholar of Afro-diasporic and Japanese political thought and studies the intellectual exchange between Black American and Japanese political actors. She is currently pursuing a PhD in Political Science at the University of California, Santa Barbara (UCSB). Her research focuses specifically on anti-racist activism and organization in the United States and Japan. Alongside an analysis of anti-racist discourse in Japan, her dissertation project explores how Japanese and American writers approach the moral question of convincing people to engage in the practice of sacrifice and disinvest from the oppressive systems they benefit from. Outside of her research, Stone-Richards has also engaged in university advocacy fighting for better housing and working conditions for graduate students at UCSB. For the academic year 2022–2023, Stone-Richards will be a Fulbright Scholar in Japan.

**JEREMY TAI** is Assistant Professor of Modern Chinese History at McGill University. He received his Ph.D. in History at the University of California, Santa Cruz in 2015. He is currently completing a book manuscript that examines how the city of Xi'an has been shaped over the past century by state programs of spatial redistribution, which have channeled capital, industry, and population from coastal to inland China in moments of crisis. His second project considers socialist critiques of racial capitalism and their legacies in contemporary China.

CPSIA information can be obtained
at www.ICGtesting.com
Printed in the USA
JSHW040242041022
31291JS00001B/17

9 781952 636295